MEDIEVAL ༄ ENGLISH ༄ THEATRE

VOLUME FORTY (2018)

MEDIEVAL ✐ ENGLISH ✐ THEATRE

VOLUME FORTY (2018)

edited by

Sarah Carpenter, Elisabeth Dutton, Gordon Kipling,
and Meg Twycross

D. S. BREWER

Medieval English Theatre is an international refereed journal publishing articles on medieval and early Tudor theatre and pageantry in all its aspects (not confined to England), together with articles and records of modern survivals or equivalents. Most issues are illustrated. Contributions to be considered for future volumes are welcomed: see the end of this volume and website for further information:
<www.medievalenglishtheatre.co.uk>

First published 2019
D. S. Brewer, Cambridge

ISBN 978 1 84384 528 7

ISSN 0143–3784

D. S. Brewer is an imprint of Boydell & Brewer Ltd
PO Box 9, Woodbridge, Suffolk IP12 3DF, UK
and of Boydell & Brewer Inc.
668 Mt Hope Avenue, Rochester, NY 14620–2731, USA
website: www.boydellandbrewer.com

A catalogue record for this title is available from the British Library

MEDIEVAL ∞ ENGLISH ∞ THEATRE

VOLUME FORTY (2018)

CONTENTS

ILLUSTRATIONS

EDITORIAL

This volume celebrates forty years of *Medieval English Theatre*. For those who were there at the first meeting in Lancaster in 1979 'to discuss the pageant waggon', this thought is both alarming and exhilarating. In the intervening decades we have travelled all over the United Kingdom, from Southampton to Edinburgh; and next year we go to Switzerland to celebrate our fortieth birthday, on what will be, by the quirk of mathematics that means that you have your first birthday a year after you were born, our forty-first meeting.

Our Fortieth Meeting on 'Performance and its Urban Context' was in Sheffield, ably hosted at the Humanities Research Institute by Charlotte Steenbrugge and her team. It was a packed day, with an interesting variety of approaches. Starting with York's Corpus Christi Play, Eleanor Bloomfield looked at the Passion sequence and its relation to the Mass; Sian Witherden spoke on the exploitation of the sense of touch, especially the implications of 'stepping in Christ's footsteps' for acts of virtual and vicarious pilgrimage; and Meg Twycross looked at 'The Sun in York' (see below). The next session considered the relationship between religious establishments and the city: Aurélie Blanc on the efforts made by the Abbess of Barking to instruct and involve the local community through drama; Olivia Robinson on the political implications of changes to the processional route at Huy in Belgium, and how the relationship of the modern nuns to their own theatrical performances casts light on that of their predecessors; and Jason Burg on the dramatic ceremonies of Lincoln (the St Anne's day procession, a possible *Ascension* play), where the Cathedral and the Guild seem to have worked together. In the afternoon, Daisy Black spoke about the unexpectedly powerful effect of silent characters in the civic plays. Mark Chambers and Gasper Jacovac recounted their discoveries about the theatrical entertainments laid on at Durham and Newcastle for James VI and I in his 1617 tour of the North. Phil Butterworth reminded us of the recalcitrance of material objects by describing the hazards to medieval street theatre from structures which were not supposed to be there. Gillian Redfern took us out of the city to consider the imagery of plays set (and possibly even acted) in the hills and dales of the

Northern countryside. Finally, Jodi-Anne George described her fascinating project to stage Henryson's masque-like *Testament of Cresseid*. Several of these papers will appear in this and subsequent editions of *METh*.

At a rough count at least seven of the original 1979 attendees were at the 2018 meeting. Some of the others had not yet been born. This is a highly encouraging situation: and the current volume, appropriately, features articles from both groups. Readers may amuse themselves by guessing which is which. Philip Butterworth and Michael Spence edit, translate, and discuss a major piece of evidence for the fifteenth-century provincial Royal Entry and the origins of the quasi-professional 'property player'. Aurélie Blanc and Olivia Robinson describe the updating by a team of seventeenth-century Belgian nuns of their extended play of the Nativity, the challenges in translating it into English, and the role that this kind of playmaking appears to have had, and still has, in their community. John Marshall considers the details of a somewhat unnerving entertainment mounted by the eighteen-year-old Henry VIII for his new-married wife, and the relationship between Robin Hood and the early morris. Clare Egan suggests that we read *Mankind* through the prism of what might almost be described as a contemporary obsession with slander and defamation, and see it as entangling the audience in a veritable spider's web of sticky suggestion and unwitting consent. Meg Twycross is dazzled by the possibilities and implications of the reflection of sunlight in the staging of supernatural illumination on the streets of York.

Staying with the theme of continuity and renewal: the current Editors welcome Elisabeth Dutton to their number. Her scholarship, skills, and range of interests and contacts make her an ideal addition to the team.

We are also delighted to name Alison Samuels as our Latin Consultant. She has been performing this role unofficially for many years and we felt that we should make an official acknowledgement of her invaluable and we hope continuing contributions.

COVER IMAGE

The cover image is a detail from the woodcut at the top of the invitation from the Antwerp Chamber of Rhetoric, the *Violeren*, to other Chambers of Rhetoric across the Low Countries to attend the 1561 *Landjuweel* (play competition). It is reproduced by kind permission of the Royal Library of Belgium: the whole image can be seen at <https://belgica.kbr.be/BELGICA/digital-viewer/c-16147621> (image 11). It was chosen by Charlotte Steenbrugge as the poster for the Sheffield meeting; their motto *Wt ionsten versaemt* means something like 'gathered together in a spirit of goodwill'. It seemed to us an excellent motto also for our society.

ONLINE LINKS

An active list of all the URLs referred to in the current volume is posted on the METh website at <http://www.medievalenglishtheatre.co.uk/URLSvol40.html>. This enables the reader to view coloured images and link to video, besides giving access where possible to online texts and articles.

COMMON ABBREVIATIONS

ANTS Anglo-Norman Text Society.

DMLBS *A Dictionary of Medieval Latin from British Sources* edited R.E. Latham, D.R. Howlett, and R.K. Ashdowne (British Academy: Oxford, 1975–2013): available online via subscribing libraries or from <http://logeion.uchicago.edu> (search by headword).

EETS Early English Text Society.
ES (extra series), *OS* (original series), *SS* (supplementary series)

MED *Middle English Dictionary*: online version © 2001, the Regents of the University of Michigan <https://quod.lib.umich.edu> available via subscribing libraries.

OED *Oxford English Dictionary*: online version © 2018 Oxford University Press <http://www.oed.com> available via subscribing libraries.

REED *Records of Early English Drama*.

PRODUCING THE JOURNAL OVER FORTY YEARS

Meg Twycross

Anyone with the good fortune to possess a complete run of *Medieval English Theatre* has on their shelves an almost complete history of desktop publishing. At the beginning it was produced on a manual typewriter with a ribbon. The text was painstakingly justified by counting the number of letters in each line and inserting double spaces accordingly. There were no italics, and no bold, and you produced underlining by going back and hitting the 'underline' key the requisite number of times. Typos were to be avoided, but small ones could be disguised with Tippex. Notes were photographed and then reduced to half size and pasted, physically, into the text (which is why for so long they were at the end of the article instead of at the bottom of the page). Black-and-white figures were glued in; photographs were screened by the printers, then also glued in. Image printing was by offset litho; the rest was essentially photocopied and reduced onto A4 from A3 sheets which were themselves made up of two A4 sheets carefully overlapped and stuck together – in the right order. You learned a lot about rectos and versos and imposition: 'Page 1 is on the right hand side of page 92, and next, back-to-back with it, comes page 2 on the left hand side of page 91'. The covers were in black and red or gold (with a separate plate for each colour) on Kaskad 'Lapwing Brown' paper; the artwork came from photocopied woodcuts or engravings, and the typography was Letraset. It was all very handicraft.

In 1983, judging from the results, we acquired a Silver Reed Electronic Memory typewriter. This had a tiny horizontal window above the keyboard which showed (part of) the line you had just typed so you could correct it before moving on to the next line, when it had gone for ever. I think it was self-justifying. It also had a daisy-wheel printer which let you do two different sizes of typeface, and bold but not italic. The spokes kept breaking off. Contributions, of course, arrived by mail in hard copy and had to be laboriously retyped.

In 1991 we dipped a toe into full-blown word processing with a dedicated programme called Vuwriter developed at Manchester. Italics made their appearance, and we solicited contributions in hard copy and on disk – but in ASCII. The earliest electronic *METh* files date from 1991, and can only be read, unformatted, on Notepad. It was a bumpy ride: the editorials keep apologising for glitches and hold-ups in production. Volumes slid up to two years out of date. Then in 1993 the arrival of Word 6 changed the face of word processing. Volume 15 (which actually appeared in 1995) invited contributions on disk, and even, somewhat nervously, by FTP. There were some drawbacks: Britain used Word for Windows, but scholars in continental Europe, Canada, and the USA mostly used WordPerfect, which was not compatible and had to be translated, with some difficulty. The format became much more professional, and I presume, judging by the lack of pasted-up sheets, that we could actually take the files to the printers on 3½-inch floppy disks, though I may be wrong. Certainly the sizing of the typeface suddenly becomes suspiciously regular: in earlier years 'reduced to half size' could vary wildly from issue to issue. In 2005 these disks were the basis of the first electronic versions deposited with EBSCO for circulation to libraries, after being updated through several versions of Word into pdfs.

From there on we slowly enter the current era. In 2000 for the first time we suggested that articles might be sent by e-mail, 'though this is not completely reliable: please send hard copy as well'. Two years later we seem more confident. Volume 22 (2000) also had our first colour illustrations, of the Japanese pageant waggons of the children's kabuki of Tonami. The first full-colour cover was for 2004, though there was a certain amount of fiddling before the background colour was stabilised.

We had also, however, entered an uncertain era in which library agents went suddenly bankrupt and sales needed much more aggressive promotion than we had time to devote to them. It had become apparent that we needed the professionals. It was our good fortune that Boydell and Brewer agreed to take on the production and publication of the journal, and we signed contracts in January 2015. Volume 37 (2015) was the first, we hope of many, to go out under their imprint.

It has been both exciting and frustrating to live through a Gutenberg equivalent in the publishing business. Possibilities have expanded to such an extent that current limitations seem even more chafing (for example, colour-printing on paper still remains very expensive; we get so much more of our information online that URLs are essential references, possibly in our discipline as essential as books, but they are daunting to copy by hand). We have tried to get round this by using the METh website as a secondary source of reference. This has had the very useful effect of allowing us to add video to our range of illustrations. The full multimedia experience lies hidden somewhere in the future, but it will doubtless come. The advertising function we started off with when we were more of a Newsletter was regretfully dropped because of timing, but has now been triumphantly taken over by e-mails and the Society's website, Facebook, and Twitter pages. We hope to develop a lively discussion strand. The website also allows us to share information with and from colleagues in other like-minded associations in their websites. Collegiality has never had it so good. The downside for print has been that fewer and fewer scholars, especially the younger ones, think of buying the paper version because they expect it to be online in their libraries, and libraries, pushed for shelf space, are also beginning to prefer the electronic version. Later history will reveal how paper and electronic books will learn to cohabit, or whether one will drive the other out; at the moment we can but juggle what we hope is the best of both worlds.

Has the nature of our contributions changed? I think computing has made us more prolix, possibly because the physical action of writing has become so much easier, and we now write much more as we speak, but also because the amount of information available to us online has multiplied exponentially, and it is sometimes difficult to prune it sensibly. The editorial process has extended because there are so many opportunities on both sides for checking corrections and having second thoughts. We need to point out more firmly to both contributors and ourselves as editors that you cannot make last-minute alterations when the book is actually at press.

The other conspicuous change has been that the volumes are no longer as themed as they used to be. When we began, the meetings were very strictly focused on the investigation of a specific topic: 'The Pageant Waggon', 'Props and Costumes', 'Characterisation', 'Place and Scaffold'. We had questionnaires, and contributors were meant to take a specific play or place and work through the questions; then we all discussed the results. This was amazingly productive. But as we went on, each of us got more interested in a particular area or areas – became specialists, in fact – and while the meetings remain themed, the themes tend to be wider, and speakers speak to their own interests. And no editor is going to refuse an excellent article because it does not fit a particular theme.

WILLIAM PARNELL, SUPPLIER OF STAGING AND INGENIOUS DEVICES, and his Role in the Entry of Elizabeth Woodville into Norwich in 1469

Philip Butterworth and Michael Spence

On 18 July 1469 Queen Elizabeth Woodville entered the City of Norwich via the Westwyk Gate (later renamed St Benedict's Gate) on the west side of the city.[1] Upon hearing of her impending visit from the 'shirreve of Norff*olk* hym silf', John Aubry, the Mayor of Norwich, had written to 'the right reuerent Ser Henry Spelman, R*ecordo*ur of the cité of Norwich' on 6 July to ask his advice about appropriate measures for the Queen's visit: 'And I desired to haue knowe of hym [*the sheriff of Norfolk*], by cause this shuld be hir first comyng hedir, how we shuld be rulyd, as well in hir resseyuyng, as in hir abidyng here'.[2] The 'shirreve of Norff*olk*' had impressed upon Aubry that the Queen 'wooll desire to ben resseyued and attendid as wurshepfully as euir was quene a-forn hir'.[3]

The principal information concerning the visit of Elizabeth Woodville to Norwich is recorded in the Chamberlains' Account Books (1469–90), held in the archives of the Norfolk Record Office, Norwich.[4] The accounts occupy folios 10^{r}–14^{r} and give full details of the financial outlay for the Queen's Entry. They were written by Geoffrey Spirleng, who was one of the Norwich Chamberlains heavily involved in the Queen's reception.[5] These costs and

1. The date of Elizabeth's entry is determined by a letter dated 6 July 1469 in the *Paston Letters and Papers of the Fifteenth Century* edited Norman Davis, Richard Beadle, and Colin Richmond, 3 vols *EETS SS 20, 21, 22* (1971) *3* 178.
2. *Paston Letters 3* 178. Spelman was at that time in London, and Aubry wished him to consult with 'them that been of counsel of that city ... that been knowing in that behalf'.
3. *Paston Letters 3* 178.
4. Norwich: Norfolk Record Office NCR 18a-2 (Treasurers and Chamberlains' accounts, 1384–1700). We have worked on photographs supplied by the Record Office although the Accounts are also recorded on Microfilm MF 783/1. See <http://www.archives. norfolk.gov.uk>.
5. Fol. 13^{v}: *Item in papero empto per G Spirleng pro hujusmodi compotis scribendis – ijd.* See Richard Beadle 'Geoffrey Spirleng (c.1426–c.1494): a Scribe of the Canterbury Tales in his Time' in *Of the making of books: medieval manuscripts, their scribes and readers: Essays*

expenses were accounted for by John Coke and William Henstede Junior, Chamberlains of the city. Folios 10^{r}–11^{r} consist of payments made by Coke and Henstede, and folios 11^{v}–12^{v} present invoices from people engaged in the preparations.[6] Itemised accounts from the notebook of Henstede occur in folios 12^{v}–14^{r}. Since selections from the accounts have often been alluded to previously but not transcribed or translated in full,[7] we have provided a full transcription and translation in our Appendix 1.

Our purpose in analysing the document is to investigate the nature and character of the reception and the role of William Parnell in creating the event. Many other people were involved in the creation and preparation of the reception but Parnell was engaged for his undoubted skill in providing the theatrical flair and colour to the proceedings. Other records beyond those

presented to M.B. *Parkes* edited P.R. Robinson and Rivkah Zim (Aldershot: Scolar Press, 1997) 116–46 at 127.

6. Their names include Burton, Massenger, Fox, Sadeler, Cambrigge, Mumford, Thorp, Carter, Godeson, Steynour, Smyth, Nichols, Benfield, Aylmere, Hagonere, Hervy, Thyxel, Neuton and Ferrour.

7. Perhaps the most extensive, yet incomplete, transcript of the Chamberlains' Account Books NCR 18a–2 is by Lucienne Cummings: it was published on the Virtual Norfolk website in 2002 and is archived by the British Library: <https://www.webarchive.org.uk/wayback/archive/20050606120000/http://virtualnorfolk.uea.ac.uk/drama/places/entries/ewoodville.html>. We disagree with some of her transcriptions and translations.

   Earlier treatments include Henry Harrod 'Queen Elizabeth Woodville's Visit to Norwich in 1469' *Norfolk Archaeology* 5 (1859) 32–7; Mark Eccles 'Ludus Coventriæ Lincoln or Norfolk?' *Medium Ævum* 40 (1971) 135–41 at 138. It seems that Eccles had intended to publish the *Chamberlains' Accounts* but this did not materialise: see note 18; R.R. Wright 'Medieval Theatre In East Anglia: a study of Drama and the Community in Essex, Suffolk and Norfolk, 1200–1580, with special reference to Game, Interlude and Play in the late 15th and early 16th Century' (unpublished M.Litt. thesis, University of Bristol, 1971); Robert R. Wright 'Parnell and Burles' *East Anglian Magazine* 33 (April 1974) 324–6; Alan H. Nelson *The Medieval English Stage: Corpus Christi Pageants and Plays* (Chicago and London: University of Chicago Press, 1974) 123; Nicola Coldstream 'The Roles of Women in Late Medieval Civic Pageantry in England' in *Reassessing the Roles of Women as makers of Medieval Art and Architecture* edited Therese Martin (Leiden and Boston: Brill, 2012) 175–94 at 190–4. She confuses John and William Parnell, 191; see 190 note 60, where she says that, 'The event is difficult to clarify since the Chamberlain's [*sic*] Accounts used by Harrod are currently untraceable in the Norfolk Record Office'. Clearly, this is not so. A translation of most of NCR18a–2 is given in Robert R. Wright 'Theatre in Late-Medieval East Anglia' (unpublished Ph.D. thesis, University of Leicester, 1992) 343–9.

of NCR 18a–2 offer additional information concerning Parnell's range of theatrical projects which enable us to consider him as what was later to be designated a 'property player'.

Although Elizabeth's visit to Norwich began on 18 July, the accounts in question were not compiled until 1472, some three years later. One month before the Queen's visit, in June, King Edward IV had visited Norwich accompanied by his brother, Richard, Duke of Gloucester, later King Richard III.[8] At this time Elizabeth did not accompany her husband. Both visits seem to have taken place under adverse weather conditions: the Queen's Entry was affected by heavy rain that caused damage to the stations and their settings. This clearly interfered with the plans of the organisers.

The King and Queen arrived through different gates on their respective visits to the city: Elizabeth arrived through the Westwyck Gate (later, St Benedict's Gate), to the west of the city and Edward entered through the Nedeham Gate (later, St Stephen's Gate), to the south of the city. Ostensibly, the accounts are primarily concerned with the Entry of Elizabeth into Norwich. However, careful analysis reveals that some invoices have been incorporated into this document from Edward's earlier Entry. The reasons for this are unclear, but it does cast doubts on the accuracy of an account that was drawn up some three years after the events that it purported to detail. The scribe himself seems to be confused about whether some payments should be attributed to the Entry of the Queen or of the King. For example, one item on fol. 10^{r} records payment for refreshments for 'the King's' Entry which is then corrected by the scribe to 'the Queen's': *Item solutum per discrecionem duorum prouisorum pro vno repastu hospitatorum domine ~~Regis~~ Regine infra mansum henrici Bradffeld viijd.* Conversely, on fol. 14^{r}, an item for the King's Entry is placed under the heading *Plus de aduentu Regine* ('More concerning the Entry of the Queen'). In another item (fol. 11^{r}), the scribe vacillates between the two, first citing the Entry of the 'King', which is then altered to the 'Queen' and then back to the 'King':

> *Item solutum Willelmo Bisshope pro duobus tiatris preparandis forma que facta fuerunt erga aduentum ~~domini Regis~~ ∧~~Regine~~ domini Regis quorum vnum ad portas fratrum predicatorum & aliud ad portas de Westwyk.*

8. Elizabeth's and Edward's routes into and through the city can be deduced from the document, but we are not aware of corroborating evidence from elsewhere. Blomefield refers to Edward being 'grandly received' in 1469, but offers no details: Francis Blomefield *Essay towards a Topographical History of the County of Norfolk* 4 vols (London: Miller, 1806) 3 716. He does not mention Elizabeth.

Even then, as the places mentioned show, the last correction is confusing; the places given refer to the Queen's route, though the patterns are presumably those drawn up for the King's reception. Because of this kind of confusion, we have extracted the accounts concerning Edward's Entry and recorded them separately in Appendix 2 to enable the reader to distinguish between the two.

The different entry points into the city of Elizabeth and Edward help us to recognise and separate the accounts that relate to the two visits. Two stations were erected for Elizabeth: one at the Westwyck Gate, and one at the gates of the Dominican Friars.[9] Similarly, two stations were built for the Entry of Edward: one at the Nedeham Gate, and one in the marketplace.[10]

Staging preparations involved the construction of two *tiatri seu staciones* ('theatres or stations'). The route of the Queen's Entry was a straight one from the Westwyk Gate down what is still called St Benedict's Street to the gates of the Dominican Friars (see FIGURE 1]. The nave of the Friary church still exists and is now called St Andrew's Hall, or The Halls.[11] At that time, as the Cuningham map (1559)[12] shows, the Friary was surrounded by a wall, though the map does not show a gate. It had, however, a preaching yard (*ortus sermonum*) to the south side (facing Princes Street) to which the gate presumably gave access.

John Aubry, the Mayor of Norwich, involved the Common Council, Chamberlains, Aldermen, and auditors in the provision and organisation of skilled staff to prepare for the Queen's Entry. Chief among these were William Bisshope and William Parnell. These two men evidently worked closely together: their skills were the same yet different. Both were carpenters and skilled with wood. But Parnell possessed additional skills for which he was engaged at Norwich. Of the two, Bisshope is described as the carpenter who appears to have conceived and built the wooden structures of the stations, whereas Parnell is described as *Pernelle de Gipewico* ('Parnelle [Parnell] of

9. Westwyck Gate: fols 10^{r}–13^{v}; Dominican friars: fols 10^{v}–12^{r}.
10. Nedeham Gate: fols 12^{r}, 14^{r}; marketplace: fols 10^{r}, 14^{r}.
11. Nikolas Pevsner and Bill Wilson *Norfolk I: Norwich and North-East* (The Buildings of England, New Haven and London: Yale University Press, 2002) 265–9, 280–1. Harrod assumes that the Queen was staying at the Friary.
12. William Cuningham *The cosmographical glasse conteinyng the pleasant principles of cosmographie, geographie, hydrographie, or nauigation* (London: John Day, 1559), foldout between fols 8 and 9. See interactive map at <http://www.norwich-heritage.co.uk/norwich_maps/1558_Cuningham_zoomify.htm>.

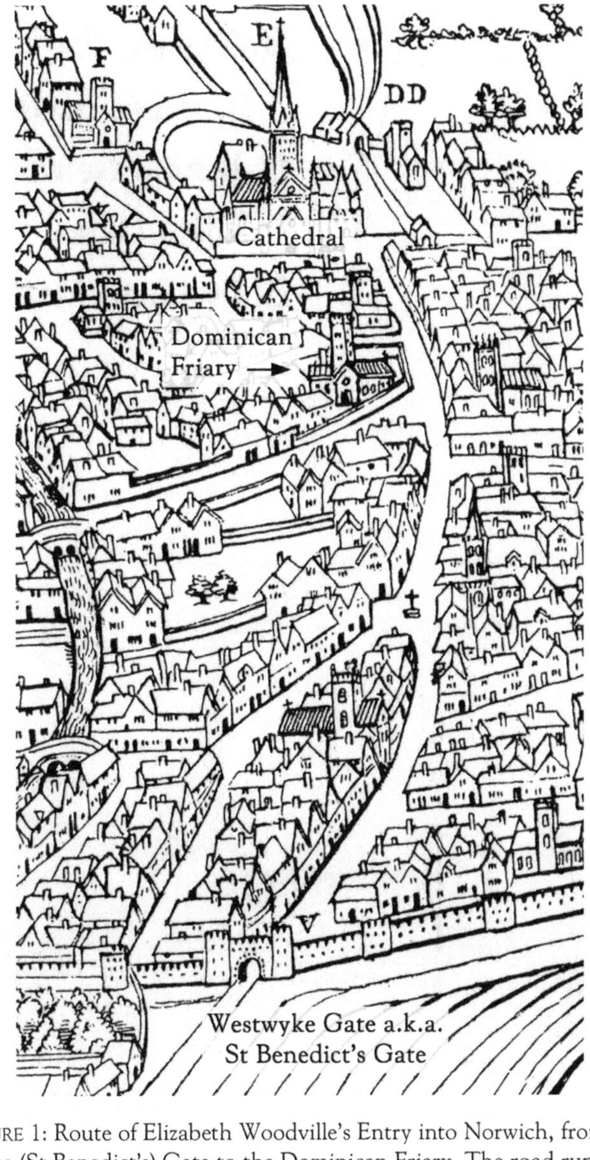

FIGURE 1: Route of Elizabeth Woodville's Entry into Norwich, from the Westwyke (St Benedict's) Gate to the Dominican Friary. The road runs roughly west to east. Base map from Cuningham's *Cosmographical Glasse* (1559). Image © Norfolk Museums Service (Norwich Castle Museum & Art Gallery).

FIGURE 2: St Benedict's (Westwyck) Gate from outside, engraved by Henry Ninham (1864) from the drawing by John Kirkpatrick (1720). Norwich Castle Museum and Art Gallery 1954.138, Todd 5, Norwich, 111b. Image © Norfolk Museums Service (Norwich Castle Museum & Art Gallery).

Ipswich')[13] *qui frequentat prouidere subtilia ludorum & stacionum* ('who regularly supplies ingenious devices for plays and stations': fol. 10^{r}). Parnell was paid 6s for his labour and travel expenses from Ipswich to Norwich: *pro suis labore & expensis de ~~Norwico~~ Gipwico usque Norwicum* (fol. 10^{r}), and 3s for board and lodging:

> *Item in mensa supradicti hominis de Gipwico vocati Pernel existentis apud Norwicum tempore preparacionis dictarum Stacionum per xij dies – ijs Item pro lecto suo per idem tempus – xijd*

> Item in board for the above-mentioned man called Pernel from Ipswich staying in Norwich for twelve days at the time of setting up the said stations: 2s Item for his lodging over the same period: 12d fol. 11^{r}

He brought a number of men to work with him: *Item in denarijs ad diuersos repastus causa reficiendi expensis super dictum Pernelle & famulos suos*[14] *ad duas vices viijd* ('Item monies paid for several meals as refreshments for the aforementioned Pernelle and his men on two occasions: 8d': fol. 10^{r}). Parnell was responsible for 'dressing' the stations and providing associated accoutrements at both locations from Thursday 6 July.

The nature of the two *tiatri seu staciones* ('theatres or stations') is not immediately obvious. An initial assumption might be that these stations consisted of some form of platform stage built out from the gate arches. Was the station at the Westwyck Gate built upon the existing stone surround of the gate or was it an independent structure positioned near the Gate? Given the associated symbolism of the Queen's 'Entry' into the City it seems more likely that the structural edifice was constructed up against and around the gate itself. Almost certainly, platform levels were involved with their lower frameworks covered, in whole or in part, with 'tapserwerk'. *Tapserwerk* is 'tapestry work': it was used to adorn the frameworks of the levels and was borrowed from the Friars Minor and cleaned by 'a certain fuller':

> *Item in locione & mundacione iiij^{or} peciarum panni de Tapserwerk pertinencium ffratribus minoribus qui ab eis fuerant conducti pro vestigijs graduum ad tiatra ascendencium sic mundatum per quendam ffullonem xd*

13. Name variously recorded as *Pernel*, *Pernell*, and *Pernelle*.

14. *Famulus* implies a household servant, possibly an apprentice.

> Item for washing and cleaning four pieces of cloth of *Tapserwerk* belonging to the Friars Minor, which were hired from them for the rising tiers at the theatres as cleaned by a certain Fuller: 10d fol. 10v

It is just possible, but unlikely, that *tapserwerk* could be used of a painted cloth.[15]

Analogous English examples of entries through city gates may be seen in the drawings of the roughly contemporaneous *Beauchamp Pageants* (c.1483–92). They record structures that make accomplished use of space, levels, and architectural features.[16] Presumably, similar care went into the Norwich stations in organising space for performers, representational figures, and architectural structures. Among John Kirkpatrick's drawings of the Norwich Gates in 1720 is one depicting an outside view of St Benedict's Gate (formerly known as the Westwyck Gate; FIGURE 2).[17] Here, walls project from either side of the arch and their respective heights reach to about half that of the gate arch.[18] The Ninham/Kirkpatrick image implies that the road up to the arch denotes the presence of the ditch, in that the adjacent buildings extend below the level of the road. One or other of these walls appears to have been damaged during construction of the station, for the accounts record:

15. See *Oxford English Dictionary Online* sv †*tapisser n*; *Middle English Dictionary* sv *tapicer* n. (b). *Tapser/tapcer* is a fairly common spelling.

16. *Pageant of the Birth Life and Death of Richard Beauchamp Earl of Warwick* K.G. *1389–1439* edited Viscount Dillon and W.H. St John Hope (London: Longmans Green, 1914); *The Beauchamp Pageants* edited and introduced Alexandra Sinclair (Donington: Richard III and Yorkist Trust/Paul Watkins, 2003); see especially the drawings on 54 (fol. 1v), 57 (fol. 2r), and 58 (fol. 2v).

17. *Views of the Ancient City Gates of Norwich, As they appeared in 1722. Drawn and etched by Henry Ninham, From Original Sketches by John Kirkpatrick*, introduction Roy Ballard (Norwich: University of East Anglia, 1982) unpaginated. The drawing itself is dated 1720 although the title states 1722.

18. There was a water-filled 8-metre ditch on that side of the city. See <https://www.norwich.gov.uk/site/custom_scripts/citywalls/17/report.php>; City Walls Survey 17: St Benedict's Gate. In 1910 an excavation report by Arthur E. Collins gave the dimensions of the remains of the surviving south side of the Westwyck gate-opening as 11ft long and about 8ft high. This did not include the arch. The tower in which the gate was set had an upper room, and access by a stairway to the roof and its crenellated parapet, which could have been useful for access.

> *Item in stipendio duorum lathamorum insimul conductorum & operancium per ij dies dimidiam pro reparacione parietum ad ingressum portarum per diem insimul xijd – ~~ijs vjd~~ iiijd – ijs vjd*
>
> Item for wages of two masons hired together and working for two and a half days to repair the wall at the entrance to the Gates, both per day, 12d: 2s 6d fol. 10^{r}

The assumption is that these ancillary walls were present in 1469 when one of them was damaged during the construction of the station. This item in the accounts adds further weight to the case for the station being built against the existing gateway. Although horizontal stage space may have been necessary for the speakers and singers, many of the payments in the accounts refer to staging accoutrements that were seemingly clustered in the available space to form some kind of three-dimensional structured edifice surrounding the gate under which the Queen entered the city.[19] Any available horizontal space seems likely to have been located on either side of the gates and above the existing arch at Westwyck.

The same sort of arrangement is probable at the gates of the Dominican Friars, where additional height and structural security appear to have been made possible by the erection and attachment of two masts at the gates: a payment of 4d is recorded to a carpenter for the putting up of two poles referred to as *lez mastes*: *solutum pro eorum labore in erigendo lez mastes pro tiatro predicto – iiijd* (fol. 11^{r}). These masts appear to be those which had already been used in the marketplace for the King's Entry:

> *Item solutum tenentibus Roperie in foro pro inhospitacione ~~duarum~~ duorum lignorum longorum & altorum prius occupatorum pro stacione in foro erga aduentum Regis & ibidem reseruatorum a pluuia – ijd*
>
> Item paid to the householders of the Ropery in the Marketplace for accommodating two long tall wooden beams previously used for the

19. An ordinance of 1276 in London required the minimum height of protruding jetties of buildings to be 9 feet in order to permit horse and rider to pass underneath: *Calendar of Letter-Books Preserved among the Archives of the Corporation of the City of London at the Guildhall, Letter-Book A. Circa A.D. 1275–1298* edited Reginald R. Sharpe (London: John Edward Francis, 1899) 217; see also *Munimenta Gildhallæ Londoniensis; Liber Albus, Liber Custumarum, et Liber Horn* edited Henry Thomas Riley, 3 parts in 4 vols (London: Longman, Green, Longman, and Roberts, 1862) *3* 89.

> stage in the Marketplace on the occasion of the Entry of the King and therein sheltered from the rain: 2d fol. 10r

An invoice presented by John Burton asks for payment for one workman digging out the pits for the masts to be placed in them: *iiijd pro stipendio vnius laborarii pro factura foraminum pro lez mastys ibidem imponendis* ('4d for the wage of one workman for making the pits to put *lez mastys* in there': fol. 11v). These masts appear to have been embedded in holes dug in the ground and surrounded by mortar in order to bind and hold them firm. The presence of mortar to bind the posts in their holes is implied by payment for mixing of burnt lime, or quicklime, which was an ingredient of mortar: *Item solutum duobus laborarijs conductis pro calce combusta temperanda viijd* ('Item paid to two labourers hired for the mixing of burnt lime: 8d': fol. 10r).[20] Payment was also made for removing the masts after the event: *Item solutum Willelmo Bisshope carpentario pro deposicione de* [space] *ij mastis a tiatro ad portas fratrum dominicalium – iiijd* ('Item paid to William Bisshope, carpenter, for taking down of [space] 2 *mastis* from the theatre at the gates of the Dominican Friars: 4d': fol. 10v). From a structural point of view, it was clearly necessary to anchor the masts in the ground but this, of itself, would not create the necessary strength and security for any other connected timbers at a higher level. The masts would also need to be secured at a higher level to the gate entablature. This principle may be seen in the modern use of scaffolding on the outside of buildings where temporary holes are cut or drilled into the fabric of the building to secure the scaffolding as it gets higher. These holes can be filled in once the scaffolding is removed. Here, the height and style of the construction are implied by payments made to three sculptors for the erection of turrets and removing them after the visit: *Item solutum tribus sculptoribus pro suis labore & expensis tempore exaltacionis turrium ad tiatrum versus portas fratrum & deposicione earundem – xijd* ('Item paid to three sculptors for their labour and expenses when putting up the turrets at the theatre at the Friars' Gates and taking them down: 12d': fol. 13v). Another payment was made to Robert Welles for providing a finial: *in denarijs solutis per filiulium Roberto Welles – ijd* (fol. 13r), though it is not clear whether this last payment was

20. *OED* sv *lime* 3.a. 'The alkaline earth which is the chief constituent of mortar; calcium oxide (CaO). It is obtained by submitting limestone (carbonate of lime) to a red heat, by which the carbonic acid is driven off, leaving a brittle white solid, which is pure lime (or quick-lime). It is powerfully caustic and combines readily with water, evolving great heat in the process, and forming hydrate of lime (*slaked lime*)'.

towards construction (or more probably repairs) at the Dominican Friars or at the Westwyck Gate. Payment for making good after the works is recorded as *Item solutum vni laborario pro implecione foraminum post remoccionem tiatri seu stacionis ad portas fratrum dominicalium impletorum cum arena – iiijd* ('Item paid to a workman for filling of holes [left] after the removal of the theatre or station at the Gates of the Dominican Friars with sand: 4d': fol. 10^{v}).

Additionally and/or alternatively, the masts may have been used to support an awning, for payment is recorded for whipcord to secure awnings: *in whipcorde empto pro velis stringendis – jd* ('Item for whipcord bought for securing the awnings: 1d': fol. 11^{r}). Payment is also recorded for badly damaged green worsted which had been used over 'extensions' (possibly awnings) which was recycled for the aldermen's seats in the preaching yard of the Friary:

> *xviijs pro j pecia de worstede viride lesata grauiter super extenciones ad tiatra & ideo empta & liberata pro sedibus aldermannorum ad ~~ser~~ ~~ortum~~ ortum sermonum infra prioratum*

> 18s for 1 piece of green worsted, badly damaged, over the extensions at the theatres and therefore purchased and delivered for the seats of the aldermen at the preaching yard within the Priory fol. 12^{v}

It is not clear at what point they decided to use awnings. Was it part of the original conception? In which case such awnings might have been considered as protection from the sun as much as the rain. Or were the awnings erected in response to the weather conditions on the day?

It is not clear whether or not the Queen passed through the Dominican Friars' Gates. The fact that the aldermen were sitting on stands *ad ortum sermonum infra prioratum* ('at the preaching yard within the Priory': fol. 12^{v}) inside the walls suggests that she did. We do not know what size the gates were: either they had sufficient height and width for horse-backed riders and/or any attendant vehicles to pass through, or the normal gates were presumably removed temporarily.

The practical construction of the stations for the Queen's entry was due to Bisshope, for the accounts record that he was paid

> *pro duobus tiatris preparandis forma que facta fuerunt erga aduentum ~~domini Regis~~ ^ ~~Regine~~ domini Regis quorum vnum ad portas fratrum predicatorum & aliud ad portas de Westwyk ex conuentione secum facta in grosso – xxxiijs iiijd*

> for two theatres to be prepared according to the constructional design [of those] which were made for the visit of the ~~Lord King~~ ^~~Queen~~ Lord King of which one at the Gates of the Preaching Friars and the other at Westwyk Gates; as agreed with him, inclusively: 33s 4d fol. 11^{r}

This item implies that Bisshope was involved in constructing the stations for the Queen but not the King, even though the Queen's stations were apparently modelled on those of the King. It is not recorded who constructed the stations at the Nedeham Gate and the marketplace for the King's visit, although their deviser/organiser was Walter Geoffrays, scrivener and alderman, who was considered to possess great experience of such things: *pro suis aduisamento discrecione & labore habitis in prouisionibus stacionum Regis qui in talibus magnam habet experienciam* ('for his advice, decisions, and work in supplying the stations of the King ... who has great experience of such things': fol. 14^{r}). He also appears to have composed the 'many and diverse texts' written on scrolls which were placed on these structures: *ac concepcionem diuersorum & plurimorum textorum positorum super tiatra ad portas de Nedeham et in foro* ('for his formulation of the many and diverse texts placed on the theatres at Nedeham Gates and in the Marketplace': fol. 14^{r}).[21]

In the fifteenth century the economic power of the city of Norwich was based on its domination of the worsted trade. It is therefore not too surprising that the account makes a number of payments for the provision of worsted as hangings for the stations. Parnell and his team made use of white worsted in the construction of the lower framework of the stations: *Item solutum pro suicione ~~de~~ quatuor peciarum albarum de worstede pro anteriore facie stacionum – xvjd* ('Item paid for the sewing of four pieces of white worsted for the front facade of the stations: 16d': fol. 10^{v}). Additional worsted used to decorate one of the stations was borrowed from John Colman:

> *Item in regardo dato Johanni Colman pro refeccione de le Calaundryng ix peciarum de worstedes ab ipso mutuatarum pro ornacione stacionum & pro mundacione ~~earund~~ earundem postquam fuerant grauiter pollute ac pro suicione diuersorum foraminum in eisdem factorum per lesiones hamorum iiijs vjd*

> Item in reward given to John Colman for redoing the pressing of 9 pieces of worsted borrowed from him to decorate the stations and for

21. These scrolls are referred to in detail on fol. 11^{r}.

> cleaning them after they were badly soiled and for sewing up several holes made in them by the piercing of hooks fol. 11r

The accounts also record payment to the Chamberlains, Reginald Harvey and Thomas Lynne, who were deputed to acquire the worsted:

> *xxijs solutis pro le Calaundryng[e] & lesione xj peciarum de worstedes vocatarum medel beddes que liberate fuerunt Reginaldo Harneys & Thome Lynne assignatis ad prouidendum Worstedes pro tiatris preparandis*

> 22s paid for the pressing and damage of 11 pieces of worsted called *medel beddes* which had been delivered to Reginald Harneys and Thomas Lynne, appointed to supply worsted for preparation of the theatres fol. 12v [22]

The worsted was damaged by exposure to the torrential rain. A number of further payments were made for drying it out and rolling it smooth (*calendaring*) once it was dry or nearly dry. Some green worsted was reused to cover seats for the aldermen in the preaching yard at the Priory:

> *xviijs pro j pecia de worstede viride lesata grauiter super extenciones ad tiatra & ideo empta & liberata pro sedibus aldermannorum ad ~~ser ortum~~ ortum sermonum infra prioratum*

22. *MED* sv *medlen* v. 1.b. 'ppl. *medled*, as adj.: (a) having a mixed constitution; (b) of cloth: = *medle* adj.; also, *medle* n. 2; *OED* sv *medley* n.: II. Specialized uses involving a mixture of component parts. 2. A type of cloth made of wools dyed (frequently in different shades or colours) and mixed before being spun; = *medley cloth* n. at Compounds.'

    OED sv *bed* n. 1 a. 'Often used by metonymy for "bedding": 1424 in F.J. Furnivall *Fifty Earliest Eng. Wills* (1882) 57 I wul þat ilk of my said childre haue a bed, þat is to say, couerlide, tapite, blankettis, too peyre schetes, matras, and canvas; (1411) *EEWills* 19/2: A reed bedde of worsteyd, with costers ... with a canvase, a materas, a pare of Blankettes, ij pare of schetys'. *MED* sv *bed* (2) 'From sv *bed* n. (1); cp. L *lectus*, a cloth or tapestry spread on the ground. (a) Cloth woven to a specified size; ?a bolt, ?a carpet or hanging'.

    Alternatively *medel beddes* might be 'beds of medium size'; see for spelling *OED* sv. *middle* adj. and n. Worsted was also sold in standard bed sizes: large beds: 14 × 4 yards; medium beds: 12 × 3 yards; small beds (these accounts *litel beddys*, fol. 12v): 10 × 2.5 yards. See Dana Durkee *Social Mobility and the Worsted Weavers of Norwich c.1450 to 1530* (Ph.D. thesis, Durham University, 2017) 164; online at <http://etheses.dur.ac.uk/12208/>. Unfortunately neither *OED* nor *MED* give these meanings.

> 18s for 1 piece of green worsted, badly damaged over the extensions [awnings?] at the theatres and therefore purchased and delivered for the seats of the aldermen at the preaching yard within the Priory
>
> fol. 12^{v}

Seven pieces of red worsted were taken to the house of the supervisors and payment was made for cleaning, drying, and rolling up of the cloth: *pro mundacione & desiccacione ac honesta revolucione* ~~*ser*~~ *septem peciarum rubiarum worstede cum portacione earundem ad domum appropriatorum ixd* ('Item paid for cleaning and drying and careful rolling up [...] of seven pieces of red worsted cloth with carrying of same to the house of the supervisors: 9d': fol. 10^{v}). Were it not for these payments, we would not know about the details of the set dressing and the probable impact of the colours.

All the costumes were also saturated, and appear to have been rescued from the Westwyk gate presentation and ultimately saved by drying them out in the solar of the Guildhall:

> *datum tribus hominibus pro suo labore & expensis portantibus omnes illas vestes ad solara* ^in *Guyhalda ibidem ad* ~~*desij*~~ *desiccandas pro eo quod grauiter* ~~*mae*~~ *madefacti fuerunt per pluuias continuas & grandes vjd ... solutum pro attendencia & pro eisdem pannis post desiccacionem voluendis vjd*

> paid to three men for their labour and expenses in carrying all these trappings to the solar in the Guildhall for drying because they had been seriously soaked by the continuous heavy rains: 6d fol. 10^{v}

There were two painted banners impaling the King's and Queen's arms, fourteen square scutcheons painted on linen, and two 'powdered' with roses and fleurs-de-lys:

> *Item pro* ~~*iij*~~ *duobus vexillis armorum domini Regis & Regine* ~~*separatorum*~~ *iunctorum in vno vexillo depingendis iiijs viijd Item similiter pro xiiij square scucheons depingendis in panno lineo viijs ijd Item similiter pro ij scucheons de powderyngges depictis cum Rosis & flourdelys – xd*

> Item, for painting 2 armorial banners bearing the ~~separate~~ impaled arms of the Lord King and Queen in one banner, 4s 8d; item similarly, for painting 14 *square* escutcheons on linen cloth, 8s 2d; item, similarly, for 2 escutcheons of powderings painted with roses and fleurs-de-lys, 10d fol. 12^{r}

Further payment is recorded *in factura xxiiij powdryngges cum coronis et rosis & flour delycez – xvjs ~~viijd~~ precium cuiuslibet viijd* ('for making up 24 *powdryngges* with crowns and roses and fleurs-de-lys: 16s ~~8d~~, price each one 8d': fol. 13r), possibly for the hangings. The *OED* defines *powdering* as 'The decorative application of a pattern of small spots, figures, heraldic devices, etc., giving the appearance of having been sprinkled or scattered over a surface; a decorative pattern of this kind; (in *pl.*) the spots or figures of such decoration'.[23]

Perhaps the largest and most precious property to be utilised in the presentation at the gates of the Friars was the throne from Norwich Priory:

> *Item solutum diuersis Carpentarijs & alijs hominibus adiuuantibus pro magna Cathedra gilde sancti luce portanda de prioratu Norwici usque tiatrum ad portas fratrum – ijs; Item solutum Simoni Tabard Carpentario pro suo labore & vij hominum suorum ad deponendam magnam Cathedram predictam pro salua preseruacione eiusdem ne lederetur – xxijd*
>
> Item paid to several carpenters and other men helping them carry the great throne of the Guild of St Luke from Norwich Priory to the theatre at the Friars' Gates: 2s. Item paid to Simon Tabard, carpenter, for his work and that of 7 of his men in taking away the aforesaid great throne for its safekeeping, lest it should be harmed: 22d fol. 11r

Clearly, the splendour of the throne was important to Parnell's vision. An immediate assumption might be that Elizabeth, herself, was intended to occupy the throne, but this seems unlikely, as the royal personage in an Entry never occupies a place on the scaffold, even if an actor is employed to present them with an image of themselves. The Queen would not have been required to descend from her horse or carriage and traipse through the mud to occupy the throne at a higher level. It is possible that the throne was incorporated into the visual conception of the station to contain an image, or person, to represent the Virgin Mary as Queen of Heaven.

Representations of angels were created. Their fittings were tied onto them: *Item in punctubus emptis pro ornamentis angelorum attachiandis – iijd* ('Item for points [laces] purchased to fasten the ornaments of the angels: 3d': fol. 10r), and *Item in vno homine conducto pro imposicione punctium & preparacione dictorum ornamentorum super dictorum angelorum corpora ijd* ('Item for one man

23. *OED* sv *powdering* II. 4. See *OED* examples.

hired to attach the points and to prepare said ornaments on the bodies of the said angels: 2d': fol. 10^r).

At the Westwyk Gate as entrance to the city, there were two giants made of wood, leather and cloth, their bodies stuffed with hay. Presumably the giants represented Samson and Hercules as guardians of the City.[24] Payment of 8d is recorded to John Norton, tailor, and three of his colleagues 'for sewing back together the giants previously made and dismantled': *Item in expensis Johannis Norton Taillour & iij sociorum suorum consuencium gigantes prius ~~factas~~ factos & diruptos – viijd* (fol. 10^r). White thread was bought for this purpose from the widow Northales: *Item in filo albo empto de vxore Northales pro eisdem consuendis – ijd* (fol. 10^r). Barrel hoops of wood formed the framework upon which the giants were constructed: *Item solutum cuidam Cowper ~~manda~~ manenti in foro Norwico pro vno cultello de ipso mutuato pro circulis ad facturam Gigancium & per operarios fracto – iijd* ('Item paid to a certain Cooper dwelling in the Marketplace at Norwich, for a knife borrowed from him for the hoops for making the Giants, and broken by the workmen': fol. 10^v). Their bodies were packed with hay and their *crests* [helmets?] were covered with gold and silver leaf:

> *in v pellibus de auro precium cuiuslibet xd & xxiiij pellibus de b[e]rmerari argenti precium cuiuslibet ijd quadrans emptis per Thomam Heruy & famulum Pernelli pro refeccione cresturarum gigancium viijs viijd*
>
> for 5 skins of gold [leaf], price of each 10d, and 24 skins of silver vermeil, price 2¼d each, purchased by Thomas Hervy and the servant of Pernelle for refurbishing the crests of the giants: 8s 8d fol. 13^v

In addition, payments are recorded for costumes for at least two patriarchs (fol. 10^v) and three Empresses: *solutum pro iij mantallis tribus sercotes & tribus coronis triplicibus pro tribus Imperatricibus preparatis & ad guyhaldam portatis ad desiccandos – jd* ('paid for 3 cloaks, three *surcotes*, and three triple crowns for three Empresses, prepared and carried to the Guildhall to be dried out: 1d': fol. 10^v). There were also twelve Apostles and sixteen virgins, all elaborately dressed:

> *solutum Johanni Thorpe ~~pro vij mantelys viij caplettis~~ per billam impositam tam pro conduccione diuersorum vestimentorum pro apostolis & virginibus*

24. See Francis Blomefield *Essay towards a Topographical History of the County of Norfolk* 4 vols (London: Miller, 1806) *4* 367; *REED: Norwich* 8–9 also records giants in pageants in 1542.

> *cum ijs pro vij mantellis & viij caplettis peioratis per grandem pluuium vjs viijd xij mantellis pro apostolis xvj mantellis cum caplettis pro virginibus & aliis diuersis vestibus*
>
> Item paid to John Thorp for ~~7 mantles, 8 chaplets~~ as presented in his invoice, as much as for rescuing several garments for the apostles and the virgins, [with] 2s; for 7 mantles and 8 chaplets damaged by the great rain, 6s 8d; 12 mantles for the apostles, 16 mantles with chaplets for the virgins and various other garments fol. 11^{v}

It is not clear how many of these were dummy figures, but the sixteen virgins were made of linen and painted: *in iij virginibus panni linei precium virginis viijd traditis dicto pernelle ad depingendum in ~~re..~~ rebus necessarijs* – ijs ('for 3 virgins of linen cloth, price per virgin 8d, brought to the said Pernelle for painting with the requisite things: 2s': fol. 13^{r}). Another seven virgins were taken to John Coke, chamberlain, for delivery to the painters (price 3d per virgin) and six more were painted by a certain Mayhew with coats of arms of the King and Queen (price 5d per virgin):

> *Item in vij virginibus panni linei traditis Johanni Coke vni Camerario ad liberandum depictoribus precium virginis iijd – xxxjd Item in vj virginibus panni linei traditis cuidam Mayhew ad pingendum scuta de armis Regis & Regine precium virginis vd – ijs vjd* fol. 13^{r}

Ten of the sixteen virgins of cloth were taken to Henry Steyn*our* to have *lez valences* fitted:

> *Item in x virginibus panni linei traditis cuidam Henry Steynour pro lez valences tam ad tiatrum ad portas fratrum quam ad portas de Westwyk [space] precium virgine vd – iiijs ijd*
>
> Item for 10 virgins of linen cloth handed over to a certain Henry Steyn*our* for *lez valences*, both at the theatre at the Friars' Gates and at Westwyk Gates, price per virgin 5d: 4s 2d fol. 13^{r}

Whether *lez valences* were veils (of *valence*) or skirts (*valances*) to mask the lower parts of the virgins is unclear.[25] They were shared between the two

25. See *OED* sv *valence* n. 'Some thin woven fabric' (both the examples given are of see-through veils); and *valance* n, our *valance*, '1. A piece of drapery attached

stations. After the presentations all the painted dummies were taken back to the upper room of the Guildhall and stored in straw: *solutum cuidam Ramseye pro stramine ad cubila depictorum fienda in alta camera* Guyhalde ('paid to a certain Ramseye for straw to make nests for the painted figures in the upper chamber of the Guildhall': fol. 13v).

An unnamed friar took part in the play/presentation of Gabriel: '*Item datum cuidam ffratri assignato ad ludum Gabriel[is] cum [d] cibo & potu ad vices – xvjd* ('Item given to a certain friar assigned to the play of Gabriel, with food and drink on several occasions, 16d': fol. 11r). The assumption is that the friar who was assigned to the play of Gabriel delivered a speech or speeches as monologue(s) in much the same sort of theatrical way as the Four Cardinal Virtues at the entry of Queen Margaret into Coventry in 1456.[26] It is interesting to note that the friar was apparently paid for taking part in this play/presentation of *Gabriel* and he, like Parnell, came from outside the immediate region, since payment is also recorded for his board, as with that of other visitors (fol. 11r). Whether this play/presentation involved other unrecorded and unpaid players is not clear. It is possible that the unnamed friar was the only speaker who delivered a monologue or an oration in character. There are no other itemised payments to anyone else involved in this *ludus* other than that of 18d (fol. 11v) to the glasier, John Munford, *pro mensa & attendencia filij sui assignati pro s monstracione Gabriel* ('for board and attendance of his son assigned to the show of Gabriel'). The age of Munford's son is not indicated and the implication is that he was engaged in an ancillary capacity or a minor performance role. The 18d may largely have been intended for his son's board. The son might, however, have been playing Mary in an Annunciation. At this time, the Queen had three daughters but no son, and an Annunciation could be a tactful hint to her, especially since, in addition, Geoffrey Spirleng, chamberlain and scribe, presented a pageant or *tableau vivant* of the Salutation of Mary and Elizabeth in which he may have operated as Expositor:

> *Item in regardo dato Galfrido Spirleng pro sua diligencia in prouisione dictarum stacionum ac pro factura loquelarum expositarum ad faciem Regine*

lengthways to a canopy, altar-cloth, or the like, so as to hang in a vertical position', especially used, as now, of a lower bed-hanging.

26. See *The Coventry Leet Book: Part One* edited Mary Dormer Harris *EETS OS 134* (1907) 285–92, at 288–9; Thomas Sharp *A Dissertation on the pageants or Dramatic Mysteries Anciently performed at Coventry* (Coventry: Merridew, 1825) 145–51.

> *ac salutacionis Marie & Elizabethe breuiter manifestate per discrecionem iam Auditorum & Superuisorum dictarum stacionum nil hic quia postea in pede*
>
> Item bonus paid to Geoffrey Spirleng[27] for his diligence in the furnishing of the said stations and for the making of expository speeches delivered to the Queen and of the salutation of Mary and Elizabeth briefly performed; through the discretion of the auditors and supervisors of the said stations; no amount shown here because included below fol. 13v

It is not clear from this payment to Spirleng whether he simply wrote the speeches or spoke them – or both. Spirleng, the scrivener, does not need to have possessed playing skill in order to deliver expository speeches. A clear voice, sufficiently audible and demonstrating understanding of the text, would carry him through an expository function. The payment to him is recorded as a bonus which may support the possibility that he also delivered his role in performance. It may have been the case that Spirleng's work was 'diligent', but when it is understood that Spirleng himself wrote this account it is clear that he was giving himself a congratulatory pat on the back.[28]

Further payment is recorded for exposition: *Item datum utrique duorum baculariorum in Theologia assignatorum pro expositoribus iijs iiijd vjs viijd* ('Item given to each of two bachelors of theology appointed as expositors, 3s 4d: 6s 8d': fol. 11r).

Choral work was provided by two separate groups of choristers at both gates: *Item in regardo dato cuidam ffakke cum pueris suis cantantibus curiose*[29]

27. Harrod records Geoffrey Spirleng as 'Gilbert'. This variation has been copied by others. See Robert Withington *English Pageantry: An Historical Outline* 2 vols (Cambridge, Mass: Harvard University Press, 1918) *1* 152–3; Coldstream 'The Roles of Women in Late Medieval Civic Pageantry in England' 191.

28. Not only did Spirleng write this account of Elizabeth Woodville's visit but he was also responsible for writing all the Chamberlains' Accounts from 1470 to 1490. See Beadle 'Geoffrey Spirleng' 127.

29. *DMLBS* sv *curiosus* 2: *cantus curiosus*, 'pricksong', c.1500. Classical Latin *curiosus* means 'taking pains' (*cura*). In the vernacular it develops a sense of 'taking extreme pains over something that requires a great deal of skill', by transference 'elaborate, complex, unusual'. This would apply to elaborate polyphony. *Prick+song* is chant that is so complex it needs to be written down ('pricked'). See *MED* sv *curious*: 'a1500 (a1460) Towneley Pl. (Hnt HM 1) 110/305: What was that sang? It was wonder curiose, with small notys emang' – of the angel singing *Gloria in excelsis*.

super tiatrum ad portas fratrum predicatorum – ijs ~~ijs~~ ('Item in reward to a certain Fakke and his boys singing pricksong on the theatre at the Gates of the Preaching Friars: 2s': fol. 11r), and *Item datum pluribus Clericis curiose cantantibus ad tiatrum ad portas de Westwyk inter se – xxd* ('Item given to numerous clerics singing pricksong at the theatre at Westwyk Gates, between them: 20d': fol. 11r). Further music was provided by a clerical organist: *Item datum cuidam clerici ludenti ad organa – viijd* ('Item given to a certain cleric for playing the organs: 8d: fol. 11r).

No doubt the Norwich Chamberlains sought to engage Parnell as rapidly as they could because of his existing and growing reputation in the provision of staging and its ornamentation. This being said, the depth and range of his work has only been referred to briefly and tangentially in existing scholarship.[30] Parnell is not only recognised in the Norwich accounts as someone *qui frequentat prouidere subtilia ludorum & stacionum* (fol. 10r), but he is also recorded in the London records as a model-maker and in the Ipswich records, as a carpenter. In 1474, William, the father, John, his son, and an apprentice, William Baker, worked together at the church of St Botolph, Billingsgate, London, on the construction of a wooden semi-automaton known as the 'Iorge'. The device depicted the encounter between St George and the Dragon. All three men came from Ipswich.

Nathaniell Bacon's *Annals of Ipswich* records in 1479, 'Willm Parnell [was] discharged of his Chamberlins accompt, because he hathe built one Dosser of Estrich board'.[31] The word *dosser* or *dorser* has three possible meanings: an ornamental cloth used to cover the back of a seat such as a throne or a chair of state; a hanging for a wall or room of state: or a panier usually carried across a horse's back, although it can also refer to one carried by a person.[32] The first and third of these meanings may be ruled out in this case. But the second meaning may be applicable as a wooden version of a usually cloth

30. Wright *Medieval Theatre In East Anglia* 84; Wright 'Parnell and Burles' 324–6; Nelson *The Medieval English Stage* 123, 199.

31. *The Annalls of Ipswiche, The Lawes Customes and Government of the same. Collected out of ye records bookes and writings of that towne by Nathaniell Bacon serving as Recorder and Town Clark in that towne Anno: Dom: 1654* edited William H. Richardson (Ipswich: printed for subscribers by H. Cowell, 1884) 143. Nathaniel Baker (brother of Francis) summarises and calendars (in English) the records which at this stage are largely in Latin.

32. *OED* sv *dosser* 1; see also *Promptorium Parvulorum Sive Clericorum, Lexicon Anglo-Latinum Princeps* edited Albert Way, 3 vols (London: Camden Society, 1843–65) *1* 125.

wall hanging;[33] this *dosser* was of 'Estrich board', timber from Norway or the Baltic region, probably what is today described as soft-wood, pine, or deal.[34] The same *dosser* may be referred to in the same accounts some two years later when 'John Alfray [was] elected ffree Burgess uppon condicon that he shall paint the Dosser wth the kings arms, and St George, and the armes of the Towne and others, and he is sworne'.[35] Reference to it as 'the' dosser suggests something of its civic significance and presumably the quality of workmanship provided by Parnell, the carpenter, and Alfray, the painter.

Later, Parnell appears to have been well known in East Anglia for his work on the Ipswich Corpus Christi pageants. The Petty and General Courts Accounts for 1490 at Ipswich record that:

> *eligerunt William Pernell Iohannem Balhed Willielmum Guykon Carpenters & Iacobum Cook ad gubernandum lez pagent & ad custodiendum omnia & singula eidem perenienes* [*pertenientes?*]
>
> they elected William Pernell John Balhed William Guykon carpenters and James Cook to be in charge of the pageants and to be responsible for all and each individual items pertaining to the same[36]

The same 1490 accounts also record *Willielmum Pernell & Iohannem Rolff pro tabernaclo Carpenteres*.[37] The sense of this record is not entirely clear. It may

33. Preparation of a piece of cloth for this purpose is recorded in 1445–46 in *The Records of the City of Norwich* edited Rev. William Hudson and John Cottingham Tingey, 2 vols (Norwich/London: Jarrold, 1906) 2 70: 'For fulling a piece of woollen cloth ordered for a dosser in the upper hall of the Guyhald, by the advice of the aldermen and supervisors, 18*d*.'
34. *OED* sv *estriche* 2. *attrib. estrich board*: 'applied to timber coming from Norway or the Baltic'. See *Memorials of London and London Life, in the XIIIth, XIVth, and XVth Centuries* edited Henry Thomas Riley (London: Longmans, Green and Co., 1868) 261; *The Medieval Records of a London City Church (St Mary at Hill)* edited Henry Littlehales (London: Kegan Paul, Trench, Trübner, 1905) 71; 'Orders of the Royal Household, Temp. Hen. VIII' *Gentleman's Magazine* edited John Mitford (January 1834) 47. In *Sir Gawain and the Green Knight*, the Green Knight's axe 'watȝ don abof þe dece, on doser to henge' (line 478). The implication is that this is a wooden *dosser*. Thanks to Sarah Carpenter for pointing this out.
35. Bacon *Annalls of Ipswiche* 145.
36. *Malone Society Collections 11* 174.
37. *Malone Society Collections 11* edited David Galloway and John Wasson (Oxford: Malone Society, 1980/1) 174; see also in general W.S. Fitch 'Notices of the Corpus

mean that Parnell and John Rolff are made responsible for the Carpenters' pageant of St Luke (*tabernaculum* is a possible term for this). But it may be that Parnell and John Rolff, carpenters, have been put in charge of the tabernacle or portable shrine of the Corpus Christi Guild. This was not a part of the pageants, but was carried in the annual procession. Two aldermen were elected annually to be wardens of the Guild of the tabernacle which when not in use at other times of the year was kept in St Mary le Tower.

The accounts for the following year, 1491, confirm Parnell's association with the Corpus Christi procession. They record *Et eligerunt Willielmum Pernell & Iohannem Balhed Ad custodiendum omnia vtencilia & ornamenta Corporis Xpi' decetero* ('And they elected William Pernell and John Balhed to be in charge of all the gear and ornaments of Corpus Christi').[38] Also in 1491, the records note:

> *Et concessum est Willielmo pernell in recompensacionem illius monete que sibi debentur pro lez pagent videlicit illos denarios quos sunt in manibus Burgenses non solutos pro prandio*[39]
>
> And it is granted to William Pernell in recompense for the moneys which are owed to him for the pageants, namely [that he should have] those moneys which are in the hands of the Burgesses [which were] not paid for the meal

The Ipswich accounts for 1479 and 1490–91 not only record William Parnell as a carpenter of refined work but also as in charge of *omnia vtencilia & ornamenta* [all the properties and ornaments] and as one among four in charge of the pageants and responsible for *omnia & singula* belonging to them. In effect, these accounts record Parnell's functions to be those of one of the quasi-professionals later (in the early sixteenth century) designated a 'property player'.

Christi Guild, Ipswich' *Proceedings of the Suffolk Institute of Archaeology and Natural History* 2: 4 (1855) 151–6; John Wodderspoon *Memorials of the Ancient Town of Ipswich, in the County of Suffolk* (Ipswich: Pawsey and London: Longman, Brown, Green, and Longmans, and J.R. Smith, 1850) 155–80.

38. *Malone Society Collections 11* 175. See also Bacon *Annalls of Ipswiche* 164.

39. *Malone Society Collections 11* 175.

John Coldewey was the first scholar to describe the generic concept of the 'property player'.[40] There appear to be four instances of the actual use of the term: the *Churchwardens' Accompts belonging to the Parish of Heybridge, near Malden, Essex* record 'Imprimis, paied to *Damyon*, the property player, for caryinge of his propertes home 0£ 1s 4d' (1508–32);[41] the accounts of the *Chyrche wardeyns of the Chyrche off* Boxford say 'the propyrte pleyer hath xxx s.' and 'there is no maner alowauns owt of this pley but onely xxx s. to the propyrte pleyer' (1535 twice);[42] '8s. paid to William Reynolds for the bording of Burles the propertie plaier this yere' (1562).[43]

The principal function of the 'property player' was clearly to provide properties for the play. Whether his task was to make the properties or simply collect and supply them, is unclear. The records at Bassingbourn, Cambridgeshire, record the following payments: 'Fyrst paid to the garnement man for garnementes and propyrtes and play booke 1£ 0s 2d', and 'Item payde for v days bord off one Pyke, propyrtes making, for hymselfe and hys servaunte one daye and for his horss' pasture vi days, summa £1 4d'.[44] These records point to both the making and supplying of properties and may well reflect the skill of Parnell.

Although Parnell is not named as a *property player* in these accounts, his functions occupy the territory of the property players recorded above at Heybridge, Boxford, Maldon, and Bassingbourn. In more recent times Burles at

40. John C. Coldewey 'The Digby Plays and the Chelmsford Records' *Research Opportunities in Renaissance Drama 18* (1975) 103–21; see also his 'That Enterprising Property Player: Semi-Professional Drama in Sixteenth-Century England' *Theatre Notebook 31: 1* (1977) 5–12.

41. John Pridden 'Churchwardens' Accompts belonging to the Parish of Heybridge, near Malden, Essex' in *Illustrations of the Manners and Expenses of Antient Times in England, in the Fifteenth, Sixteenth and Seventeenth Centuries, deduced from the Accompts of Churchwardens, and other authentic documents, collected from various parts of the Kingdom, with explanatory notes* edited John Nichols (London: Society of Antiquaries, 1797) 156.

42. *Boxford Churchwardens' Accounts 1530–1561* edited Peter Northeast (Suffolk Records Society 23; Woodbridge: Boydell Press, 1982) 19.

43. W.A. Mepham 'Municipal Drama at Maldon in the Sixteenth Century' *Essex Review* 56 (1947) 34–41 at 41.

44. *The Churchwardens' Book of Bassingbourn, Cambridgeshire 1496–c.1540* edited David Dymond *Cambridgeshire Records Society 17* (Cambridge: Cambridgeshire Records Society, 2004) 75.

Chelmsford (1562);[45] Thomas Felsted of London at Maldon (1540);[46] Richard Gibson at Lydd, Kent (1526); and Gover Martyn at New Romney, Kent (1560)[47] have all been labelled 'property players' by scholars, even though they are not called so at the time. Thus their functions have been permitted to extend the range of those at Heybridge, Boxford, and Bassingbourn.[48] These references all post-date those to William Parnell and his work from 1469 to 1491.

Coldewey, as the first writer in modern times to identify the role of the 'property player', did not include either William or John Parnell in his list.[49] Similarly, Robert R. Wright did not identify William or John Parnell as 'property players' in his 1971 M.Litt. thesis.[50] Thus, William Parnell had not

45. Archdeacon Mildmay 'Extracts from an Old Chelmsford Parish Account Book, Extending from 1557, the Last Year of Queen Mary, down to 1668' in *Transactions of the Essex Archæological Society 2* (Colchester: The Essex and West Suffolk Gazette Office, 1863) 211–28 at 226–7; Karl Pearson *The Chances of Death and Other Studies in Evolution* 2 vols (London: Edward Arnold, 1897) 2 Appendix 2 413–23 at 415, 417: the accounts of Archdeacon Mildmay and those of Karl Pearson differ. Mildmay records the services of Burles as 'fixinge' the play whereas Pearson records Burles as 'suinge' the play. Both words should be read as '*suruinge*' ('serving').

46. A. Clark 'Maldon Records and the Drama' *Notes and Queries, Tenth Series 7* (January–June 1907) 181–3; W.A. Mepham 'Municiple Drama at Maldon in the Sixteenth Century' *The Essex Review 55* (October 1946) 169–75; Meg Twycross 'Felsted of London: Silk-Dyer and Theatrical Entrepreneur' *Medieval English Theatre 10: 1* (1988) 4–16; John Pridden 'Churchwardens' Accompts belonging to the Parish of Heybridge, near Malden, Essex' in *Illustrations of the Manners and Expenses of Antient Times in England* edited John Nichols (London: Society of Antiquaries, 1797) 156.

47. *REED Kent: Diocese of Canterbury* edited James M. Gibson, 3 vols (University of Toronto Press and London: British Library, 2002) 2 681–2, 684–7, 768, 770, 3 945, 955–6, 1348–9, 1361.

48. Pyke appears to have been from outside the area for he was found accommodation for five days while working on the Bassingbourn Play of Saint George in 1511; Stephen Doree 'The Bassingbourn St George Play of 1511' *Hertfordshire's Past 33* (Hertford: Hertfordshire Archaeological Council/Hertfordshire Association for Local History, Autumn 1992) 36–44 at 37; The Churchwardens' Book of Bassingbourn also includes payment towards an assistant for Pyke on one day, 75. See above.

49. Coldewey 'The Digby Plays and the Chelmsford Records' 103–21; Coldewey 'That Enterprising Property Player' 5–12. Alan Nelson referred to William Parnell but did not designate him as a *property player*; Nelson *Medieval English Stage* 199.

50. Indeed, Wright confused William with a Thomas Parnell who is also mentioned in the Ipswich records, although there is no evidence of Thomas's connection with theatrical presentations.

been considered as a property player until Wright made the tentative link in his University of Leicester Ph.D. thesis in 1992.[51]

It might be said that Parnell was the earliest of the burgeoning band of East Anglian property players were it not for a record from 1445 of the work of John Causton on the Ipswich Corpus Christi Pageant:

> John Causton admitted, and sworne free Burgess, uppon condition that for seven yeres next following, he shall mantaine the ornam^{ts} belonging to Corp' Xi pageant, and the stages, receiving the Charges thereof from the farmers of the Common Marshe, and the Portmens medow as the Bayliffs for the time being shall think meete.[52]

In the light of currently available evidence, the work of John Causton might be regarded as the earliest in establishing the role and function of the property player, although his role may have been limited to taking care of the Corpus Christi Guild's ornaments and the stages for the play.

William Parnell's involvement in the Corpus Christi Pageants at Ipswich does not appear to be recorded beyond 1491. However, his son John seems to have taken over some of his father's responsibilities.[53] He is recorded at Ipswich in 1505 as finding the 'ornaments' for Corpus Christi play: 'Granted to John Stangilts, 20^{s} 8^{d} yerely for 12 yeres, to finde the stageing for Corp' Chr'i play. And to John Parnell, 33^{s} 4^{d}, to find the ornam^{ts} during suche time, and collectors named of assessm^{ts} for the play'.[54] Here, a distinction is

51. 'In each of its three performance arenas the 'N-Town' Play demanded the presentation of technically difficult "miracles". These, it seems, were so important that they urge me to claim that craftsmen and theatre professionals (property-players) were employed to construct and efficiently operate the necessary technical devices. We know of several such craftsmen and have already met one, Parnell of Ipswich, who was employed by Norwich in 1469': Wright 'Theatre in Late-Medieval East Anglia' 174.
52. Bacon *Annalls of Ipswiche* 103.
53. There has been some confusion over the respective identities of the Parnells. Harrod appears to have been responsible for the initial confusion when he by implication conflated the identities of father, William, and son, John. He quoted the record concerning the work of John at Ipswich in 1505 as a footnote to the name of Parnell; Harrod 'Queen Elizabeth Woodville' 34 note.
54. Bacon *Annalls of Ipswiche* 177; Wodderspoon *Memorials of Ipswich* 170; Malone Society *Collections 11* 178, where the editor notes that this portion of the original accounts is badly damaged. This entry summarises what were presumably three separate entries in the original. See also Victor Scherb *Staging Faith: East Anglian Drama in the Later*

made between payments for the staging of the play and its decoration. The working relationship between the roles of John Stangilts and John Parnell in Ipswich seems to mirror that between William Bisshope and William Parnell at Norwich in 1469. Evidently, John Parnell acquired some of the skills and interests of his father, since his aptitude and expertise, like his father's, was in demand beyond his Ipswich base.

Confirmation of the relationship between William and John Parnell is found in a manuscript in the London Metropolitan Archives that records the details of the 'Iorge': 'And Alle thes foresaid werkes were wrowgt by the handwerk of wyll*ia*m P*ar*nell & wyll*ia*m Baker hys prentys, & Iohn p*ar*nell hys sonne Dwellyng in Epyswych in the schyre of Sowthffolke'.[55] This hitherto-unknown evidence of William Parnell's work on automata is investigated in the article by Philip Butterworth with Eric Williamson in *Medieval Theatre Performance* (2017), together with a consideration of the possible identities of the various Parnells and their apprentice.[56]

John Parnell is also recorded as operating some 40 miles away from his Ipswich base in Great Dunmow, Essex. Here, the *Churchwardens' Accounts* for

Middle Ages (London: Associated University Presses, 2001) 35 and 210 note 66. Scherb is also unclear about the relationship between William and John Parnell. He mis-transcribes both Bacon and Wright in declaring this account to be from 1502.

55. London Metropolitan Archives, P69/ BOT3/ D/001 (formerly Guildhall Library, MS 00059) fol. 47^{r}.

56. Philip Butterworth with Eric Williamson 'The Mechanycalle Ymage off Seynt Iorge at St Botolph's, Billingsgate, 1474' in *Medieval Theatre Performance: Actors, Dancers, Automata and their Audiences* edited Philip Butterworth and Katie Normington (Cambridge: D.S. Brewer, 2017), 215–38. References to the two Parnells are recorded from 1469 to 1527. During this period, in 1505, a third Parnell, Thomas, is recorded at Ipswich as one of three men who were 'elected and sworne in the number of 24'. However, it is recorded for November 12, 1518 that 'They discharged Tho: Parnell out of theire number of the 24'. A further record of one month later determines that in December 1518, Parnell 'received £23 6s 8d for losses in the king's service'. Do 'losses' in this record refer to injuries? Was Thomas Parnell invalided out of the King's service and simultaneously no longer able to fulfil his duties as a member of the 24? He was certainly paid a lot of money. Whatever the predicament in which Thomas Parnell found himself there appear to be no available records that connect him to the theatrical work of William and John Parnell; see R.R. Wright *Medieval Theatre In East Anglia*. Wright confused William and Thomas Parnell both in 'Parnell and Burles' and his 'Community Theatre in Late Medieval East Anglia' *Theatre Notebook 28: 1* (1974) 24–39 at 38 note 13.

1527/8 record: 'for lyne, and pakthrede, and whepcorde, whan Parnell made the pagantes on corpuscrysti daye, 4d'.[57] The date of this record appears to mark the end of John Parnell's work on pageants of this kind, some fifty-four years after assisting his father on the automaton of St George and the Dragon at St Botolph's, Billingsgate.

Just as it is appropriate to consider William Parnell's skills as craftsman and provider of staging and ingenious theatrical devices so too is it with his son John. The same case may be made for John Parnell in respect of the range of his functions. Both William and John Parnell were paid specialists, with sought-after skills, which local and church authorities were prepared to import and pay for. Their working territory ranged throughout East Anglia and as far as London. They may be seen to join that broad group of other paid craftsmen, tradesmen, and supervisors now designated 'property players', who put on, or caused to be put on, plays and presentations during the late fifteenth and early sixteenth centuries throughout East Anglia and south-east England.

University of Leeds

Acknowledgements: The authors would very much like to express their gratitude to Meg Twycross, the team of Editors, and the Reader for their carefully considered suggestions in helping us to improve our transcription and translation. Meg Twycross was instrumental in providing us with the final page of the NCR document which had not been included in the photographs provided for us by the Norwich Record Office. All concerned have demonstrated much more interest, enthusiasm, and understanding than their editorial roles require.

57. W.T. Scott *Antiquities of an Essex Parish; or, Pages from the History of Great Dunmow* (London: H.S. King, 1873) 43; Andrew Clark 'Great Dunmow Revels 1526–1543' *Essex Review 19* (1910) 189–98 at 194; W.A. Mepham 'Mediæval Drama in Essex: Dunmow' *Essex Review 55* (1946) 57–65 at 60; J.W. Robinson 'Three Notes on the Medieval Theatre' *Theatre Notebook 16: 2* (1961/2) 60–2; Wasson 103.

APPENDIX ONE
Transcription of NCR 18a–2: Norwich Chamberlain's Accounts

Notes:

1. Italics indicate extensions of abbreviated or contracted forms in the manuscript, although intended gender, number and case of extensions are not always unambiguous from the text; occasional square brackets supply letters implied by the context but not contracted or abbreviated; unidentified words or letters are enclosed in [ ].
2. These accounts are written continuously but for ease of reference they have been separated into items.

Fol 10r **Norwic[um]**

Iste Quat*er*nus declarat et exprimit om*n*es custus et Expens*as* h*ab*it*os* et solut*os* *per* Joh*ann*em Coke et Will*elmu*m Henstede Juniorem Cam*er*arios istius Ciuitatis erga aduentu*m* Excellentissime Regine Elizabeth*e* que venit ad hanc Ciuitatem Anno regni Illustrissimi Regis Edwardi quarti sponsi sui nono

In prim*is* solut*um* cuidam Pernelle de Gipewico qui frequentat p*ro*uidere subtilia ludo*rum* & staci*o*nu*m* p*ro* suis labore & expen*sis* de ~~Norwico~~ Gipwico vsq*ue* Norwicu*m* p*er* aduisamentu*m* & discreci*o*nem Will*elm*i Swayn ald*er*manni Joh*ann*is Welles Joh*ann*is Burton Ed*mund*i Redknape Will*elm*i London et alio*rum* – vjs

It*em* in denar*ijs* ad diu*er*sos repast*us* *causa* reficiendi expen*sis* sup*er* d*ictu*m Pernell*e* & fam*u*los suos ad duas vices viijd

Item in expen*sis* d*ictorum* cam*er*ario*rum* Reginaldi Harneys Thome Cambrigge Thome Lynne Galfr*idi* Spirleng & alio*rum* elect*orum* p*er* co*mmun*em Consiliu*m* Ciuitatis ad om*n*ia p*re*missa p*ro*uidenda v*idelicet* una vice in domo Joh*ann*is Kar Sherman temp*ore* sup*er*uidendi portas de Westwyk erga aduentu*m* Regine – iiijd

APPENDIX ONE
Translation of NCR 18a–2: Norwich Chamberlain's Accounts

Note:

1. Arabic numerals are given where the accounts give Roman ones. In accordance with usual practice, abbreviations for coinage have been left unexpanded.

Fol. 10^r **Norwich**

This Booklet discloses and expresses all the costs and expenses incurred and paid by John Coke and William Henstede Junior, Chamberlains of this city, in relation to the Entry of her most excellent majesty Queen Elizabeth who came to this city in the ninth year of the reign of her husband the most illustrious King Edward IV

Firstly, paid to a certain Pernelle of Ipswich, who regularly supplies ingenious devices for plays and stations, for his labour and expenses from Ipswich to Norwich, by advice and at the discretion of William Swayn alderman, John Welles, John Burton, Edmund Redknape, William London, and others: 6s
Item monies paid for several meals as refreshments for the aforementioned Pernelle and his men on two occasions: 8d
Item expenses of the said chamberlains, Reginald Harneys, Thomas Cambrigge, Thomas Lynne, Geoffrey Spirleng and others elected by the Common Council of the city to supervise all the prearrangements, namely on one occasion in the home of John Kar, shearman, at the time of overseeing the Westwyk Gate on the occasion of the Entry of the Queen: 4d

It*em* sol*utum* tenentib*us* Rop*er*ie in foro p*ro* inhospitac*ione* ~~duarum~~ duo*rum* ligno*rum* longo*rum* & alto*rum* prius occupato*rum* p*ro* stac*ione* in foro erga aduentu*m* Regis & ib*idem* res*er*uato*rum* a pluuia – ijd
It*em* sol*utum* p*er* discrecio*nem* duo*rum* prouiso*rum* p*ro* vno repast*u* hospitato*rum* d*omi*ne ~~Regis~~ Regine infra mansu*m* henr*ici* Bradffeld viijd
It*em* in refecc*ione* diu*er*so*rum* laboranc*ium* in ereccio*ne* tiatro*rum* vna vice – viijd in bero
It*em* in claui*s* maiorib*us* & minorib*us* empt*is* & tradit*is* fam*ulis/o* d*ic*ti p*er*nell*e* – vjd
It*em* in repastu Joh*annis* Newton cu*m* soc*ijs* ad vnu*m* repastu*m* infra mansu*m* Henr*ici* Bradfeld qui erant associati cu*m* d*ic*tis p*ro*uisorib*us* ad p*re*missa p*ro*uidenda – iiijd
It*em* in expens*is* Joh*annis* Norton Taillo*ur* & iij soc*iorum* suo*rum* consuencium gigantes prius ~~factas~~ fact*os* & diruptos – viijd
Item in filo albo empto de vx*or*e Northales p*ro* eisd*em* consuendis – ijd
It*em* in stip*endio* duo*rum* lathamo*rum* insim*ul* conduct*orum* & op*er*anc*ium* p*er* ij dies dimi*diam* p*ro* rep*ar*ac*ione* p*ar*ietu*m* ad ingressu*m* porta*rum* p*er* diem insim*ul* xijd – ~~ijs vjd~~ iiijd – ijs vjd
It*em* in stip*endio* vn*ius* hom*in*is s*er*uient*is* d*ic*tis lathamis p*er* tempus p*re*d*ic*tum p*er* diem ~~insimul~~ ad tasc*am* iiijd – xd
It*em* sol*utum* duob*us* laborarijs conduct*is* p*ro* calce combusta temp*er*and*a* viijd
It*em* in bero empto alia vice exp*enso* sup*er* ffamulos d*ic*ti p*er*nell*e* – ijd
It*em* in claui*s* ferre*is* empt*is* & disposit*is* alia vice in caus*is* p*re*d*ic*tis – iijd
It*em* in cordul*is* seu capistris empt*is* p*ro* teatris corroborand*is* & voluend*is* jd
It*em* in punctub*us* empt*is* p*ro* ornamentis angelo*rum* attachiand*is* – iijd
It*em* in vno ho*m*ine conducto p*ro* imposic*ione* punct*ium* & p*re*parac*ione* d*ic*to*rum* ornamento*rum* sup*er* d*ic*to*rum* angelo*rum* corpora ijd
It*em* sol*utum* p*er* aduisam*entum* & discrecio*nem* p*ro*uiso*rum* ...

summa probata xvs jd

Item paid to the householders of the Ropery[1] in the Marketplace for accommodating two long tall wooden beams previously used for the stage in the Marketplace on the occasion of the Entry of the King and therein sheltered from the rain: 2d
Item paid at the discretion of the two stewards for a meal at the house of Henry Bradfield for the procurers of accommodation for the ~~King~~ Queen: 8d
Item refreshments for various labourers on the erection of the theatres on one occasion: 8d in beer
Item for large and small nails purchased and delivered to the servant[s] of the said Pernelle: 6d
Item for a meal for John Newton and associates, at a meal in the house of Henry Bradfield, who were associated with the said suppliers in providing for the prearrangements: 4d
Item for expenses of John Norton, tailor, and three of his colleagues, for sewing back together the giants previously made and dismantled: 8d
Item for white thread purchased from the wife [of] Northales for sewing the same: 2d
Item for wages of two masons hired together and working for two and a half days to repair the wall at the entrance to the Gates, both per day 12d: 2s 6d
Item for wages of one man, apprentice to the said masons, for the aforementioned period, at the rate of 4d [per day]: 10d
Item paid to two labourers hired for the mixing of burnt lime: 8d
Item for beer purchased on one occasion for the men of the said Pernelle: 2d
Item for iron nails purchased and used for the aforementioned purposes: 3d
Item for cords or halters purchased for reinforcing and draping the theatres: 1d
Item for points purchased to fasten the ornaments of the angels: 3d
Item for one man hired to attach the points and to prepare said ornaments on the bodies of the said angels: 2d
Item paid by advice and discretion of the stewards ...

Sum ^{checked} 15s 1d

1. The Ropery: 'Bethel-Street was formerly called Over or Upper Newport, and that part lying within this parish [*St Peter Mancroft*] was called the Ropery, because the cord and rope makers anciently dwelt there'; Philip Browne *The History of Norwich* (Norwich: Chipperfield, 1814) 191.

Fol. 10^{v} Plus de aduentu Regine

... ffamulo dicti Pernelle ad eius recessum de Norwico vsque Gippewicum pro labore suo videlicet ad hoc consencentibus Willelmo Swayn aldermanno Edmundo Redknape aldermanno Johanne Burton Johanne Welles Galfrido Spirleng Johanne Munford Thoma Lynne & alijs vjs vjd
Item in regardo eidem dato per discrecionem dictorum superuisorum xvjd
Item solutum Stephano Skynner pro imposicione ~~v~~ duarum penularum in duobus Capellis pro Patriarchis super stacionem – vjd
Item solutum Johanni Waters Skynner pro imposicione duarum penularum in alijs duobus Capellis – vjd
Item solutum Reginaldo Godfrey Skynner pro imposicione iij penularum in alijs tribus Capellis – xd
Item solutum pro suicione ~~de~~ quatuor peciarum albarum de worstede pro anteriore facie stacionum – xvjd
Item in famulis Willelmi Londen & Philippi Curson conductis pro puteis fiendis pro fundo tiatri ad portas fratrum ~~Carmel~~ predicatorum quasi per vnum diem viijd
Item in auro empto pro armis Regine depingendis vijs
Item in locione & mundacione iiij^{or} peciarum panni de Tapserwerk pertinencium ffratribus minoribus qui ab eis fuerant conducti pro vestigijs graduum ad tiatra ascendencium sic mundatum per quendam ffullonem[1] xd
Item in expensis diuersorum prouisorum ~~& superuisorum~~ ac plurimorum laborariorum & artificum videlicet in pane & ceruisia in manso cuiusdam Cissoris ad portas de Westwyk xijd
Item solutum cuidam ffremason pro emendacione crestoure fontis in angulo boriali Cimiterij ecclesie sancti andree – vjd
Item solutum pro deposicione omnium vestimentorum preparatorum pro honorabili stacione ad portas de Westwyk – iiijd
Item datum tribus hominibus pro suo labore & expensis portantibus omnes illas vestes ad solara ^{in} Guyhalda ibidem ad ~~desij~~ desiccandas pro eo quod grauiter ~~mae~~ madefacti fuerunt per pluuias continuas & grandes vjd

1. In this entry and the next – *quendam ffullone*, *cuiusdam Cissoris* – it is impossible to tell whether the scribe intends to indicate the person's craft or his surname (possibly both?). He gives capitals (i.e. double *f*, capital C) but the Latin form of the occupational word/surname, not the English. Then we have *cuidam ffremason*, also with a capital double *f* (not a surname for us, but possibly then?), and four lines down *cuidam Cowper*, whose surname must be the same as his trade, from what he is supplying.

Fol. 10^{v} More concerning the Entry of the Queen

... to a servant of a certain Pernelle for his return to Ipswich from Norwich for his labour, those agreeing to this being William Swayne alderman Edmund Redknape alderman John Burton John Welles Geoffrey Redker Geoffrey Spirleng John Mumford Thomas Lynn and others: 6s 6d
Item in reward given to the same at the discretion of the said supervisors: 16d
Item paid to Stephen Skinner for fitting two fur trimmings[1] to the caps of two patriarchs at the station: 6d
Item paid to John Waters, skinner, for fitting fur trimmings to two other caps: 6d
Item paid to Reginald Godfrey, skinner, for fitting fur trimmings on another three caps: 10d
Item paid for the sewing of four pieces of white worsted for the front facade of the stations: 16d
Item for hiring the workmen of William Londen and Philip Curson to dig pits for the base of the theatre at the Preaching Friars' Gates, one-day equivalent: 8d
Item for gold purchased for the painting of the coat of arms of the queen: 7s
Item for washing and cleaning four pieces of cloth of *Tapserwerk* belonging to the Friars Minor, which were hired from them for the rising tiers at the theatres as cleaned by a certain Fuller: 10d
Item in expenses of sundry suppliers ~~and supervisors~~ and of many workmen and craftsmen as in bread and ale at the establishment of a certain Tailor at Westwyk Gates: 12d
Item paid to a certain Freemason for repairing the coping[2] of the well in the northern corner of the cemetery of the church of St Andrew: 6d
Item paid for the removal of all the trappings prepared for the triumphal station at Westwyk Gates: 4d
Item paid to three men for their labour and expenses in carrying all these trappings to the solar in the Guildhall for drying because they had been seriously soaked by the continuous heavy rains: 6d

1. See *DMLBS* sv *penna* [ME, AN *panne*, *penne*], *paena* [assoc w. CL *paenula*], 'garment made of or lined with fur, fur lining'. Probably fur trimmings on prophets hoods? All the workmen involved are skinners.
2. *DMLBS* sv *crestura*, v. *cristatura*: (arch.) cresting, coping.

Item solutum pro attendencia & pro eisdem pannis post desiccacionem voluendis vjd
Item solutum pro mundacione & desiccacione ac honesta revolucione ~~ser~~ septem peciarum rubiarum worstede cum portacione earundem ad domum appropriatorum ixd
Item solutum cuidam Cowper ~~manda~~ manenti in foro Norwico pro vno cultello de ipso mutuato pro circulis ad facturam Gigancium & per operarios fracto – iijd
Item solutum vni laborario pro implecione foraminum post remoccionem tiatri seu stacionis ad portas fratrum dominicalium impletorum cum arena – iiijd
Item in vno tribulo mutuato et deperdito & elongato – iijd
Item in dimidio barelle de beer empto de Johanne peterson pro refeccione & potu diuersorum hominum super stacionem monstrancium – xijd
Item solutum pro iij mantallis tribus sercotes & tribus coronis triplicibus pro tribus Imperatricibus preparatis & ad guyhaldam portatis ad desiccandos – jd
Item in custubus trium famulorum domini Ducis Norffolk vocatorum Johannis Dauy / Cokessen & Greneacras existentium ad vnum repastum in Aurora et [*blank space*] aliorum superuenientium – xxd
Item solutum Willelmo Bisshope carpentario pro deposicione de [*space*] ij mastis a tiatro ad portas fratrum dominicalium – iiijd

Summa huius partis – xxvijs probata

Fol. 11r **Plus de aduentu regine**

Item in whipcorde empto pro velis stringendis – jd
Item in pane ceruisia & caseo expensis super diuersos operarios & laborarios tempore deposicionis tiatri & stacionis ad portas ffratrum dominicalium – iiijd
Item in mensa supradicti hominis de Gipwico vocati Pernel existentis apud Norwicum tempore preparacionis dictarum Stacionum per xij dies – ijs
Item pro lecto suo per idem tempus – xijd
Item datum in regardo Bedello gilde sancti Luce Euangeliste pro sua attendencia tempore predicto vjd

Item paid for their diligence and for rolling up the same cloths after they had been dried out: 6d
Item paid for cleaning and drying and careful rolling up [...] of seven pieces of red worsted cloth with carrying of same to the house of the supervisors: 9d
Item paid to a certain Cooper dwelling in the Marketplace at Norwich, for a knife borrowed from him for the hoops for making the Giants, and broken by the workmen: 3d
Item paid to a workman for filling of holes [*left*] after the removal of the theatre or station at the Gates of the Dominican Friars with sand: 4d
Item for one shovel, borrowed, misplaced, and lost: 3d
Item for half a barrel of beer purchased from John Peterson for refreshment and drink to sundry men [working] on the station of the displays: 12d
Item paid for 3 cloaks, three *surcotes*, and three triple crowns for three Empresses, prepared and carried to the Guildhall to be dried out: 1d
Item for the expenses of three servants of the Lord Duke of Norfolk, called John Davy, Cokessen, and Greenacres, being present at a meal at the 'Aurora';[1] also [*blank space*] of other visitors: 20d
Item paid to William Bisshope, carpenter, for taking down of [*space*] 2 *mastis* from the theatre at the Gates of the Dominican Friars: 4d

Subtotal – 27s checked

Fol. 11r More concerning the Entry of the Queen

Item for whipcord bought for securing the awnings: 1d
Item for bread, beer, and cheese spent on sundry workmen and labourers at the time of dismantling of the theatre and station at the Gates of the Dominican Friars: 4d
Item for board for the above-mentioned man called Pernel from Ipswich staying in Norwich for twelve days at the time of setting up the said stations: 2s
Item for his lodging over the same period: 12d
Item given in reward to the Beadle of the Guild of St Luke the Evangelist for his attendance at the aforementioned time: 6d

1. Name of the public house? Possibly 'The Rising Sun'?

It*em* sol*utum* Will*elm*o Bisshop*e* p*ro* duob*us* tiatris preparand*is* forma que f*ac*ta fuerunt erga aduentu*m* ~~domini Regis~~ ^~~Regine~~ *domini* Regis q*uorum* vnu*m* ad portas fr*atru*m p*re*dicator*um* & aliud ad portas de Westwyk ex con*uentione* secu*m* f*ac*ta in grosso – xxxiijs iiijd

It*em* in regardo dat*o* Joh*ann*i Colman p*ro* refecc*i*on*e* de le Calaundryng ix pecia*rum* de worsted*es* ab ipso mutuat*arum* p*ro* ornac*i*on*e* stac*i*onum & p*ro* mundac*i*on*e* ~~earund~~ ear*un*dem postq*uam* fuerant gr*a*uit*er* pollut*e* ac p*ro* suic*i*on*e* diu*er*sor*um* foraminu*m* in eisdem f*ac*tor*um* p*er* lesiones hamor*um* iiijs vjd

It*em* dat*um* utriq*ue* duor*um* bacularior*um* in Theologia assign*atorum* p*ro* expositorib*us* iijs iiijd vjs viijd

It*em* in vno Rastro ferreo voc*ato* a Rake mutuat*o* de Thoma Cambrigge & elongat*o* et dep*er*dit*o* in cui*us* negligencia ignorat*ur* – vd d*ic*t*o* Thome restitut*um*

It*em* dat*um* cuidam ffr*atr*i assign*ato* ad ludu*m* Gabriel[*is*] cum ~~d~~ cibo & potu ad vices – xvjd

It*em* in mensa sua cu*m* alijs sup*er*ueni*entibus* q*ua*si p*er* iij dies vjd

It*em* sol*utum* Joh*ann*i Thixtel ad restituendu*m* Thome Cambrigge p*ro* lesione vni*us* pentyce vbi erectu*m* fuit tiatru*m* – xvjd

It*em* in conducc*i*on*e* Organor*um* cum cust*ubus* portac*i*on*is* usq*ue* portas de westwyk – xijd

It*em* in potu sup*er* eos adtunc expens*o* – ijd

It*em* p*ro* portac*i*on*e* eor*un*dem reducend*o* post ingressu*m* Regine vjd

It*em* in regard*o* dat*o* cuidam ffakke cu*m* pueris suis cantant*ibus* curiose sup*er* tiatru*m* ad portas fr*atru*m p*re*dicator*um* – ijs ~~ijs~~

It*em* dat*um* cuidam cl*er*ic*i* ludenti ad organa ~~ibidem~~ – viijd

It*em* dat*um* pluribu*s* Cl*er*icis curiose cantantibu*s* ad tiatru*m* ad portas de Westwyk int*er* se – xxd

It*em* sol*utum* diu*er*sis Carpentar*ijs* & alijs ho*min*ibu*s* adiuuantibu*s* p*ro* magna Cathedra gilde s*anc*ti luce portand*a* de p*r*ioratu No*rwici* usq*ue* tiatru*m* ad portas f*ratrum* – ijs

It*em* solutu*m* Simoni Tabard Carpent*ario* p*ro* suo labore & vij ho*minum* suor*um* ad deponend*am* magna*m* Cathedra*m* p*re*d*ictam* p*ro* salua p*re*seruac*i*on*e* eiusd*em* ne lederet*ur* – xxijd

It*em* sol*utum* p*ro* eo*rum* labore in erigendo lez mastes p*ro* tiatro p*re*d*ic*t*o* – iiijd

It*em* in refecc*i*on*e* potu*um* eor*un*dem adtunc temp*or*is vjd

Item paid to William Bisshope for two theatres to be prepared according to the constructional design [of those] which were made for the Entry of the ~~Lord King~~ ^~~Queen~~ Lord King of which one at the Gates of the Preaching Friars and the other at Westwyk Gates; as agreed with him, inclusively: 33s 4d

Item in reward given to John Colman for redoing the pressing of 9 pieces of worsted borrowed from him to decorate the stations and for cleaning them after they were badly soiled and for sewing up several holes made in them by the piercing of hooks: 4s 6d

Item given to each of two bachelors of theology appointed as expositors, 3s 4d: 6s 8d

Item one iron rake, called 'a Rake', borrowed from Thomas Cambrigge, misplaced and lost, by whose negligence is not known: 5d to the said Thomas in recompense

Item given to a certain friar assigned to the play of Gabriel, with food and drink on several occasions: 16d

Item in board for him and for other visitors, equivalent to three days: 6d

Paid to John Thixtel for recompensing Thomas Cambrigge for damage to a pentice where the theatre was erected: 16d

Item for hire of the organs, with the costs of portage to Westwyk Gates: 12d

Item for drink spent on for those [present] at that time: 2d

Item for carriage of the same in taking them back after the entry of the Queen: 6d

Item in reward to a certain Fakke and his boys singing pricksong[1] on the theatre at the Gates of the Preaching Friars: 2s

Item given to a certain cleric ~~there~~ for playing the organs: 8d

Item given to numerous clerics singing pricksong at the theatre at Westwyk Gates, between them: 20d

Item paid to several carpenters and other men helping them carry the great throne of the Guild of St Luke from Norwich Priory to the theatre at the Friars' Gates: 2s

Item paid to Simon Tabard, carpenter, for his work and that of 7 of his men in taking away the aforesaid great throne for its safekeeping, lest it should be harmed: 22d

Item paid for their labour in erecting *lez mastes* for the aforesaid theatre: 4d

Item in liquid refreshment for them at that time: 6d

1. R.E. Latham *Revised Medieval Latin Word-List from British and Irish Sources* (London: Oxford UP for the British Academy, 1999): *cantus curiosus*, 'pricksong', c.1500.

Item solutum duobus Carpentarijs cum ij famulis pro suis laboribus & expensis in deponendo tiatrum ad portas de Westwyk cum ijd in ceruisia viijd
Item solutum pro ij magnis gigantibus portandis a tiatro ad portas de Westwyk vsque altam Cameram infra Guyhalde – ijd
Item pro portacione magne Cathedre gilde sancti luce a tiatro ad portas fratrum predicatorum vsque ad prioratum Norwici – ijd
Item solutum pro portacione iiij^or vestimentorum magnorum ~~ae~~ ad domum ffratrum minorum jd

probata
Summa huius partis ~~lxiijs ixd~~

Fol. 11^v

billa Burton:[1] Item solutum Johanni Burton pro diuersis minutis parcellis per ipsum solutis cum vjd pro ij circulis & ij sparres pro tiatro ad portas fratrum predicatorum iijd pro suicione ij frondeletes ibidem ijd pro suicione vnius frenge ibidem & vjd pro mensa laborariorum ibidem ac iiij^d pro stipendio vnius laborarij pro factura foraminum pro lez mastys ibidem imponendis Sic in toto per billam dicti Johannis Burton – xxjd

billa massenger: Item solutum cuidam Simoni massenger pro minutis custubus apud portas de westwik per billam impositam – xd.

billa ffox: Item solutum cuidam Willelmo ffox pro minuta soluta & custubus ^per billam impositam pro preparacione vnius tiatri ibidem – xijd. Item solutum cuidam [space] Lyntok pro suo labore & expensis equitando precepto maioris usque Wyndesore ad afferendum certitudinem de aduentu domini Regis exeundo & redendo per vj dies per diem xvjd, viijs. Item eidem alia vice equitando precepto maioris causa predicta ~~eq~~ vsque Bury sancti edmundi moram trahente per iij dies iiijs per diem ut supra vna Summa – xijs

billa Sadeler: Item solutum cuidam Johanni Sadeler equitando precepto maioris erga adventum Regine ad informandum familie sue super suo Itinere ad ingrediendam ciuitatem per portas de Westwik per billam impositam – ijs.

1. All these subheadings are written in the margin, and the main text is indented.

Item paid to two carpenters with their two servants for their labour and expenses in dismantling the theatre at Westwyk Gates, with 2d in beer: 8d
Item paid for carrying the 2 great giants from the theatre at Westwyk Gates to the upper chamber within the Guildhall: 2d
Item for the carriage of the great throne of the Guild of St Luke from the theatre at the Gates of the Preaching Friars to Norwich Priory: 2d
Item paid for the carriage of 4 great garments to the House of the Friars Minor: 1d

checked
Subtotal ~~63s 9d~~

Fol. 11v

Burton Invoice: Item paid to John Burton for sundry small items paid for by him: with 6d for 2 hoops[?] and 2 *sparres* for the theatre at the Gates of the Preaching Friars; 3d for sewing of 2 frontals (*frondelets*) there; 2d for sewing of one ornamental border (*frenge*) there; and 6d for the board of the workmen there and 4d for the wage of one workman for making the pits to put *lez mastys* in there. Thus in total as per the invoice of the said John Burton: 21d

Massenger Invoice: Item paid to a certain Simon Massenger for small expenses at Westwyk Gates as presented in his invoice: 10d

Fox Invoice: Item paid to a certain William Fox for small sums paid [by him] and for expenses, as per the invoice presented for preparation of one theatre there: 12d; Item paid to a certain [*space*] Lyntok for his services and expenses in riding on the Mayor's instructions to Windsor to ascertain the facts of the Entry of His Majesty the King, 6 days in going and returning at 16d per day: 8s; Item to the same person for another ride to Bury St Edmunds on the Mayor's instructions on the same business, spending 3 days at 4s a day, as above; in total: 12s

Sadeler Invoice: Item paid to a certain John Sadeler riding on the Mayor's instructions in relation to the Entry of the Queen to brief her household on her itinerary upon entering the city through Westwik Gates; as presented in his invoice: 2s billa Cambrigge: It*em* sol*utum* Thome Cambrigge p*er* billa*m* imposit*am* cu*m* ijs iiijd p*er* ips*u*m solut*um* cuidam [*blank*] p*ro* suis expens*is* & labore equit*ando* in diu*er*sas p*ar*tes in comit*atu* Norff*olk* ad afferend*um* ~~eq~~ certum de p*ro*gressu Regine p*er* j diem & di*midium* iiijd. p*ro* exp*ensis* eiusd*em* ~~ad le~~ equit*ando* v*er*sus Walsyngh*am* ad loquend*um* cu*m* subvic*ecomite* Norff*olk* & cu*m* iijd in pane & ceruis*ia* exp*ensis* sup*er* ffr*atr*es ffrat*er*nitat*is* s*an*cti luce cu*m* punctub*us* empt*is* & tradit*is* eisd*em* p*ro* angel*is* p*re*parand*is* Sic in toto ijs xjd

billa munford: It*em* solut*um* Joh*anni* Mundford p*er* billa*m* imposit*am* cu*m* ijs p*ro* stip*endio* suo & mensa p*er* iij dies xviijd p*ro* mensa & attendencia filij sui assignati p*ro* ~~s~~ monstrac*ione* Gabriel[*is*] jd p*ro* claui*s* jd p*ro* whipcord jd p*ro* p*ar*cell*is* loquele scribend*is* & jd p*ro* tynfoyle vn*a* *Summa* iijs xd.

billa Thorp: It*em* sol*utum* Joh*anni* Thorp*e* ~~pro vij mantelys viij caplettis~~ p*er* billam imposit*am* tam p*ro* conducc*ione* diu*er*so*rum* vestim*entorum* p*ro* ap*osto*lis & virginib*us* cum ijs p*ro* vij mantellis & viij caplett*is* peiorat*is* p*er* grandem pluuium vjs viijd xij mantell*is* p*ro* ap*ost*olis xvj mantel*lis* cu*m* caplett*is* p*ro* virg*in*ib*us* & aliis diu*er*sis vestib*us* [...]

probata
Summa xxiiijs iiijd

Fol. 12ʳ **Plus de Adventu Regine**

et cu*m* ijs p*ro* labore & expens*is* d*icti* Joh*ann*is Thorp*e* p*er* iij dies p*ro* causis p*re*d*ic*tis vn*a* *Summa* xs viijd

billa Couper: It*em* sol*utum* Joh*anni* Carter Coup*er* p*ro* ij pec*ijs* m*er*emij p*ro* gigantib*us* – p*er* billa*m* affilat*am* xijd

billa Godeson: It*em* sol*utum* Joh*anni* Godson Carter p*ro* cariac*ione* ij xijd carect*ata* arene & iij vjd carect*atas* de Coldre p*ro* impleac*ione* vie ad portas de Westwik – xviijd p*er* billa*m* imposit*am*

Cambrigge Invoice: Item paid to Thomas Cambrigge according to his invoice; 2s 4d paid by him to a certain [*blank*] for his expenses and labour riding into diverse parts of the County of Norfolk to ascertain the facts of the progress of the Queen, for 1 day and a half: 4d. For expenses of the same in riding towards Walsingham to speak with the Under-Sheriff of Norfolk; with 3d in bread and beer expended on the friars of the Fraternity of St Luke, and purchase of points delivered to them for the preparation of the angels. In total: 2s 11d

Munford Invoice: Item paid to John Mundford as presented in his invoice; 2s for wages and board over 3 days; 18d for board and attendance of his son assigned to the show of Gabriel; 1d for nails; 1d for whipcord; 1d for writing out the 'parcels' of the speech; and 1d for tinfoil; in total: 3s 10d

Thorp Invoice: Item paid to John Thorp for ~~7 mantles, 8 chaplets~~ as presented in his invoice, as much as for rescuing several garments for the apostles and the virgins, [with] 2s; for 7 mantles and 8 chaplets damaged by the great rain, 6s 8d; 12 mantles for the apostles, 16 mantles with chaplets for the virgins and various other garments [*something missing*]

checked
Total 24s 4d

Fol. 12^{r} More concerning the Entry of the Queen

and for 2s for labour and expenses of the said John Thorp for 3 days engaged in the aforementioned tasks; in total: 10s 8d

Cooper Invoice: Item paid to John Carter, cooper, for 2 pieces of timber for the giants, per the attached invoice: 12d

Godeson Invoice: Item, paid to John Godson, carter, for carriage of 2 cartloads [12d] of sand and 3 [6d] cartloads of rubble[1] for spreading on the road at Westwik Gates: 18d, per invoice as presented

1. The word *colder* appears in the *Promptorium Parvulorum* with the gloss: 'This word prob. means "clippings of stone". It is perhaps identical with the word *colder*, used in East Anglia, according to Forby and Moor, in the sense of ears not separated from the chaff by ordinary threshing': *Promptorium Parvulorum* edited A.L. Mayhew *EETS ES 102* (1908) 579–80.

billa Steynour: Item solutum Johanni Stonhale Steynour per billam impositam cum xvijd ob pro stipendio & mensa scilicet per ij dies & dimidium operante in arte sua diuersis de causis iiijd pro coloribus ab eo emptis & ijs pro iiij scutis vocatis scochons de armis Regine Summa in toto – iijs ixd ob

billa Smyth: Item solutum Jacobo Smyth pro clauis ferreis ab eo emptis pro tiatro ad portas fratrum per billam viijd

billa Nichols: Item solutum cuidam Johanni Nichols per billam suam impositam cum vs xd pro suo labore & expensis per xiiij dies ad ~~operandum~~ attendendum super famulum Pernelle qui preparauit magnam partem stacionis ac similiter attendente super nunc Computatores jd pro whipcord ijd pro clauis jd pro sero ob pro cervisia [*margin*: plus ijd] & ijd pro vna hasta. Sic in toto per billam predictam vjs ijd ob

billa Beufeld ~~Nichols~~: Item solutum dicto ~~Johanni Nichols~~ Thome Beufeld per aliam billam ut in auro sibi liberato ad pingendum xviijd

billa Aylmere: Item solutum Roberto Aylmere per billam impositam cum xijd ~~pro~~ dictis tribus Imperatricibus apparentibus ^erga aduentum domini Regis ad portas de Nedham & ijd pro pu[n]ctris[1] vna Summa xiiijd

billa Sadeler: Item solutum Ricardo Sadeler per billam impositam pro correo vocato leder hungry pro gigantibus ijs

billa hagonere: Item solutum Roberto Hagoner equitando precepto Thome Cambrigge ad loquendum cum Plumstede nuper Armigero gladij maioris pro j penone remanente in manibus suis per billam impositam cum viijd et similiter equitando ad cognoscendum tempus aduentus domine Regine & per quam viam intenderet aduenire xijd vna Summa xxd

billa Roberti Heruy: Item in stipendium Roberti Hervy Steynour per iij dies depingentis in diuersis causis notarijs xvjd ~~tet~~ Item pro ~~iij~~ duobus vexillis armorum domini Regis & Regine ~~separatorum~~ iunctorum in vno vexillo depingendis iiijs viijd Item similiter pro xiiij square scucheons depingendis in panno lineo viijs ijd Item similiter pro ij scucheons de powderyngges depictis cum Rosis & flourdelys – xd Item similiter pro pictura vnius Rotuli longi in fronte tiatri ad portas fratrum xijd & alterius ad frontem tiatri ad portas viijd & pro j viser ~~le~~ reficiendo pro angelo rubeo iiijd & pro suicione dicti Rotuli ad le battelment jd & pro brasile expenso in reparacione gigancium

1. Sic: *punctis?*

Stainer Invoice: Item paid to John Stonhale, stainer, per invoice as presented, for 17½d for wages and board for 2 days and a half applying his skills to sundry tasks; 4d for colours purchased from him; and 2s for 4 shields called *scochons* bearing the arms of the Queen; in total: 3s 9½d

Smyth Invoice: Item paid to James Smyth, for iron nails purchased from him for the theatre at the Gates of the Friars, per invoice presented: 8d

Nichols Invoice: Item paid to a certain John Nichols per his invoice as presented, for 5s 10d for his labour and expenses for 14 days for looking after the employee of Pernelle who prepared most of the station, and similarly waiting on the current accountants; 1d for whipcord; 2d for nails; 1d for a handle; ½d for beer;[1] and 2d for a pole; so in total for the aforementioned invoice: 6s 2½d

~~Nichols~~*Bewfeld* Invoice: Item paid to ~~John Nichols~~ Thomas Bewfeld per another invoice, as delivered to him in gold, for painting: 18d

Aylm*ere* Invoice: Item paid to Robert Aylmere per invoice presented: 12d for three Empresses appearing in relation to the Entry of the Lord King at Nedeham Gates; and 2d for points, total: 14d

Sadeler Invoice: Item paid to Richard Sadeler, per invoice presented, for leather called 'Hungary-leather' for the giants: 2s

Hagonere Invoice: Item paid to Robert Hagoner, for riding on the instruction of Thomas Cambrigge to speak with Plumstede, former sword-bearer of the mayor for 1 pennant remaining in his possession, per invoice, 8d; and similarly riding to discover the time of the Entry of the Lady Queen and by which road she intended to travel, 12d; total: 20d

Robert Hervy Invoice: Item in wages for Robert Hervy, stainer, for 3 days painting motifs for sundry items, 16d; item, for painting 2 armorial banners bearing the ~~separate~~ impaled arms of the Lord King and Queen in one banner, 4s 8d; item similarly, for painting 14 *square* escutcheons on linen cloth, 8s 2d; item, similarly, for 2 escutcheons of powderings painted with roses and fleurs-de-lys, 10d; item, similarly for painting of one long scroll at the front [*facade*] of the theatre at the Friars' Gates, 12d; and of another at the front of the theatre at the Gates, 8d; and for repairing 1 mask for the red angel, 4d; and for stitching the said scrolls to the battlement, 1d; and for brasile [*scarlet cloth*] used to repair the giants, 7d; and the labour

1. Marginal gloss: 'plus 2d'.

vijd et pro labore & expensis dicti Roberti ad portas de Westwik per ij dies & pro iij paruis Rotulis pro Imperatribus de texto Intende &c Natura &c vjd vna *Summa* in toto xixs ijd ut per billam suam liquet manifeste

probata

verte *summa* xlix s iiijd

Fol. 12^{v} **Plus de Adventu Regine**

billa Thixel: Item solutum Johanni Thixelle Carpentario pro denarijs prius solutis Thome Cambrigge pro lesione vnius pentyce mesuagij ~~sue~~ sui facta per tiatrum supradictum – ~~xvjd~~ prout supra per billam affilatam

billa Neuton: Item solutum per mandatum maioris Johanni Neuton pro suo labore & expensis equitando versus Gipwicum pro quodam Pernelle ad prouidendum stacionem erga aduentum Regine – ijs ijd per billam impositam Item solutum Andree Davy pro cariacione xij carectarum materie corrupte extra vicum de Westwik erga aduentum Regine – ijs

Item solutum Jacobo ffoster pro cumulacione eiusdem per iij dies ad tascam – xijd per billam affilatam Item in vno ^equo conducto pro Willelmo Brightwayte equitaturo versus Notyngham per securitatem Roberti Welles pro extraneis negocijs inquirendis &c per x dies per diem iiijd – iijs iiijd

billa R fferrour: Item in denarijs solutis Ricardo fferrour ⱡ aldermanno per billam affilatam cum xiijs iiijd per ipsum solutis pedestribus domini Regis in regardo xiijs iiijd solutis pedestribus domine Regine vjs viijd datis clericis Justiciarij domini Regis ad le Oyer determynere xxijs solutis pro le Calaundryng[e] & lesione xj peciarum de worstedes vocatarum medel beddes que liberate fuerunt Reginaldo Harneys & Thome Lynne assignatis ad prouidendum Worstedes pro tiatris preparandis iijs vjd solutis pro le Calaundryng vij pecias de Worstedes traditas & liberatas Johanni Coke &

and expenses of the said Robert at Westwik Gates for 2 days, and for 3 small scrolls for the Empresses with the texts of *Intende &c* and *Natura &c*,[1] 6d; in total, 19s 2d, as clearly shown per his invoice.

checked
turn over total 49s 4d

Fol. 12^v More concerning the Entry of the Queen

Thixel Invoice: Item paid to John Thixelle, carpenter, for monies previously paid to Thomas Cambrigge for damage incurred to a pentice of his messuage by the above-mentioned theatre: ~~16d~~ as above, per invoice attached

Neuton Invoice: Item paid by order of the mayor to John Neuton for his labour and expenses in riding to Ipswich for a certain Pernelle to furnish a station on the occasion of the Entry of the Queen, per invoice presented: 2s 2d
Item paid to Andrew Davy for carriage of 12 cartloads of waste material away from the district of Westwik relating to the Entry of the Queen: 2s
Item paid to James Foster for gathering up the same [rubbish] for 3 days at the rate of 12d per day, per attached invoice: [*no amount*] Item for one ^horse hired for William Brightwayte, to ride to Nottingham, on the security of Robert Welles, inquiring about non-local business &c, for 10 days, at 4d per day: 3s 4d

Invoice R. Ferrour: Item in monies paid to Richard Ferrour, alderman, per invoice attached: for 13s 4d paid by him to the footmen of the Lord King as a bonus; 13s 4d paid to the footmen of the lady queen; 6s 8d given to the clerks of the King's Justiciar at the [*court of*] Oyer [*and*] Determiner; 22s paid for the pressing and damage of 11 pieces of worsted called *medel beddes* which had been delivered to Reginald Harneys and Thomas Lynne, appointed to supply worsted for preparation of the theatres; 3s 6d paid for the pressing of 7 pieces of worsted delivered to John Coke and

1. Apparently lifted wholesale from the Coronation Entry of Henry VI into London 1432: see John Lydgate *Minor Poems Part 2* edited H.N. MacCracken *EETS OS 192* (1934) 630–48, lines 106–222. The 'Empresses' were Nature, Grace, and Fortune, they were accompanied by 14 virgins representing the Seven Gifts of the Holy Spirit and the seven spiritual gifts bestowed on the king by his coronation. A placard declared *Intende prospere et regna*, 'Proceed prosperously and reign'; Psalm 44: 5 Vulgate version and Douay translation (AV Psalm 45).—MT

Will*elmo* Henstede Cam*erarijs* iam computat*is* xviijs p*ro* j pec*ia* de worstede virid*e* lesat*a* grauit*er* sup*er* extenc*io*nes ad tiatra & ideo empt*a* & lib*er*ata p*ro* sedib*us* aldermanno*rum* ad ~~ser ortum~~ ortum sermonu*m* infra prioratu*m* xxiiijs p*ro* ij p*ar*uis pec*ijs* de worsted*es* virid*ibus* voc*atis* litel beddys lesis & confract*is* lib*er*at*is* d*ic*tis Cam*er*arijs ijs solut*is* p*ro* lesione & fracc*io*ne vni*us* medlebed virid*is* appropriatori relib*er*at*e* & viijd pro J sera pro australi ostio Guyhalde vn*a* su*mm*a in toto Ciijs vjd

modo de parcell*is* content*is* in paruo quat*er*no Will*elmi* Henstede uni*us* Cam*er*ario*rum*

It*em* in vino expens*o* sup*er* sup*er*uisores stac*io*num ad tab*er*nam Burton vna vice ~~iijd~~ iiijd

It*em* in c*er*uisi*a* expens*a* sup*er* depingentes & alios artifices circa p*re*parac*io*nes tiatri ad portas fra*trum* cu*m* jd dato adtunc carpentarijs ib*ide*m – vijd

It*em* in vj ~~yn~~ virg*inibus* panni line*i* tradit*is* depictorib*us* p*ro* scutis & alijs reb*us* p*re*parand*is* p*re*ci*um* virg*inis* vjd iijs

Item in stipen*dio* Joh*ann*is Neuton p*er* iij dies op*er*ant*is* c*ir*ca p*re*d*ic*tam xijd

p*ro*b*ata*
cxvjs xjd
S*umm*a hui*us* p*ar*tis ~~cxvijs iijd~~

Fol. 13r **Plus de Aduentu Regine**

It*em* solut*um* Joh*ann*i Neuton p*ro* su*o* labore & exp*en*s*is* equit*ando* vsq*ue* Gipwicu*m* ad quendam Pernell*e* adducend*um* p*ro* p*ro*uisione stac*ionum* – xxd

It*em* in iij virg*inibus* panni line*i* p*re*ci*um* virg*inis* viijd tradit*is* d*ic*to pernell*e* ad depingend*um* in ~~re..~~ rebus necess*ar*ijs – ijs

Item in 1 q*uart*a hollond tradita Joh*ann*i Stonhalle Steyno*ur*[1] c*ir*ca p*re*d*ic*tam – ijd

It*em* in vij virg*inibus* pa*nn*i line*i* tradit*is* Joh*ann*i Coke vni Cam*er*ari*o* ad lib*er*and*um* depictorib*us* p*re*ci*um* virg*inis* iijd – xxxjd

It*em* in vj virg*inibus* pann*i* line*i* tradit*is* cuidam Mayhew ad pingend*um* scuta de armis Regis & Regine p*re*ci*um* virg*inis* vd – ijs vjd

1. One who works on 'stained cloths', apparently painted with water-based pigments, as opposed to the oils used by painters. See *OED* sv *stained* adj.

William Henstede, chamberlains, already accounted for; 18s for 1 piece of green worsted, badly damaged, over the extensions at the theatres and therefore purchased and delivered for the seats of the aldermen at the preaching yard within the Priory; 24s for 2 small pieces of green worsted called *little beddys*, damaged and torn, and delivered to the said Chamberlains; 2s paid for damage and tearing of one green *medlebed* returned to the supervisor; and 8d for a bolt for the south gate of the Guildhall. Of which, sum in total: 103s 6d

Now from the itemised accounts in the small notebook of William Henstede, one of the Chamberlains.

Item in wine spent on the supervisors of the stages at Burton's tavern on one occasion: 4d

Item in beer for the painters and other craftsmen involved in the preparations of the theatre at the Gates of the Friars, and 1d given to the carpenters there: 7d

Item for 6 virgins of linen cloth delivered to the painters for the preparation of shields and other items, price per virgin 6d: 3s

Item: in wages for John Neuton for 3 days working on these tasks: 12d

checked
116s 11d
Total for this part ~~117s 3d~~

Fol. 13^{r} More concerning the Entry of the Queen

Item paid to John Neuton for his labour and expenses in riding to Ipswich to bring a certain Pernelle for the supply of the stations: 20d

Item for 3 virgins of linen cloth, price per virgin 8d, brought to the said Pernelle for painting with the requisite things: 2s

Item for 1 quarter of holland cloth handed over to John Stonhalle, stainer, for the same: 2d

Item for 7 virgins of linen cloth handed over to John Coke, one of the Chamberlains, for delivering to the painters, price per virgin 3d: 21d

Item for 6 virgins of linen cloth handed over to a certain Mayhew for painting the coats of arms of the King and Queen, price per virgin 5d: 2s 6d

It*em* in denar*ijs* tradit*is* eidem in p*ar*tem soluc*ionem* stipend*ii* sui – xijd
It*em* in x virg*inibus* panni lin*ei* tradit*is* cuidam Henry Steyno*ur* p*ro* lez valence*s* tam ad tiatru*m* ad portas fr*atrum* q*uam* ad portas de Westwyk [*space*] p*recium* virg*ine* vd – iiijs ijd
It*em* in feno empt*o* p*ro* implec*ione* pectoris gigant*is* – ijd It*em* in vino ad ij vices expens*o* sup*er* xij p*ro*uisores stac*ionum* qua*rum* vna vice xijd & alia vice viijd in Tab*er*na Burton – xxd
It*em* sol*utum* Ric*ardo* fferrour ald*ermanno* p*ro* allac*ione* ~~de~~ v pecia*rum* de Worstede*s* voc*atas* bedde*s* ad tiatru*m* v*er*sus portas fr*atru*m & v pecia*rum* alia*rum* ad portas de Westwik & iiij pecia*rum* alia*rum* ad prisones infra Guyhald ib*id*em suenda*rum* – iiijd
It*em* in clauis voc*atis* patenayles[1] empt*is* & disposit*is* in p*re*parac*ione* stac*ionum* [*sic*] ad portas de Westwik ijd
It*em* in punctib*us* empt*is* p*ro* p*re*parac*ione* angelo*rum* iiijd
It*em* in c*er*uis*ia* expens*a* & dat*a* p*er* Thomam Cambrigge ad op*er*arios stac*ionum* reficiendos iijd
It*em* sol*utum* iiij^{or} hom*in*ibus p*ro* ~~deposicione~~^{preparacione} omn*ium* vestim*entorum* stac*ionis* ad portas de Westwik post demonstrac*ionem* ac p*ro* ~~adducione~~ ^{reducione} ij giganc*ium* v*er*sus altam cam*er*am Guyhalde viijd
It*em* in stipend*io* Will*elm*i Glou*er*e Carpentar*ij* p*er* j diem op*er*ant*is* in f*ac*tura tiatri ad d*ic*tas portas vjd
It*em* in denar*ijs* solut*is* p*er* filiuliu*m* Rob*er*to Welles – ijd
It*em* in clau*is* ferro & filo empt*is* & expens*is* ijd
It*em* p*ro* portac*ione* vni*us* scale d*ic*ti Will*elm*i Hensted ad portas de Westwik – jd
It*em* in f*actura* xxiiij powdryngge*s* cu*m* coronis et rosis & flour delycez – xvjs ~~viijd~~ p*recium* cuiusl*ibet* viijd
It*em* in expens*is* in vigiland*o* p*er* ij ~~dies~~ noctes vt*raque* nocte jd – ijd
It*em* in vno caseo empto & expens*o* sup*er* op*er*arios – ijd
It*em* in stipend*io* vni*us* laborarij [*blank*]

p*ro*b*ata*
S*umma* xxxiiijs jd

1. See *OED* sv *patten*: apparently originally tacks for wooden clogs.

Item in cash handed over to the same in part payment of his wages: 12d
Item for 10 virgins of linen cloth handed over to a certain Henry Steyn*our* for *lez valences*, both at the theatre at the Friars' Gates and at Westwyk Gates, price per virgin 5d: 4s 2d
Item for hay purchased for stuffing the chest of the giant: 2d
Item for wine on 2 occasions, for 12 stewards of the stations, of which at one time 12d, and the other time 8d, in Burton's Tavern: 20d
Item paid to Richard Ferrour, alderman, for bringing 5 pieces of worsted called *beddes* to the theatre by the Friars' Gates, and 5 other pieces to Westwik Gates, and of 4 other pieces to be sewn up by the prisoners within the Guildhall: 4d
Item for nails, called *patten nails* purchased and used in the preparation of the stations [*sic*] at Westwik Gates: 2d
Item for points purchased for the preparation of the angels: 4d
Item for beer purchased by Thomas Cambrigge and given to the workmen of the stations for refreshment: 3d
Item paid to 4 workmen for ~~taking down~~ arranging all the trappings [*vestimenta*] of the station at Westwik Gates after the exhibition, and for ~~bringing~~ taking back the 2 giants to the high chamber [at] the Guildhall: 8d
Item in wages for William Glouere, carpenter, for 1 day working on the construction of the theatre at the said Gates: 6d
Item for monies paid out [for repairing?] a pinnacle[1] to Robert Welles: 2d
Item for nails, iron and wire, bought and used: 2d
Item for carrying one ladder of the said William Henstede to Westwik Gates: 1d
Item for making up 24 *powdryngges* with crowns and roses and fleurs-de-lys: 16s ~~8d~~, price each one 8d
Item paid out for watching for 2 ~~days~~ nights, each night 1d: 2d
Item for one cheese bought and expended on the workmen: 2d
Item in wages for one of the workmen: [*blank*]

checked
Total 34s 1d

1. *DMLBS* gives one example of this translation of *filiolus*, also suggesting 'column, turret'. The English word is *filiole* (no Latin source recorded).

Fol. 13^{v} Plus de aduentu Regine

Item iam Computatores petunt allocacionem pro vna scala perdita ad portas de Westwik xijd

Item solutum tribus ~~Ð~~ sculptoribus pro suis labore & expensis tempore exaltacionis turrium ad tiatrum versus portas fratrum & deposicione earundem – xijd

Item in punctubus alia vice emptis pro preparacione angelorum vltra *iiijd supra* – vjd

Item in vna domo conducta iuxta portas de Westwik pro omnibus ornamentis imponendis tempore magne pluuie tunc contingentis – vijd

Item solutum Thome Heruy pro auro ab eo empto pro refeccione & depiccione diuersarum rerum vijs

Modo de alijs parcellis in quaterno Johannis Coke[1]

Item solutum pro expensis in hospicio henrici Bradfeld ad vnum repastum mane videlicet super diuersos auditorum ^compoti Jam Computancium de custubus aduentus ^domini Regis facti scilicet Ricardi Brasier Walteri ffornfeld Ricardi fferrour aldermannorum Thome Cambrigge G Spirleng & aliorum xxjd

Item solutum per billam affilatam Nicholao Noble pro expensis cuiusdam Pernel de Gippewico operantis in prouisione stacionum erga aduentum domine Regine cum famulo dicti Pernelle – ijs jd

Item in expensis Johannis Coke vnius iam Computatorum Augustini Boys & Galfridi Spirleng mense Decembris anno xij^{o} existentium in Guyhald pro scriptura partis compoti presentis – xiijd ob

Item[2] solutum Johanni Bekles ffletcher pro denarijs sibi debitis per Communitatem tempore Thome Elys nuper maioris videlicet in precio xvj sheef sagittarum precium xxxijs & xij duodena de stryngges precium iiijs missis ad artellaria domini ^Regis versus guerras in Comitatem Eboraci – Regis ~~xxxvjs~~[3]

Item solutum Edwardi Cutiller maiori pro regardo quod dedit cuidam Nuncio domini Regis afferenti litteras privatas domini Regis – vs

Item solutum Thome Bokenham vni vice pro regardo quod ~~deit~~ dedit eidem Nuncio sic solutum per mandatum dicti maioris – vs

1. Marginal gloss: *quere in iij^{o} folio patet* 'look [where it] appears on the third folio'.
2. Marginal gloss: *quere* [?] *in pede* 'look at the foot'.
3. Marginal gloss: *Regis* 'of the king'.

Fol. 13v More concerning the Entry of the Queen

Item the current accountants claim reimbursement for one ladder lost at Westwyk Gates: 12d
Item paid to three sculptors for their labour and expenses when putting up the turrets at the theatre at the Friars' Gates and taking them down: 12d
Item for points purchased on another occcasion to dress the angels, in addition to the 4d above: 6d
Item for one house rented near Westwyk Gates to accommodate all the ornaments at the time the great rains occurred: 7d
Item paid to Thomas Hervy for gold bought from him for restoring and decorating various objects: 7s

Now from other itemised accounts in the notebook of John Coke:

Item paid for expenses incurred at the inn of Henry Bradfeld for an early morning meal, namely for several of the auditors of the accounts just [then] being calculated of the costs of the Lord King's Entry, namely Richard Brasier, Walter Fornfield, Richard Ferrour, aldermen, Thomas Cambrigge, G[eoffrey] Spirleng and others: 21d
Item paid per attached invoice to Nicholas Noble for the expenses of a certain Pernel from Ipswich working on the furnishing of the stations for the Queen's Entry with a servant of the said Pernelle: 2s1d
Item for the expenses of John Coke, one of the accountants, of Augustine Boys and Geoffrey Spirleng, in the month of December in the 12th year[1] being at the Guildhall for the writing up of part of the present account: 13½d
Item paid to John Bekles, fletcher, for moneys owing to him from the community since the time of Thomas Elys as mayor,[2] namely, for 16 sheaves of arrows, price 32s and 12 dozen bowstrings, price 4s, sent to the King's munitions for the wars in the county of York, [expenses] of the king: ~~36s~~
Item paid to Edward Cutiller, Mayor,[3] for the reward he gave to the messenger of the Lord King bearing private letters of the Lord King: 5s
Item paid to Thomas Bokenham on one occasion for the reward he gave to the same messenger, as paid by command of the said Mayor: 5s

1. 1472.
2. Thomas Ellis was Mayor of Norwich for the years 1460, 1465, and 1474; A.D. Bayne *A Comprehensive History of the City of Norwich* (London: Jarrold and Sons, 1869) 690–1.
3. Edward Cutler was Mayor of Norwich for the year 1470 (Bayne *History of Norwich* 690).

Item in papero empto per G Spirleng pro hujusmodi compotis scribendis – ijd per billam Boys:[1] Item solutum per quamdam billam augustini Boys cum iijd ob pro deposicione ij altarum mastis pro tiatro in foro erga aduentum domini Regis ijd pro portacione duorum scutorum armorum domini Regis a Guyhalda vsque portas de Coslany erga recessum domini Regis ijd solutum cuidam Ramseye pro stramine ad cubila depictorum fienda in alta camera Guyhalde & jd pro sparcione arene ad finem de Sporyrowe Sic in toto – viijd ob
Item in regardo dato Galfrido Spirleng pro sua diligencia in prouisione dictarum stacionum ac pro factura loquelarum expositarum ad faciem Regine ac salutacionis Marie & Elizabethe breuiter manifestate per discrecionem iam Auditorum & Superuisorum dictarum stacionum nil hic quia postea in pede
Item in v pellibus de auro precium cuiuslibet xd & xxiiij pellibus de b[e]rmerari argenti precium cuiuslibet ijd quadrans emptis per Thomam Heruy & famulum Pernelle pro refeccione cresturarum gigancium viijs viijd

probata
Summa huius partis xxxiiijs vijd

Fol. 14r **Plus de aduentu Regine**

Item in denarijs petitis per Walterum Geffreys aldermannum pro suis aduisamento discrecione & labore habitis in prouisionibus stacionum Regis qui in talibus magnam habet experienciam ac concepcionem diuersorum & plurimorum textorum positorum super tiatra ad portas de Nedeham et in foro ut in billa sua imposita coram iam auditoribus inter alia affilata liquet aperte nil hic quia postea in pede

probata ~~iiijd~~
Summa de Custubus aduentus Regine per iam computatores – ~~xv li xiiij s ix d~~ ~~xvij li xvjs iijd~~ xviijli iiijs xjd

1. Marginal gloss.

Item for paper purchased by G. Spirleng to write accounts of this kind: 2d
For the Invoice of Boys: Item paid for a certain invoice from Augustine Boys, as to 3½d for the taking down of 2 tall *mastis* for the theatre in the Marketplace for the Entry of the Lord King: 2d for carrying two shields of arms of the Lord King from the Guildhall to Coslany Gates for the departure of the Lord King; 2d paid to a certain Ramseye for straw to make nests for the painted figures in the upper chamber of the Guildhall; and 1d for spreading sand at the end of Spurrier Row. In all: 8½d
Item bonus paid to Geoffrey Spirleng for his diligence in the furnishing of the said stations and for the making[1] of expository speeches delivered to the Queen and of the salutation of Mary and Elizabeth briefly performed; through the discretion of the auditors and supervisors of the said stations; no amount shown here because included below.
Item for 5 skins of gold, price of each 10d, and 24 skins of silver vermeil, price 2¼d each, purchased by Thomas Hervy and the servant of Pernelle for refurbishing the crests of the giants: 8s 8d

checked
Total for this part 34s 8d

Fol. 14r More concerning the Entry of the Queen

Item, cash requested for his advice, decisions, and work in supplying the stations of the King, by Walter Geffreys, alderman, who has great experience of such things, also for his formulation of the many and diverse texts placed on the theatres at Nedeham Gates and in the Marketplace, as set out in his invoice, deposited with others in the presence of the then auditors; paid separately, no amount shown here because included below.

Checked ~~4d~~
Total costs of the Entry of the Queen by the current accountants ~~£15 14s~~ 9~~d~~
~~£17 16s 3d~~ £18 4s 11d

1. This could mean 'delivering' or 'composing'.

Fol. 14v[1]

xiiij s ij d ob
~~vjd ob~~

S*umm*a Om*nium* Soluci*onum*	Cxxx iiij li ~~vs iiij ob~~
[Sum]mis & Expens*is*	p*robata*
Cum Cust*ubus* Regine	~~Cxxxij li iij s vd ob~~

[*Margin*] ~~iiij li xiiijs iijd ob q~~

Et sic debent*ur* ~~iiij li~~

De quibus allo*cantur* iam Comput*o* pro facienda vni*us* spere in domo Computator*um* [camer] vs It*em* in lez batelment ib*idem* fiend*is* cu*m* clau*is* ferr*eis* vj d [camer*arij*[?]] It*em* in tab*ulis* empt*is* p*ro* lez shelves in eadem [a] xiij d Item p*ro* f*act*ura eo*run*dem cu*m* lez cletys iiij d [a] It*em* sol*utum* Willelmo Cosyn p*ro* ij staplez p*ro* ostio claudendo in le paretos[2] eundent*e* inter domum Comput*atorum* & domum Thesaur*ii* ac p*ro* claue p*ro* le hetche ad summam partem gradu*um* v*ersus* ~~do~~ ostiu*m* domus Consilij & p*ro* emend*is* sere eiusde*m* et p*ro* f*act*ura de le hagoday ferre*i* dom*us* Computo*rum* [a] viij d It*em* p*ro* xiiij par*ibus* cerotecarum p*ro* Angel*is* in d*ic*t*is* stac*io*nibus – xiiijd vna S*umm*a viiijs ixd Et sic debent*ur*.

1. Although the final page of the document appears to wind up the account of the Queen's Entry in financial terms, it also seems to incorporate costs from a much wider sphere. It is unclear how these additional costs relate, if at all, to the Queen's Entry, and it is therefore with some caution that we present this final page. The gloves for the angels seem an afterthought.
2. *Pertuis*? OF 'Narrow passage way'.

Fol. 14^{v}

		14s 2½d
		~~6½d~~
Total of all payments	£134 ~~5s 4½d~~	
Totals & Expens*es*	checked	
Including the costs of the Queen	~~£132 3s 5½d~~	

[*Margin*] ~~£4 14s 3¾d~~

And thus ~~£4~~ are owing

Of which: they have allocated to the current account to make a screen in the Counting House: chamberlains? 5s. Item for making the battlements of the same with iron nails: 6d. chamberlains? Item for planks bought for the shelves [cupboards?] in the same: 12d. Item for making the same with the pegs: 4d. Item paid to William Cosyn for two staples to close the door in the pertuis going between the Counting House and the Treasurer's House, and for a key for the hatch at the highest part of the stairs over against the gate of the Council Chamber, and to mend the bolts of the same, and for making the iron ring-latch[1] of the Counting House: 8d. Item for 14 pairs of gloves for the angels in the said stations, 14d. Total: 8s 9d. And so there are owing.

1. *OED* defines *haggaday* as 'a kind of door latch'. L.F. Salzman *Building in England* (Oxford: Clarendon Press, 1952) 299, cites examples showing it to be the ring used to raise a latch, as on many church doors. Nineteenth-century antiquarians used it (wrongly) of a sanctuary knocker, as at Durham or Adel, and this has been taken up by modern commentators.

APPENDIX TWO
References to the Entry of King Edward IV

[Fol. 10^{r}]

It*em* sol*utum* tenentib*us* Rop*er*ie in foro p*ro* inhospitac*ione* ~~duar*um*~~ duo*rum* ligno*rum* longo*rum* & alto*rum* prius occupato*rum* p*ro* stac*ione* in foro erga aduentu*m* Regis & ib*ide*m res*er*uato*rum* a pluuia – ijd
It*em* sol*utum* p*er* discrec*ionem* duo*rum* prouiso*rum* p*ro* vno repast*u* hospitato*rum* d*omi*ne ~~Regis~~ Regine infra mansu*m* henr*ici* Bradffeld viijd

[Fol. 11^{r}]

It*em* sol*utum* Will*el*mo Bisshop*e* p*ro* duob*us* tiatris p*re*parand*is* forma que f*act*a fueru*n*t erga aduentu*m* ~~domini Regis~~ ∧~~Regine~~ domini Regis q*uorum* vnu*m* ad portas fr*atru*m p*re*dicato*rum* & aliud ad portas de Westwyk ex con*uentione* secu*m* f*act*a in grosso – xxxiijs iiijd

[Fol. 11^{v}]

billa ffox: It*em* sol*utum* cuida*m* Will*el*mo ffox p*ro* minut*a* solut*a* & cust*ubus* per billam imposit*am* p*ro* p*re*parac*ione* vni*us* tiatri ib*ide*m – xijd. It*em* solut*um* cuidam [*space*] Lyntok p*ro* suo labore & expens*is* equit*ando* p*re*cept*o* maioris usq*ue* Wyndesore ad afferend*um* certitudi*n*em de aduentu d*omi*ni Regis exeundo & redendo p*er* vj dies p*er* die*m* xvjd, viijs. It*em* eidem alia vice equit*ando* p*re*cept*o* maioris caus*a* p*re*dicta ~~eq~~ vsq*ue* Bury s*an*cti edm*undi* moram trahent*e* p*er* iij dies iiijs p*er* diem ut sup*ra* vn*a* S*umm*a – xijs

[Fol. 12^{r}]

billa Aylm*er*e: It*em* sol*utum* Rob*er*to Aylm*er*e p*er* billa*m* imposit*am* cu*m* xijd ~~pro~~ dict*is* trib*us* Imp*er*atricib*us* app*ar*entib*us* ∧erga aduentum d*omi*ni R*egi*s ad portas de Nedh*am* & ijd p*ro* pu[n]ctris vn*a* Summa xiiijd

APPENDIX TWO
Translations

[Fol. 10^{r}]

Item paid to the householders of the Ropery in the Marketplace for accommodating two long tall wooden beams previously used for the stage in the Marketplace on the occasion of the Entry of the King and therein sheltered from the rain: 2d
Item paid at the discretion of the two stewards for a meal at the house of Henry Bradfield for the procurers of accommodation for the ~~King~~ Queen: 8d

[Fol. 11^{r}]

Item paid to William Bisshope for two theatres to be prepared according to the constructional design [of those] which were made for the Entry of the ~~Lord King~~ ^~~Queen~~ Lord King of which one at the Gates of the Preaching Friars and the other at Westwyk Gates; as agreed with him, inclusively: 33s 4d

[Fol. 11^{v}]

Fox Invoice: Item paid to a certain William Fox for small sums paid [by him] and for expenses, as per the invoice presented for preparation of one theatre there: 12d; Item paid to a certain [*space*] Lyntok for his services and expenses in riding on the Mayor's instructions to Windsor to ascertain the facts of the Entry of His Majesty the King, 6 days in going and returning at 16d per day: 8s; Item to the same person for another ride to Bury St Edmunds on the Mayor's instructions on the same business, spending 3 days at 4s a day, as above; in total: 12s

[Fol. 12^{r}]

Aylm*ere* Invoice: Item paid to Robert Aylmere per invoice presented: 12d for three Empresses appearing in relation to the Entry of the Lord King at Nedeham Gates; and 2d for points, total: 14d

billa R fferrou*r*: It*em* in denar*ijs* solut*is* Ric*ardo* fferrour ‡ aldermanno p*er* billam affilat*am* cum xiijs iiijd p*er* ips*um* solut*is* pedestrib*us* d*omi*ni Reg*is* in regardo

[Fol. 13v]

It*em* solut*um* p*ro* expen*sis* in hospicio henr*ici* Bradfeld ad vnu*m* repastu*m* mane v*idelicet* sup*er* diu*er*sos audito*rum* ^compoti Jam Computancium de custub*us* aduentus ^domini Regis facti *scilicet* Ric*ar*di Brasier Walt*er*i ffornfeld Ric*ardi* fferro*ur* aldermanno*rum* Thome Cambrigge G Spi*r*leng & alio*rum* xxjd

It*em* sol*utum* Joh*anni* Bekles ffletcher p*ro* denar*ijs* sibi debit*is* p*er* Com*mun*itatem temp*ore* Thome Elys nup*er* maioris vi*delicet* in p*re*cio xvj sheef sagitta*rum* p*recium* xxxijs & xij duoden*a* de stryngges p*recium* iiijs miss*is* ad artellar*ia* d*omi*ni ^Regis v*er*sus guerras in Com*itatem* Ebor*aci* – Regis ~~xxxvjs~~

It*em* sol*utum* Edward*i* Cutiller maiori p*ro* regardo quod dedit cuidam Nuncio d*omi*ni Regis afferenti l*itt*eras pr*i*vatas d*omi*ni R*egis* – vs

It*em* solut*um* p*er* qu*am*dam billam aug*ustini* Boys cum iijd ob p*ro* deposic*ione* ij altar*um* mastis p*ro* tiatro in foro erga aduentu*m* d*omi*ni Reg*is* ijd p*ro* portac*ione* duo*rum* scuto*rum* armo*rum* d*omi*ni R*egis* a Guyhalda vsq*ue* portas de Coslany erga recessu*m* d*omi*ni R*egis* ijd ...

[Fol. 14r]

It*em* in denar*ijs* petit*is* p*er* Walteru*m* Geffreys alderm*annum* p*ro* suis aduisam*ento* discrec*ione* & labore h*abitis* in p*ro*uisionib*us* stac*ionu*m Regis qui in talib*us* magna*m* h*ab*et exp*er*ienciam ac concepc*ionem* diu*er*so*rum* & plurimo*rum* texto*rum* posito*rum* sup*er* tiatra ad portas de Nedeh*am* et in foro ut in billa sua imposit*a* coram iam auditorib*us* int*er* alia affilat*a* liquet ap*er*te n*il* hic q*uia* postea in pede

Invoice R. Ferrour: Item in monies paid to Richard Ferrour, alderman, per invoice attached: for 13s 4d paid by him to the footmen of the Lord King as a bonus

[Fol. 13v]

Item paid for expenses incurred at the inn of Henry Bradfeld for an early morning meal, namely for several of the auditors of the accounts just [then] being calculated of the costs of the Lord King's Entry, namely Richard Brasier, Walter Fornfield, Richard Ferrour, aldermen, Thomas Cambrigge, G[eoffrey] Spirleng and others: 21d

Item paid to John Bekles, fletcher, for moneys owing to him from the community since the time of Thomas Elys as mayor, namely, for 16 sheaves of arrows, price 32s and 12 dozen bowstrings, price 4s, sent to the King's munitions for the wars in the county of York, [expenses] of the king: ~~36s~~

Item paid to Edward Cutiller, Mayor, for the reward he gave to the messenger of the Lord King bearing private letters of the Lord King: 5s

Item paid for a certain invoice from Augustine Boys, as to 3½d for the taking down of 2 tall *mastis* for the theatre in the Marketplace for the Entry of the Lord King: 2d for carrying two shields of arms of the Lord King from the Guildhall to Coslany Gates for the departure of the Lord King; 2d

[Fol. 14r]

Item, cash requested for his advice, decisions, and work in supplying the stations of the King, by Walter Geffreys, alderman, who has great experience of such things, also for his formulation of the many and diverse texts placed on the theatres at Nedeham Gates and in the Marketplace, as set out in his invoice, deposited with others in the presence of the then auditors; paid separately, no amount shown here because included below.

THE *HUY NATIVITY* FROM THE SEVENTEENTH TO THE TWENTY-FIRST CENTURY
Translation, Play-Back, and Pray-Back

Aurélie Blanc and Olivia Robinson

In the early seventeenth century in Huy (present-day Belgium), one or more anonymous Carmelite nuns embarked upon a piece of theatrical translation.[1] Using a medieval vernacular playbook which had been copied in Walloon French within their own convent around a hundred years before, in the second half of the fifteenth century, they set about adapting two of the short plays they found in it (which together cover the narrative of the Nativity, Epiphany, Rage of Herod, and Purification of the Virgin) into a single, new French-language play.[2] They, or two of their sisters collaborated to copy this play into a separate manuscript. The Huy convent's medieval playbook is now owned by the Musée Condé at Chantilly (Chantilly, Condé MS 617); however, the early-seventeenth-century play has remained in the convent's archive, alongside their surviving administrative and financial documentation (Liège, Archives d'Etat, Fonds Dames Blanches de Huy [hereafter 'Fonds DBH'], doc. 386bis). 386bis's play (hereafter the *Huy Nativity*) translates, reworks, and expands the material comprising the first play in Chantilly 617 and the first part of that manuscript's second play. It thus presents the Nativity, Epiphany, and part of Herod's Rage, omitting the Purification and other non-Biblical episodes found in Chantilly 617's Play Two. (We provide a detailed synopsis of the *Huy Nativity* as an appendix.) However, the script breaks off unfinished, suggesting that it might well have gone on to include – in another copy, or in performance – further material from Chantilly 617's second play, and/or from elsewhere.

1. The research presented in this article has been undertaken with the financial support of the FNS (Fonds National Suisse de la Recherche Scientifique), grant no. 100015_165887.

2. Maurice Delbouille established that the later play was directly adapted from the earlier ones: 'Essai sur les nativités Wallonnes de Chantilly, et sur leur adaptation française du xvii siècle' *Mélanges de linguistique romane offerts à M Jean Haust* (Liège: H. Vaillant-Carmanne, 1939) 97–128, at 128.

Minor alterations include changes of spelling or grammatical construction, that reflect changes in linguistic and orthographic practice (e.g. *les anges du ciel* for *les angle de ciel*); more major revisions include for example, the addition of entirely new characters. Sometimes, however, the script is much more radically revised at a structural level, including, for example, the addition of entirely new characters. One such character is the Sibyl, who does not appear at all in the medieval play, but who is sent for by Herod in the *Huy Nativity* to confirm his pre-eminence. In an episode which was certainly known as far back as the Middle Ages (it appears in the *Golden Legend*) the Sibyl experiences a vision of a virgin holding an infant in her arms. In the play, this vision enables her to confirm the birth of Jesus and deny that Herod is all-powerful.[3] The insertion of her vision parallels the vision of the star seen by the Three Kings, and creates a further layer of prophetic foreshadowing and interpretative activity around the birth of Christ.

In 2017, the Medieval Convent Drama project[4] undertook a translation into present-day English of the *Huy Nativity*, as part of our ongoing investigation of the theatrical culture within the Carmelite women's house at Huy that is central to our research project. Although MCD focuses primarily on the medieval period, and thus on the plays in Chantilly 617 and their contexts, we were interested in understanding some of the ways in which a *post*-medieval generation of sisters approached their own convent's medieval history of playmaking and in investigating the kinds of translatorly decisions which they had made.[5] We undertook this study in part through our own, contemporary translation practice, a practice which necessitated close, careful reading, and collaborative discussion about semantics, tone, register, and formal features. Our position as a pair of translators working together (both

3. We discuss the Sibyl further in Matthew Cheung Salisbury, Elisabeth Dutton, and Olivia Robinson 'Medieval Convent Scripts: Translating Scripture and Transforming the Liturgy' forthcoming in *A Companion to Medieval Translation* edited Jeanette Beer (Kalamazoo, MI: Medieval Institute Publications).

4. Online at <http://medievalconventdrama.org>. We here use the term *convent* in its non-specialist sense, to signify a women's religious house of any order, rather than its academic sense, signifying a house (male or female) of one of the mendicant orders.

5. The *Huy Nativity* has never, to our knowledge, been fully edited. Our translation is based on Robinson's unpublished transcription of 386bis, which we also cite in this article. We retain manuscript spelling, lineation, capitalisation, and distinction between *u* and *v*. We have silently expanded abbreviations and have added accents to tonic *e* where appropriate, to facilitate comprehension (e.g. *cité* for *cite*, 'city').

medievalists; one native English speaker and one native French speaker; but each also proficient in the other's native language) mirrored, in some respects, what we know of the play's copyists (who may possibly have been its translators and adaptors): in doc. 386bis, as Thomas-Bourgeois has shown, the *Huy Nativity* is copied collaboratively by at least two different hands, working together to shape and order the material.[6] We were also interested in exploring the ways in which the *Huy Nativity* might have worked in performance and the spaces, pace, and types of movement it might have utilised: our translation, therefore, was designed to be the subject of a staged read-through at the 2017 METh conference in Glasgow. This article comprises some of our reflections on these processes and experiences, both translation and performance, and on the ways in which they have helped us to approach the medieval-inspired *Huy Nativity* in terms of its adaption, its *mise-en-scène*, and its signification in the context of conventual memorial practices.

We also hope that it will serve to open up the Huy sisters' dramatic activities (both medieval and post-medieval) to a wider audience. Within the medieval English tradition, very little convent drama of any kind has survived, but especially not of the sort of play which the Huy Carmelites' manuscripts seem to preserve: that is, performative activities which do *not* seem to have been designed to be an embedded part of a particular liturgical celebration, but which may have taken place as stand-alone events at different times and in different spaces within the nunnery.[7] However, we possess hints that such drama did, indeed, take place in England, in both male and female

6. A.C. Thomas-Bourgeois 'Le Drame religieux au Pays de Liège, avec documents inédits' in *Etudes de dialectologie romane dédiées à la mémoire de Charles de Grandgagnage* (Paris: Droz, 1932) 283–313, at 297–304. This collaborative copying, intriguingly, also mirrors the way in which the two fifteenth-century source-plays in Chantilly 617 were copied (discussed by Olivia Robinson 'Mystères as Convent Drama' in *Les Mystères: Studies in Genre, Text, and Theatricality* edited Peter Happé and Wim Hüsken (Amsterdam: Rodopi, 2012) 93–118, especially 98–103, and by Ernest Hoepffner 'Date et Composition des Jeux dramatiques de Chantilly' *Romania* 48 (1922) 62–92): playmaking and copying play-scripts may, perhaps, have formed a collaborative, creative recreational activity within the convent over a long period of time.

7. Two Latin *Visitatio Sepulchri* ceremonies are extant from English convents: one from Barking Abbey and one from Wilton Abbey. Unlike the Huy plays, they do not seem to be targeted purely at women but rather towards a mixed congregation: see Margaret Aziza Pappano 'Sister Acts: Conventual Performance and the *Visitatio Sepulchri* in England and France' in *Medieval Constructions in Gender and Identity* edited Teodolinda Barolini (Tempe AZ: Arizona Center for Medieval and Renaissance Studies, 2005)

religious houses, and that it may have operated as a recreational as well as a liturgical or para-liturgical activity, even if no complete scripts now survive. In 1526, to give one example, visitation records show that the Benedictine nuns of Carrow Priory in Norwich were enjoined not to undertake their Christmas entertainment in which one (or more) of the younger nuns would perform as an Abbess:

> *Item habent in festo Natalis Domini juniorem monialem in abbatissam assumptam, jocandi*[8] *gratia; cujus occasione ipsa consumere et dissipare cogitur quæ vel elemosina vel aliorum amicorum largitione acqusierit.*[9]
>
> Item: At the feast of the Nativity of our Lord, they have a young nun taking on the role of Abbess, for the sake of play; on which occasion it is thought that they ate up and squandered what had been acquired, either as alms or through the generosity of other friends.[10]

This description, along with the precision that the entertainment took place at the feast of the Nativity, both suggest a form of 'Girl Abbess' ceremony or

43–67 and Dunbar H. Ogden *The Staging of Drama in the Medieval Church* (London: Associated University Presses, 2002).

8. The *Dictionary of Medieval Latin from British Sources* suggests a correction to the original editor's reading here, proposing *jocandi gratia* for *vocandi gratia*. See *Dictionary of Medieval Latin from British Sources* edited R.E. Latham, D.R. Howlett and R.K. Ashdowne (Oxford: British Academy, 1975–2013) sv *abbatissa*, sense b.
9. *Visitations of the Diocese of Norwich, A.D. 1492–1532* edited Rev. A. Jessopp (Camden Society, 1888) 209; we are grateful to Veronica O'Mara for drawing our attention to this document. James Stokes gives many further examples of nuns' involvement in dramatic activities in the diocese of Lincoln: 'Women and Performance: Evidence of Universal Cultural Suffrage in Medieval and Early Modern Lincolnshire' in *Women Players in England, 1500–1600* edited Pamela Allen Brown and Peter Parolin (Aldershot: Ashgate, 2005) 25–43, at 36–7. David Klausner has recently discussed an example of monks undertaking extra-liturgical theatrical activities: 'Playing the Crucifixion in Medieval Wales' *METh 38* (2015) 57–67. Abigail Young has suggested that sisters within Canonsleigh Abbey in Devon may have been leaving the convent to attend lay 'spectacles' or performances, a practice which was discouraged by their Visitor in 1329: 'Theatre-Going Nuns in Devon?' *Early Theatre 22* (1997) 25–9. These various examples suggest that the nature and purpose of performative activities undertaken or attended recreationally within and by members of medieval religious houses was very wide-ranging indeed.
10. Our thanks to Sarah Carpenter for help with this translation.

game. The emphasis placed on the consumption and dissipation of resources suggests that the Carrow sisters took the opportunity to indulge in an extended festive role play which perhaps involved food, drink, and communal entertainment alongside the traditional reversal of ceremonial and liturgical roles between senior and junior members of the community.[11]

While it does not, of course, 'stand in' unproblematically for lost English scripts and detailed documentation, the evidence from Huy provides us with a more precise sense of what we might provisionally term the recreational drama taking place in English women's religious houses may have been like. For this reason, the Huy Carmelite plays are a particularly important set of materials for students of medieval English theatre. The precise performance contexts, purposes, and audiences of this kind of convent theatre are difficult to recapture; the convent at Huy, for example, may have used its plays in a number of ways and played them before quite different audiences. The medieval source-play in Chantilly 617 specifies *tresdouche suers* ('sweet sisters') as its primary audience, suggesting, at that stage, members of the convent *only* as both participants *and* audience, and situating the plays as a community exercise in creative devotion. Surviving account books, however, show that the Huy Carmelites operated a school at the time the medieval manuscript was copied, a fact which opens up the possibility that the fifteenth-century scriptural plays (and, indeed, the other plays which accompany them in the Chantilly manuscript) may have been used in an educative context and that the performers may have been the nuns' pupils rather than the sisters themselves.[12] The seventeenth-century *Huy Nativity* begins with an *Anoncemant d'iciluy Jeux* ('announcement of this play') which addresses the *Reverande Dame Prieure* ('reverenced Lady Prioress') and the *chere Dames* who

11. See Marilyn Oliva, *The Convent and the Community in Late Medieval England* (Woodbridge: Boydell, 1998) 72–3.

12. The essays in *Drama and Pedagogy in Medieval and Early Modern England* edited Elisabeth Dutton and James McBain (Swiss Papers in English Language and Literature 31; Tübingen: Narr Francke Attempto, 2015) discuss the widespread overlap between theatrical and pedagogical practices in the late medieval and Tudor periods. Andrea Knox documents a sixteenth-century manuscript which makes reference to a play about the life of St Mary Magdalen written by female pupils in the Irish Dominican convent of Valladolid, Spain (founded 1545): 'Her Book-lined Cell: Irish Nuns and the Development of Text, Translation and Literacy in Late Medieval Spain' in *Nuns' Literacies in Medieval Europe: The Kansas City Dialogue* edited Virginia Blanton, Veronica O'Mara, and Patricia Stoop (Turnhout: Brepols, 2015) 67–86, at 75.

make up the audience. We translated this as 'dear sisters', since 'dear ladies' struck us as a trifle patronising in tone, in contemporary usage, yet it is worth remembering that 'dear sisters' skews our sense of the audience members towards nuns alone, when the word *dames* (unlike the medieval plays' *suers*) might also include other, lay women.[13]

Translating the Play's Language

A first section of this article will reflect on language and the implications its translation has on the transmission both of the play's theological content and of its performative characteristics. The initial questions we encountered regarding language which needed to be addressed at the outset mainly related, in one way or another, to establishing the degree of modernisation or acculturation which it might be best to aim for. Our choices here would influence the performance given by the actors and the perception of the play by the audience. In translating a piece of early Burgundian theatre composed in Walloon French into contemporary English, we were faced with a double foreignness or 'distance': temporal *and* geographic. Simon Gaunt has discussed the translation of medieval texts into contemporary English in terms of the ethical difficulties inherent in smoothing out or eliding specificities relating to time, place, linguistic identity, and form in an attempt to accommodate the linguistic and cultural norms of a contemporary audience.[14] We agreed

13. Delbouille documents an alternative *anoncemant* for the *Huy Nativity*, copied roughly contemporaneously on a loose sheet of paper rather than in its manuscript booklet, 'De l'intérêt des nativités Hutoises de Chantilly et de Liège' *Mélanges d'histoire du théâtre du Moyen-Age et de la Renaissance offerts à Gustave Cohen, professeur honoraire en Sorbonne par ses collègues, ses élèves et ses amis* (Paris: Librairie Nizet, 1950) 75–84, at 83. This alternative prologue, intriguingly, addressed the play to '*Madame la reine*' as well as the Prioress and '*dames*': evidently, the sisters at some point intended to play, or actually played, the piece before a visiting queen (Delbouille identifies a possible candidate, Marie de Medici, who in the end did not make her proposed visit to Huy in 1638). The slip of paper preserving this reworked prologue is no longer held directly alongside doc. 386bis: we hope that further searches will unearth it elsewhere in the Fonds DBH.

14. Simon Gaunt 'Untranslatable' in *Rethinking Medieval Translation: Ethics, Politics, Theory* edited Emma Campbell and Robert Mills (Cambridge: D.S. Brewer, 2012) 243–55. Discussing idiomatic, facing-page modern English translations of medieval texts, Gaunt writes: 'shouldn't it be *difficult* and *challenging* to access a different culture, and isn't being confronted with the alterity of a strange language part of this process?' (255).

in principle with this position and initially felt a desire to preserve the *Huy Nativity*'s foreignesses rather than sacrifice them to make the play more palatable to our audience. Yet we also needed to produce a text that would be readable and quickly assimilated: the read-through at METh would involve non-professional actors, some entirely unfamiliar with medieval French, who had little preparation time and no rehearsals. Because of these practical constraints, we chose to punctuate our script with modern punctuation and uniformly added speech markers where they were absent, making decisions about attributing speeches to characters where the manuscript was unclear.[15] We added regular scene divisions, in order to help our actors and to underscore the movements between different time frames and spaces presented within the play.[16] In the case of unreadable words, or words we found it impossible to gloss satisfactorily, we emended to give a contextually plausible alternative.[17]

We also swiftly realised, as the translation process got under way, that we could find no satisfactory way of retaining the *Huy Nativity*'s *francophonie* without making the translation sound parodic. Preserving the play's syntax struck us as a possible solution but we felt that this might just sound very odd, rather than specifically Walloon or French. Attempting to include French accents would risk sounding like the BBC 'wartime' comedy *'Allo 'Allo*. We thus decided not to emphasise the play's geographical location in our translation. We did, however, seek to preserve its 'time'. The play is now

15. On taking into account the particular contexts and medium of a play's anticipated delivery when translating for the theatre, see the comments on translating Pirandello for radio performance in Susan Bassnett 'Still Trapped in the Labyrinth: Further Reflections on Translation and Theatre' in *Constructing Cultures: Essays on Literary Translation* edited Susan Bassnett and André Lefevere (Clevedon: Multilingual Matters, 1998) 90–108, at 98.
16. One scene division exists in the seventeenth-century manuscript; it comes after the adoration of the Shepherds and the introduction of the three kings and moves the action of the play to Herod's court. It is preceded by a blank folio (fol. 4^{v}) and starts on fol. 5^{r} with *Cy Commence le Jeux/D'Herode* ('Here starts the Play/Of Herod').
17. For example, we struggled with the term *bolet*, in the phrase *prennons bolet et bourdon* ('grab your [?] and your staff', spoken by a Shepherd preparing to travel to the manger). In all the examples of usage which we found for this noun, it signified 'mushroom' (and still does in contemporary French). We translated the term 'bundle' as an alternative which made sense in the context of the scene, but we have found no independent textual evidence to support this. It is of course possible that the reading *bolet* is incorrect: the first two letters of the word are partially obscured by an ink smudge in 386bis (fol. 3^{r}).

triply in the past – our translation deals with a seventeenth-century version of a medieval imagining of a scriptural past. As our translating work progressed, however, it became increasingly clear to us how much the seventeenth-century version of the play highlights the fact that its performance is taking place in a *contemporary* time frame. Its opening moments, in which the *Anoncemant* marks or charts the transition from real world into play world, are marked by ambiguity as to who is performing and who is part of the audience. Joseph's first words address an individual or a group of people, asking for lodgings, but the only other person who speaks 'onstage' is Mary:

> Joseph et Marie vons logis cherchans
>
> [Joseph]
> *Hé bon ians loge nous ceans*
> *ie vous prie nous loger*
> *cet nuit seulement*
>
> Marie
> *Bonne Dame au non de Dieu*
> *loge nous icy nous ne scavons que d'en enquerir*
>
> Joseph and Mary go looking for lodgings
>
> *Joseph:*
> Good people, are there lodgings here?
> I beg you to shelter us
> Just for tonight.
>
> *Mary:*
> Good lady, in the name of God
> Give us lodgings here: all we can do is beg.

No one answers.

It is highly likely that the 'people' and 'good lady' addressed here are the audience of Prioress and nuns and, if they were present, other women too. This immediately implicates the watching community in the action onstage, drawing them into the scriptural past as active participants. They become, for that moment, the hostile residents who will not shelter the fleeing couple, rather than the safe refuge which might be more readily associated with a monastic house. The play is, therefore, deeply anchored from the very start in its own present moment, and we chose to underline this by avoiding wherever possible obviously archaic formulations. Our initial, theoretical, desire to keep the text's foreignesses thus had to be altered as we undertook the practical business of translation. We wanted our script to have a similar contemporary relationship with its actors and audience to the one that it appears to have had at the time of its initial performance: a careful bringing into the present time of a past narrative (the Nativity) and a past performance heritage *within* the convent. While we did very occasionally use specific archaisations for local effects,[18] we largely aimed to construct a more contemporary idiom and style.

Our wish to archaise only very sparingly led to some difficulties, which caused us to question our own stylistic preconceptions and assumptions concerning contemporary dramatic language. Some of these issues were simply a case of not wishing to sound needlessly parodic to a contemporary ear. For example, we struggled to find a term to equate to *dame* when it was used as a title from one shepherdess to another: 'lady' in Modern English sounded too elevated for a shepherdess and 'mistress' evoked Mistress Quickly and cod-Shakespearean comedy. Similarly, we translated *Compagnons et berger*, an address by one shepherd to the others, as simply 'friends' because we felt that 'Friends, shepherds' sounded too close to a parody of *Julius Caesar*, while 'Friends and shepherds' seemed to imply, in present-day English, two different groups of people. Perhaps unsurprisingly, given his centrality in both school and university English Literature courses, both of these difficulties were determined by the lasting influence of Shakespeare's dramatic language on our own sense of theatrical decorum and parody.

Our desire not to archaise also made us aware of the poverty of present-day English vocabulary in certain domains that were key to the play's action and modes of expression. As we tried to free our translation from old-fashioned phrases, we rapidly exhausted our options. Predictably, a particular challenge was presented by the French differentiation between *tu* and *vous*, which we expressed through changes in register, present-day English lacking a

18. Our best example of this was Mary's announcement that she is about to give birth: *Mon père l'eur et venue maintenant | Que je doit anfanter mon anfant*. This we translated as: 'Father, I am nearing my time | The birth of my child is close at hand', where the old-fashioned euphemism 'nearing my time' was used largely for reasons of its associated decorum: the Virgin Mary does not speak about Christ's birth colloquially or graphically. The verb *anfanter* still exists in present-day French (spelled *enfanter*), although its use would, today, sound very archaic: we deployed an equivalent archaism to translate it which replicates the effects of *enfanter* for a contemporary French speaker.

grammatical distinction between formal and colloquial 'you'. Other instances in which we struggled to find a modern English translation included: *Hé las noble dame!* We rendered this as 'Oh noble lady' instead of using the now comically archaic 'Alas!'. While the expression 'Oh' arguably does not convey the same strength of feeling as *Hé las*, we struggled to come up with an English expression that would encapsulate sorrow and despair at a turn of events and which did not sound ridiculous.[19]

Creating an appropriately decorous style in which to render the play's sometimes complex treatment of theological subject matter was also especially difficult. Translation has the power to affect audience perception of the play as either foreign or familiar, but it can also influence the audience's understanding and reception of its content. As we have noted, it was important to us to avoid a sense of parody in our translation (although there were certainly moments in the play intended to be humorous) because we felt that the expansions and rewordings undertaken in the *Huy Nativity*, when compared to its medieval counterpart, often tended to explore particularly complex theological or devotional questions, questions which were evidently perceived as important by the play's creator(s). Words which might carry particular theological resonance, then, necessitated careful translation. One intriguing example is the term *nourisons*; this is applied to Joseph, who is addressed as: *vous, nourisons | de l'anfant*. Cotgrave's 1611 *Dictionarie*, Richelet's 1680 *Dictionnaire françois*, and the 1762 *Dictionnaire de l'Académie françoise* all accord in giving a definition for the noun *nourrisson* which suggests that the term refers unambiguously, in the seventeenth and eighteenth centuries, to a child who is being fed, rather than an adult who feeds a child.[20] Clearly, though, this usage does not fit with how the word is used when it is applied to Joseph. *Nourisons* differs from the equivalent term used in the medieval version

19. Readers suggested terms or expressions such as 'dear', 'gee', 'woe', 'dear me', and 'too bad', synonyms generated by a thesaurus. None of these appeared to do justice to Joseph's feelings in these lines without sounding comedic.

20. Randle Cotgrave *A Dictionarie of the french and english tongues* (1611): *Nourrission*; Pierre Richelet *Dictionnaire françois* (1680): *Nourrisson, norrisson*. Both consulted online via the Classiques Garnier Numériques database: <https://www.classiques-garnier.com/numerique-bases/index.php?module=App&action=FrameMain>, accessed 25 September 2017. *Le Dictionnaire de l'Académie françoise* (Paris: Brunet, 1762); consulted online at <http://catalogue.bnf.fr/ark:/12148/cb351535262>, accessed 21 September 2017. *Le Trésor de la langue française* gives an attested example for this usage dating to 1538: <http://atilf.atilf.fr/tlf.htm>, accessed 21 September 2017.

of this scene, which gives *norisseur*. This is a well-attested medieval word meaning 'one who feeds, one who brings up or provides for'. It is, therefore, a theologically precise definition of Joseph's relationship to Mary's child which highlights both Christ's paternal Divinity and Joseph's unique and privileged experience within the Holy Family, and which emphasises the role which *Joseph*, specifically, plays in contributing to the bodily nourishment, care and bringing-up of the Christ-child.[21] Highlighting this foster-paternal source of nourishment and education may even have eucharistic implications: Joseph contributes to the feeding and nurturing of Christ's body, which will in turn 'nourish' the bodies of the faithful, both spiritually and literally, at the moment of communion. We chose to translate the address to Joseph fairly neutrally as: 'you, Joseph, who provide for this child', although a translation which was more explicit about Joseph as Jesus' foster-father would also have been possible: clearly, this is what the medieval play is suggesting, and the *Huy Nativity* is, presumably, aiming for something similar.

Its adaptors' decision to use the word *nourisons* to suggest this meaning is intriguing, however; particularly so since the medieval noun *nourrisseur* was apparently still in use in the seventeenth century: the adaptors could simply have retained this term.[22] It is, of course, possible that the use of *nourisons* is simply a mistake, and that the copyist meant to write *nourrisseur*. However, it is also possible that the sisters deliberately chose to employ this word and that it was selected to sound consciously old-fashioned or strange. The *Anglo-Norman Dictionary* lists an uncommon Anglo-Norman noun which is much closer to that used in the *Huy Nativity*: *nuriçun*. It gives a primary meaning

21. See *DMF* sv *nourrisseur*, sense A and B; consulted online at <http://www.atilf.fr/dmf/>, accessed 21 September 2017. The honouring of Joseph's particular role as foster-parent and provider for Jesus appears to have been embedded in the Huy Carmelites' liturgical practices: Joseph's feast day is marked in their surviving Obituary with the very unusual entry *Sancti ioseph* ***nutricij domini*** ('Saint Joseph, *foster-father of the Lord*'; Fonds DBH doc. 43, page 24). On the Latin verb *nutrire*, suffix *nutri-*, and related medieval terms designating the contemporary practice of fosterage, see Anita Guerreau-Jalabert '*Nutritius/Oblatus*: parenté et circulation d'enfants au Moyen Âge' in *Adoption et Fosterage* edited Mireille Corbier (Paris: de Boccard, 1999) 263–90, at 266–8.

22. It is attested in Cotgrave (1611) and in Richelet (1680): in both dictionaries, it refers to an adult who raises a child but who is not their parent. Social practices of fosterage appear to have continued from the early medieval period into the seventeenth century: see Guerreau-Jalabert '*Nutritius/Oblatus*' and Tracy Adams 'Fostering Girls in Early Modern France' in *Emotions in the Household, 1200–1900* edited Susan Broomhall (Basingstoke and New York: Palgrave Macmillan, 2008) 103–18.

of 'nourishment, sustenance', for this noun, but also one example (dating to the late fourteenth century) of a secondary meaning: 'foster-child' *or* 'foster-father', in line with the associations attached to the much more commonly attested medieval word *no[ur]risseur*.[23] Anita Guerreau-Jalabert, citing the *Altfranzösisches Wörterbuch*, likewise highlights the Old French term *norriçon*'s use to mean 'educateur, tuteur, "père adoptif"'.[24] It would seem likely that the *Huy Nativity*'s unusual seventeenth-century use of the word *nourisons* to designate Joseph responds to the theological significance of the way his role and relationship to Jesus – that of foster-father – is clearly articulated in the medieval source-play. And it is, perhaps, possible that this response is expressed in a word which consciously created an archaic or dated tone, looking back to the source of the play in the convent's medieval past. Our translation, we found, could not express these potential nuances in effect.

We had similar difficulty in conveying the description of God's activity and presence within the human world which is articulated by the three Shepherds upon their arrival at the stable, when they describe the wonder of the Incarnation:

> *Voicy le lieu qui est bien reluisant*
> *ou nostre Dieu et sur le foin gisant*
> *voiez la lumier de Dieu eternele*
> *oeuure singulier du grand Dieu*
> *immortele*
>
> Here is the most radiant place
> Where our God is lying on the hay.
> See the light of God eternal,
> Incomparable sign of our great God
> immortal.

23. See *AND*, s. *nuriçun*, sense 1 and 2, and commentary. Consulted online at <http://www.anglo-norman.net>, accessed 21 September 2017. *Nuriçun* only appears in one citation with the possible meaning 'foster-father', which dates to 1388. As the *AND* editors note, if this example does *not* denote a foster-father, it denotes a foster-child. For more instances of related terms meaning 'foster-child', see *AND*, sv *nuriçune*. For the *medieval* French term *nourrisson* (which carries a primary meaning 'food' or 'nourishment' and a secondary meaning 'those brought up by an individual', or 'the education, upbringing of, e.g., a child), see *DMF* sv *nourrisson*.

24. '*Nutritius/Oblatus*' 268.

The adjective *singulier* expresses at once the uniqueness and the extraordinary nature of God's *oeuure*. *Oeuure* (present-day French *œuvre*) itself also proved difficult to translate. Its formal register made us discard the literal translation of 'work'. After trying various alternatives, including 'unique making', 'unique achievement', and 'incomparable act', we decided to highlight the fact the Shepherds were here discussing the light (*la lumier de Dieu eternele*) rather than the event of the Nativity itself (although that, too, is clearly an *oeuure singulier*, and the term would, therefore, seem to refer to both). 'Sign' for *oeuure* appeared to us to be the best possible choice, although this unambiguously associates its referent with the light. We finally settled upon 'incomparable sign'.

The words of the Angel to the Shepherds presented challenges in translating theological language of a different nature:

Gloria jn excelcis deo
Tres chere frere et amy
grande ioie je vous annonse
car au iourdhuy vous est né le sauve[*ur*]
qui est crist et seigneur
allez vous en betleem la sité
la vous le truueré en la creche
de drapelet enuelloppez

Gloria in excelsis deo!
Dearest brothers and friends
I bring you news of great joy
For unto you is born this day
A saviour which is Christ the lord.
Go to the city of Bethlehem
You will find him there wrapped in swaddling clothes,
Lying in a manger.

The speech begins with the liturgical Latin *Gloria*, signalling a shift into a heavenly register, which we imagined as highly traditional and formal. The close similarity of the Angel's words to Luke 2: 11–12 led us to base our translation on these verses from Luke, and thus to reverse the order in which the manger and cloths are mentioned. Furthermore, we decided to cite these words as they appear in the King James Bible: although clearly anachronistic in the context of the play's action, this choice gives a present-day academic audience an instantly recognisable Biblical effect and formal register. Even at the time of its translation, the King James Bible was conservative in its lexical and grammatical choices, and it now represents an archaic English that is nonetheless familiar to most listeners from (for example) Christmas readings. It has become 'traditional', formal, and culturally prestigious: we decided that it would form a legible way of translating the shift in register which the Angel brings to the scene.

The sisters' affective piety, too, gave rise to some terms which were a challenge to translate, such as the verb *a[d]orer* and its associated adjective *adorable* (used relatively frequently within the play to denote the attitude and feelings of the visiting Shepherds and Kings towards Jesus). The modern English terms that have developed from the same etymological roots now have a rather different register from the medieval French: *adorable* in contemporary English usually connotes a kind of trivial, cutesy excitement about something like a puppy. The profound, more spiritual implications that the verb carries in the *Huy Nativity* are largely lost. We used the doublet 'love and worship' to express characters' sense of affective devotion but also reverence and honour. At times, we used *love* or *worship* alone if it seemed one emotion was being more insisted on than the other in a particular context. The difficulty presented by *adorer* demonstrates how the theological sense of a word can be lost through a shift in register over time, even if that word has remained recognisably in the language.

Startling shifts in register and tone were also deployed by the dramatists as a theatrical technique within the play. We sought to preserve such shifts and focused on grammar, form, and tone to do so. Changing them would influence the actors' performance, their understanding of the characters, and the effect of these characters on the audience. Beyond its role in the transmission of the play's content, translation thus has an impact on the transmission of some of its textual features which play a central role in performance. We tried to maintain the original variations from informal to formal register indicated in the script through the use of the distinction *tu/vous*, and of regular rhymes and polysyllabic words. The Magi's language is a perfect example of formal register: flowery, courteous, and extremely repetitive almost to the point of parody, it features many repeated rhymes and terms, and its metre, while not perfectly regular, is sustainedly more so than in the speech of other characters in the play. These characteristics are particularly obvious in the Kings' introductions to one another:

Jaspar
Mon non meseigneur volontier
vous diray san mantir
iay non iaspar et suy Roy
darabie et par plusieur iour
me suy partit sachez que naie
austre volonté que dadorer le Roy
nouvaux nay.

My name, my lords, I will gladly
Reveal to you:
I am called Jaspar and am king
Of Arabia, and it has been many days since
I left there.
I would make known to you that I have
No other wish than to worship
The newborn king.

Melchior
Je suis audit attandant
de lescresture qui dit avant
de iacob lestoille aistreroit
les filïs dis[r]*ael a nous vindroit*
qui tout les regne terriens
auroit tres biens en se main
sachez que ie suy dune cité
Roialle, qui est dit cité de thar[s]*e*
et suit par droit non appellez
Melchior bien renomé.

I follow the many sayings
Of those who have prophesied before
That the star of Jacob will be set shining in the sky;
The son of Israel will come to us
Who will hold all the principalities of the earth
Firmly in his hand.
I make known that I come from a royal city, which is named
The city of Tharse;
And I am by right name known as
Melchior, the well-renowned.

Balthazar
Sachez mes seigneur
que mon non est balthazar
et suy Roy couronnet
de la cité de Saba
cy aie une estiolle veut
qui au ciel et apparue
la quel ma issy droit amennez
pour trouuer le Roy nouvaux nay.

I make known, my lords,
That my name is Balthazar
And I am crowned king
Of the city of Saba.
There I beheld a star
Which appeared in the sky
And which has brought me directly to this place
To find the newborn king.

Clearly, we were unable in our translation to reflect the rhythmical and formal features of these lines. We tried, however, in our choice of lexis to convey the ponderous and aristocratic tone taken by the Three Kings; we wondered whether they are characterised deliberately as slightly pompous, or whether this is simply an example of poor style. However, we decided to attempt to retain their tone because of the various possibilities of characterisation it offered the actors. For example, we translated *sachez* ('know', second person imperative, used repeatedly in the play from one king to another to signal the conveying of information) formally and performatively as 'I make known that ...' every time it was used by the Kings; the past tense of the verb *voir* as 'I beheld' rather than 'I saw'; and the expression *issy droit amennez* as 'brought directly to this place' rather than (for example) 'brought straight here'. Very occasionally, we were able to recreate particular rhymes in English. For example, we replicated the rhyme that concludes Balthazar's moving description of Jesus's poverty, emphasising the opposition between Christ's earthly poverty and their own wealth as earthly kings: *nous abonsdons en richesse / et nostre Roy est mit en la chreche* ('We abound in treasure / While our king lies in the manger'). Our half-rhyme couplet provides a sense of conclusion and summary familiar to more modern audiences from Shakespeare's frequent use of rhyming couplets to conclude a scene.

The most challenging characters to translate were Herod and his Fool, because of their profound rudeness to one another. Herod, for instance, aggressively insults and silences the Fool: *Taisé vous gloutin.* Colloquialisms, as well as the distinction between *tu* and *vous* are key to expressing the transgressive familiarity of the Fool to his superiors. The casual terms in which he addresses the Magi – *Hé, brave gent* – were translated as the similarly colloquial 'Oi, lads!'. When he proceeds to insult Herod, we needed to get across not only his rudeness, but also the marked shift from *vous* to *tu* in the middle of the speech:

> *Ha sire a vostre parolle*
> *on antan bien que vous est un tré*
> *bon homme de bien*
> *comant osse tu panser le parole*
> *que tu dit*
> *avec ces noble Roy il ont grande*
> *puissans et san nombre de ian d'arme*
> *et ne vous craing nulemant.*

We decided that the *vous* (*vostre parole*) at the start of the speech was mockingly deferential, and that the shift in register to *tu* (*comant osse tu*) at its centre was very marked. We conveyed the Fool's disrespect with sudden use of colloquialism and obscenity:

> Oh, oh my gracious Lord, one can understand by your words
> That you are a most excellent and noble gentleman!
> But seriously, you idiot, how do even dare imagine the crap that you spout
> About these noble kings?
> They are incredibly powerful and command plenty of armed men:
> They in no way fear you!

By contrast, the adoration of the Shepherds and Shepherdesses, with its repetition and enumeration of Jesus' body parts, proved difficult to translate because of its highly sentimental tone. Gushing over Jesus, they call him *tendrelet*, a cute and tender colloquialism that expresses their closeness to the child. In our search for a modern equivalent, we went from 'little chap' to the more generic 'little one', but were dissatisfied with both. The intimacy and affection of the tone often sound sentimental when replicated in Modern English; some of the work is already done in French by the pronoun *tu*, used to an intimate or equal, with which the Shepherds address Jesus. We further struggled to mirror the Shepherds' physical, bodily devotion to the baby Jesus in a language that did not sound parodic to a modern audience. A prime example was *o joyeux fron*, which signifies literally 'O happy forehead' and which seemed to recall almost inevitably Shakespeare's mechanicals. Our translation of this and other similar passages, while avoiding the most egregious oddities (we chose 'joyful face' over 'happy forehead'), retained a sense of deep emotional and affective engagement with Jesus's status as a baby which still, in a contemporary context, at times struck us as sounding exaggerated.

The kinds of discussion which we had about specific words or expressions and which we have explored in this section sensitised us to the ways in which the seventeenth-century sisters may have approached their adaptation work. This is particularly true for moments at which terms or expressions are altered between medieval and seventeenth-century play in a more substantive fashion than modernisation of spelling. For example, the Fool's insult to Herod, which we cite above, largely follows the language of the equivalent medieval passage closely. Alterations mainly take place at the level of orthography (e.g. *penser* for *penseir*, or *osse* for *ouse*); however, the final line of the insult has been reworded: instead of in no way fearing Herod, the medieval kings do not consider him worth a button, or a button's worth (*il ne vous priesent pont ung botton*). The meaning of the Fool's words remains broadly the same across the two scripts: he asserts that the Kings are unimpressed and undaunted by the prospect of Herod's anger. Yet the later adaptors evidently decided to alter the expression in which that sentiment was conveyed. Clearly, it is impossible to say categorically why this change was made: reflecting on the discussions which we had as we translated cannot simply reveal the reasoning of our seventeenth-century counterparts. However, the range of conversations and dilemmas which formed a core part of our collaborative translation process, and which were often at the level of particular words or expressions, offered us valuable imaginative insights into the *kinds* of discussion and shared decision which may have led the Huy adaptors to reword certain passages in the ways that they did. For example, the *botton* analogy may simply have sounded too archaic or too obscure to the seventeenth-century adaptors. Or, more interpretatively, perhaps the sisters felt a desire to tone down slightly the transgressive humour of the Fool's words at this moment: *il ... ne vous craing nulemant* is a statement of fact; a much less challenging, creative, and evocative image than *il ne vous priesent pont ung botton*. Our own work, therefore, led us to think more creatively about the kinds of conversation and process which may lie behind the seventeenth-century play-text as it currently survives.

Embedding Direction in Translation

Translating dramatic texts such as this one presents challenges and opportunities. We have seen how specific decisions about the translation of language and tone can affect characterisation and performance. More than words only, however, the voices, gestures, costumes, and props, lighting, sound effects, and the architecture, decoration, and facilities of the venue as a whole all convey meaning during a dramatic performance, as Susan Bassnett reminds us.[25] Bassnett argues that the theatrical translator is responsible for the words of the script *only* ('the linguistic and paralinguistic aspects of the text that are decodable and re-encodable').[26] However, as we were translating, we realised that we could not function as 'words only' translators, in the way outlined by Bassnett. Perhaps due to our shared experiences as theatre practitioners, rather than translators for the theatre, we found ourselves imagining *mises-en-scène* as we worked, and this exerted an impact on our lexical choices. The times at which our imagination was especially vivid might be conceptualised as a conscious taking on of the role of directors as well as translators, embedding an imagined performance *into* the translated text. This was the case, for instance, with Joseph's words to Mary:

> Joseph a Marie:
> *Noble Dame cet soy sy*
> *ie voy biens que on ne nous veuss*
> *loger nulement.*
> *ie voy iscy un viel estable:*
> *Loger il nous faudra dedans.*
> *He las noble dame!*
> *que vous faut til? A mon sanblans*
> *vous estre moult belle et resplandissante*

25. Susan Bassnett 'Theatre and Opera' in *The Oxford Guide to Literature in English Translation* edited Peter France (Oxford UP, 2000) 96–103, at 96.
26. Bassnett 'Still Trapped' 107.

Joseph to Mary
Noble lady
I can see that no one is willing to shelter us tonight.
Here is an old stable:
We will have to take refuge within it.
O noble lady, how can I look after you?
In my eyes you glow with beauty.

Our close reading and discussion of Joseph's lines, as we considered how best to translate them, drew apparent disconnections and non sequiturs to our attention. His speech shifts from the logical discussion of shelter in the stable, to a question about Mary's needs, to a statement about her glowing beauty. The latter two elements appear in a new folio of the manuscript (fol. 2^{r}), even though there is a gap at the end of fol. 1^{v} which could have contained them: perhaps, then, these changes in tone might in part be due to the scene being composed over a space of time. Nonetheless, the overall effect is one of rather abrupt changes of subject matter. We imagined what might occur onstage to give rise to this: Joseph is in despair because of the poor treatment shown to his wife, a tired and heavily pregnant woman struggling to sit and get comfortable in a stable. We therefore translated Joseph's words to her as both reassuring and tender, rendering *que vous faut til* as 'how can I look after you?' to give a sense of 'how can I make this space comfortable for you in your condition?', 'how can we make the best of this?'

His next words, a sudden suggestion that Mary is *resplandissante*, very probably draw on a rich, apocryphal, and typological field of imagery describing the Virgin as a source of supernatural light, which was understood at both a figurative and a literal level.[27] Twycross's discussion of occurrences of this motif and its significations offers several points of connection with the *Huy Nativity*'s Joseph; the most pertinent of these, perhaps, relates to Mary's virgin conception and birth. As Twycross summarises, 'the apocryphal motif of Mary's shining face [*was*] ... integrated into the imagery of light surrounding the Incarnation ... She is like a semi-transparent vessel through which the light of God glows'.[28] Within the *Huy Nativity*, Mary herself will

27. Meg Twycross has traced this imagery and the ways in which it was glossed and understood exhaustively: 'As the sun with his beams when he is most bright' *METh 21* (1990) 34–79.

28. Twycross 'As the sun' 52, 58.

very explicitly parallel the moment of Christ's incarnation with the moment of His birth:

> *Mon pere, Ainsy qu'a la con-*
> *ception nul creature n'y fus*
> *chose du monde,*
> *pareillemant ne fera a la*
> *nativité*
>
> Father, just as at the moment of conception
> No human acted in any way,
> So no one will at the Nativity.

She will also refuse Joseph's offer to fetch the midwives who, traditionally, test and confirm her continued virginity after the birth. Her apparently radiant appearance, in the moments prior to this happening, underlines the connection between Incarnation and Nativity, and the assertion of her continued chastity throughout. The fact that it is Joseph who comments on her radiance also connects this moment suggestively to the role sometimes attributed to Mary's dazzling brightness in quashing Joseph's doubts about her pregnancy: 'a confirmation of Joseph's intuition that she is the chosen one of God'[29] and, therefore, a depiction of Joseph which underlines his humility and his comprehension of Mary's role in God's divine plan. The motif of Mary's radiance also appears in the N.Town *Mary Play*, again experienced and voiced by Joseph (although, unlike in the *Huy Nativity*, his recognition of this light takes place at the moment at which he returns to find Mary pregnant, not at the Nativity). This led Twycross to wonder whether and how the radiance was physically staged.[30] The *Huy Nativity* does not provide stage directions for this moment, nor any explicit suggestion that Mary's *resplandissante* appearance is anything other than figurative (nor does the earlier Chantilly manuscript's medieval play-text). Nonetheless, our feeling when translating these lines was that the shift in subject matter from one moment to the next was sudden and unexpected enough to suggest a possible nonverbal action of some kind from Mary, triggering Joseph's words about her brightness; following Twycross, we imagined Mary's appearance *literally* altered on stage and wondered whether she was somehow suddenly bathed in light.

29. Twycross 'As the sun' 61.

30. Twycross 'As the sun' 65–6.

A different example of imagined performance occurred as we were translating the scene introducing Herod and his court, where the question of interpreting and translating comedy was central. Although locating humour is always an interpretive and potentially subjective act, we felt that we were justified in assuming that this scene should be played as much for laughs as possible, and in cueing actors to produce this kind of performance within our script. Other medieval plays featuring the character of Herod are known for their parodic portrayal of him. Later in the *Huy Nativity*, too, Herod is given the opportunity for some physical comedy, as he is involved in slapstick confrontations with his Fool, who openly mocks him, presumably to comedic effect. We thus sought to give to the speeches of Herod and his courtiers an exaggeratedly bombastic tone. For example, we translated the Messenger's qualification of Jesus's birth as *chose inennarable*, literally 'an unnarratable thing', as 'something unspeakable'. The word *unspeakable* in contemporary English brings with it a sense of taboo, of something so shocking it cannot be named, and was a deliberate attempt on our part to accentuate the comedy. The lines of the Clerk who discusses Jesus's birth with Herod were also translated to comic effect: his description of Bethlehem as *assez pres de Jeruasalem* struck us as giving the opportunity for a kind of pedantic over-exactitude: we rendered these lines as: '*relatively* near to Jerusalem'. Herod's verbatim echo of these exact words in his later speech to the people only reinforces the comedy. The choices we made here were suggested by the text, yet still afforded the actors a certain liberty of interpretation, as will become clear in our discussion of the performance.

The Performance at METh 2017

After the pre-performance in our imagination, we witnessed the actual performance of our translation at the Medieval English Theatre Conference in March 2017. In this section, we reflect on the insights this performance brought us, both in terms of our work as translators, and in terms of the possible staging of the *Huy Nativity* in the seventeenth century. This staged reading was co-ordinated by Elisabeth Dutton and performed in Glasgow University's James Arnott Theatre. The setting was of course not a convent, and the participating academics were not nuns, but they included a core group who have worked together for many years and who have built strong personal as well as professional relationships with each other. The fact that actors and audience members belonged to the same group of people gave the performance a communal spirit. Spectators enjoyed seeing friends and colleagues play well-known biblical figures, and actors sometimes broke character when delivering a line they knew would amuse their audience. In this respect, if in no other, they perhaps embodied some part of the dynamic that might have been found within a convent. Not only were the participants familiar with one another, they also possessed an extensive knowledge of the medieval period and of its drama in particular. Their expertise gave some of them a predetermined view of how their roles ought to be played. The actors playing Herod and Joseph, for instance, were aware of these figures' depiction in medieval drama, respectively as a raging yet often comical tyrant, and as a caring old man. Our Sybil and Shepherds confirmed that their knowledge of the medieval representation of their characters influenced their movements. The participants were given minimal costumes and props, and were asked to read through the script beforehand, but were offered no explicit direction, as the aim was to see how the cast, all expert readers of medieval drama, would respond to our script alone.

As we have noted, many decisions which we made about word-choice within our translation frequently involved us thinking about staging and interpretation of the play in terms of tone, register, and nonverbal actions. Ultimately, our translation is a critical reading of the play, which will inevitably promote a certain kind of production. Once performed, however, we saw that this was not the whole story. While our translation did indeed encode some presupposed interpretative decisions, which were reflected in the actors' performances, certain moments in the play did not pan out as we expected, and performers were able to bring their own interpretation to the piece. The performance provided us with a fresh approach to the play and a fresh approach to the decisions we had made as translators.

The audience laughed at the comedy we had emphasised and the actors concerned responded to the way we had translated (for example) Herod's speeches to his court, delivering them for laughs. However, when arriving at the stable, Joseph's words did not seem to be directly triggered by Mary's nonverbal helplessness in the precise way in which we, when translating, had imagined. In spite of that, the actor playing Joseph afterwards commented that the translation had clearly communicated to him that this scene should be solemn and gentle. Additional dignity and pathos was created by the fact that Joseph, in accordance with medieval tradition, was considerably older than Mary. She was able to reach the stable before him, which emphasised his own inability to assist her.

The Shepherds, too, surprised us in performance. What had seemed to us the extremely saccharine language used about the baby Jesus did not trouble the audience, who found it humorous rather than off-putting; but, crucially, still appreciated the emotional effect of the Shepherds' sincerity of feeling towards the baby: much, perhaps, as we can laugh at Shakespeare's Thisbe and still be strangely moved by her despair. The fact that women played all of the Shepherds heightened the near-maternal affection shown by these characters to the baby, and audience members discussed afterwards the many possible effects which this aspect of the play might have had when the women playing these roles were nuns.

The Three Kings made a rather different impression. The performance emphasised the characters' lack of emotional depth as well as their heavily presentational speeches and movements to an even greater extent than was evident while we were translating. We noticed also that our King-actors rushed to give Jesus their gifts, only to realise after a few further speeches had elapsed that they were in fact meant to acknowledge the baby much later, and that there was a very long stretch of dialogue provided to accompany their movement to the manger. For the actors playing these parts to perform their roles accordingly, then, they would need either a large performing space around which to move slowly, or regular stops throughout their journey. We would suggest that the latter is perhaps more likely, considering the highly choreographed way in which the Kings' dialogue is composed: each speaks in order, in carefully patterned speeches, and each is apparently followed by a retinue of some sort (Balthazar, for example, is described by Jaspar as arriving with *si grand convoye*, 'such a great entourage', an allusion which recalls lavish late medieval depictions of the journey of the Magi such as those found on the walls of the Magi Chapel in the Palazzo Medici Riccardi, Florence). Each stop might, therefore, form a tableau for the audience to behold. Their slow and choreographed approach towards the Holy Family, via Herod's palace, might well also recall a liturgical procession, characterised by movement between various stations upon a spiritual journey towards the sacred.[31]

31. On religious and civic procession in a European context see the essays in *Moving Subjects: Processional Performance in the Middle Ages and the Renaissance* edited Kathleen Ashley and Wim Hüsken (Amsterdam and Atlanta, GA: Rodopi, 2001). Anne Bagnall Yardley discusses liturgical processions in medieval English convents, arguing that processions unite 'pomp and piety' and are at once lavish events and 'spiritual journeys'; see *Performing Piety: Musical Culture in Medieval English Nunneries* (New

Importantly, this liturgical effect was already suggested in the medieval script, through the use of sung Latin liturgical citations within parts of the Kings' dialogue. Elsewhere, we have argued that this feature forms a sophisticated and creative reflection upon the complex temporal qualities of the liturgy, and its rootedness in both scriptural past and living present: this is a quality which the adaptors of the *Huy Nativity* have retained.[32] They further underscored its processional effects by occasionally lengthening each King's speeches and heightening their stateliness.

The buildings of the convent at Huy are no longer standing, and (to date) we have not located any archaeological reports which might map the known topography of the convent architecture in detail. We do not, therefore, have much concrete data about the spaces in which the play may have taken place: given the liturgical tenor of the *Huy Nativity*, most especially the processional aspects of the Three Kings' scenes, the church and the immediately surrounding areas are a distinct possibility. Surviving buildings accounts from the late fifteenth century show that the then newly refurbished conventual church was equipped with at least two side chapels – one dedicated to St Michael and one to the Virgin Mary. The latter had two parlours, as well as a small room behind it.[33] There are several references in the accounts to

York: Palgrave Macmillan, 2006) 113–14. For example, the Palm Sunday procession of the Benedictine priory of St Mary's at Chester, preserved in the early-sixteenth-century *Chester Processional*, started with the nuns going from the church door to 'Jerusalem' while singing *Cum approprinquaet dominus*. Once in 'Jerusalem', they would continue singing before moving to the 'hye crosse in the churcheyarde', and then to the 'crosse on the northe halff' where the gospel was read by a deacon. Finally, the nuns moved back to the church door where the *Gloria Laus* was sung (see Yardley *Performing Piety* 126–7). Processions were also part of the performative tradition of the Huy Carmelite house and its associated organisations; a 1660 letter from the prioress, which survives in the convent archive, requests permission from the dean and chapter of the collegiate church of Nôtre Dame in Huy for the procession of the Confraternity of the Holy Scapular (which was attached to the convent) to change its habitual route, and instead start above the bridge and go around the marketplace (Fonds DBH doc. 388).

32. Cheung Salisbury, Dutton, and Robinson 'Medieval Convent Scripts'; also Olivia Robinson 'Feminizing the Liturgy: The N-Town Mary Play and Fifteenth-Century Convent Drama' in *Drama and Pedagogy* edited Dutton and McBain 71–88, at 79–86.

33. The church was again refurbished in the late seventeenth century (see Alain Orbain 'Vestiges d'Architecture Hutoise: Les églises St Martin d'Outremeuse et St Germain' *Bulletin de la commission royale des monuments et des sites* 8 (1979) 76–89 note 36). It is unclear how much it had changed in the interim period, when the *Huy Nativity* was

stone *greis* (steps) which lead up to the chapels, and in 1479 the sisters had *les fourmes de hour* (the structure of the platform) built. This *hour* – a term which can refer to all kinds of wooden platform or dais and which is sometimes used in a theatrical context to denote a stage[34] – is mentioned several times in the accounts, often with chairs, very probably indicating a wooden gallery within the church, with appropriate seating. It was linked to a dormitory, which was situated above the chapter house and next to the church, by a small doorway or wicket, and to the ground floor interior of the church by a wooden staircase. There was, therefore, quite a complex distribution of space available to be exploited within the conventual church which might make processional performance within it particularly effective.

Experiencing the performance of our script as actors and audience members reignited our reflections on the process of translation. It demonstrated how perceptions of tone can vary from page to stage. We had worried about the Shepherds' speeches, yet their sentimentality did not disturb a contemporary audience. The Kings' stateliness and pomp also emerged more strongly than anticipated. These unexpected differences in perception drew our attention to the subjectivity of translators: performance firmly confirmed that translation is always the product of one or more subjective individuals. Presumably, this was also true for the sisters who adapted the *Huy Nativity*. Our rendition of the tones and registers we had perceived seemed to be at times successful, for instance in the case of comical elements. It became obvious, however, that we had lost control over what was no longer a text on a page. Some of the directions we had embedded in the script were taken up, but actors and audience alike brought their own ideas and sensitivities to the performance. We had, to a certain extent, envisioned our work as directorial and were confronted with the tangible realisation that theatre truly is a collaborative art form, where multiple people open unexpected and enriching possibilities of interpretation.[35]

copied. The fifteenth-century buildings accounts are found in Fonds DBH, doc. 333. A brief narrative account of the construction and renovation of some of the convent buildings soon after its arrival in Huy is also found at the opening of the community's Obituary book, Fonds DBH doc. 43.

34. See *DMF* sv *hourd* (1), sense I. Consulted online at <http://www.atilf.fr/dmf/>, accessed 28 June 2018.

35. Bassnett 'Still Trapped' 107.

Performing this script at METh additionally helped us to reflect on the seventeenth-century staging of the Huy play. We could not gain indisputable answers from witnessing this *mise-en-scène*, but we were made aware of certain practical issues of performance and of certain effects the plays might have had on their audience. The playful interactions between audience and actors, as well as the Magi's liturgical movements, are potent examples of unforeseen staging possibilities, revealed by contemporary performance.

Theatre as Commemorative Practice

As we have seen, our reflections on our own translation practice and the realisation of our translated script in performance provided us with practice-based, experiential perspectives from which to consider the work of the seventeenth-century nuns. The parallels between the nature of our work and that of the Huy nuns prompted us to reflect on the nuns' creative decisions and potential difficulties while adapting a medieval play, but they also prompted questions concerning sisters' relationships with their own conventual past and its cultural productions: why might a seventeenth-century community choose to undertake this adaptation? There are, of course, differences between our relationship to the text we translated, and that of its authors to their medieval source-manuscript. In our case, there is a significant temporal and emotional or identity-related distance between translators and seventeenth-century script. We were not rewriting a cultural artefact from our own past or that of a community or group to which we belonged. Not only was the opposite true of the sisters who adapted the play in MS Chantilly 617, there is also evidence to suggest that the medieval play-script itself was potentially still in use a long time after its copying. The manuscript's final folio (fol. 27^{v}) contains the signature of a sister Eliys de Potiers who is known to have been in the convent between 1583 and 1612.[36] Eliys' signature suggests that the plays within the medieval manuscript may have been known to several generations of sisters. The *Huy Nativity* may not have been the result of a sudden desire to rework an object from the distant past; rather, its adaptors may have been updating a medieval text and event which was still familiar to the community because frequently reiterated. Alternatively, Eliys' signature may mark a new interest in a play which had been discovered or rediscovered among community

36. See *Mystères et Moralités du Manuscrit 617 de Chantilly* edited Gustave Cohen (Paris: Champion, 1920) c–ci.

possessions. In either case, the seventeenth-century Huy nuns clearly chose to use and actualise their own predecessors' work rather than to create an entirely new piece of theatre. In this final section, therefore, we consider *The Huy Nativity* alongside conventual and formal memorial strategies, exploring the ways in which the play might be conceptualised as a communal act of commemoration.

The seventeenth-century nuns' awareness of their convent's past literary culture and traditions, and their desire to keep these alive are attested to by Eliys de Potiers' signature on Chantilly 617 and by the existence of The *Huy Nativity*. We have not uncovered any other examples of a post-medieval religious community reworking or repurposing an earlier entertainment as a form of commemoration or a new performance. However, it is clear that established institutions of all kinds consolidated their sense of communal identity by evoking past members and their activities more broadly through a variety of means, and that the memory of an earlier heritage was often deployed and cultivated as part of this endeavour during the sixteenth and seventeenth centuries. At Balliol College, Oxford, for example, a Fellow named John Atkinson recorded the names and obits of his institution's medieval benefactors in the back of the College Register in 1568.[37] This act is an example of a deliberate deployment of a shared institutional past which constructs or performs a Catholic heritage for his institution in the context of the English Reformation.

Many, if not all, medieval religious houses celebrated and commemorated their history, heritage, and past members as part of their identity through a range of ritual and cultural practices; at times, as in the case of Huy, through creative activities. *The Ordinale and Customary* of Barking Abbey contains, for instance, numerous feasts tailored specifically to this convent. Such modifications of the liturgy are, as Anne Bagnall Yardley asserts, acts of 'creative engagement' driven by the nuns and particularly by the abbesses, even if not verifiably composed by them.[38] These feasts repeatedly commemorate, for an audience of nuns and at times for the laity, the abbey's

37. John Jones *Balliol College: A History* (Oxford UP, 1997) 75.

38. Anne Bagnall Yardley 'Liturgy as the Site of Creative Engagement: Contributions of the Nuns of Barking' in *Barking Abbey and Medieval Literary Culture: Authorship and Authority in a Female Community* edited Jennifer N. Brown and Donna Alfano Bussel (York: York Medieval Press, 2012) 267–82, at 267–8.

prestigious past association with holy figures and its cultural heritage.[39] Burial traditions at Barking Abbey continued to celebrate the nuns' history and to render it visible in the present: some abbesses were buried, as the *Ordinale* indicates, in various parts of the conventual church.[40] Walking in this space daily, the nuns would be physically confronted with the tombs of their predecessors.[41]

Commemorative practices in the Huy Carmelite house, too, straddled past and present in important ways, emphasising a kind of a-temporal continuity within the community even as they engaged with specific, local moments of rupture or change, and so acknowledged the specificity of a particular moment in time. The convent's Obituary survives in its archive and preserves entries from soon after the foundation of the Huy house (in 1466) to the seventeenth century and later.[42] The book records the anniversaries of saints, and integrates them with obits of prominent members of the Carmelite order and the convent's own sisters, along with their families, lay donors, and friends.[43] The *familia* in whose centre the convent sits is thus commemorated through appropriate anniversary prayers or reading out of names.[44] The structure of the Obituary facilitates *repeated* commemoration, keeping the past present.

39. The principal feasts of St Ethelburga (11 October) and St Erkenwald (30 April), for example, celebrate, respectively, the first abbess and the founder of Barking abbey (*The Ordinale and Customary of the Benedictine Nuns of Barking Abbey* edited J.B.L. Tolhurst (London: Harrison, 1927–28) 319, 221, 10, 4).

40. *The Ordinale and Customary* 361–2.

41. Alison Findlay *Playing Spaces in Early Women's Drama* (Cambridge UP, 2006) 151.

42. Fonds DBH doc. 43. For the particular structuring of Obituaries according to liturgical calendar rather than chronological date, see, e.g., Charlotte Stanford *Commemorating the Dead in Late Medieval Strasbourg: The Cathedral's Book of Donors and its Uses (1320–1521)* (Farnham: Ashgate, 2011) xv.

43. The Obituary situates its commemorative entries specifically in the context of the history of the house at Huy: it opens with a short chronicle detailing the arrival of the first sisters from Dinant, and the foundation and building of the convent. This mixing of liturgical with self-referential content is a common feature of such manuscripts; see David Carrillo-Rangel, Blanca Garí, Núria Jornet-Benito 'The Devotional Book in Context and Use: Catalan Poor Clares and English Birgittines: Spaces, Performance, and Memory' in *Religious Practices and Everyday Life in the Long Fifteenth Century (1350–1570)* edited Ana Maria S.A. Rodrigues and Ian Johnson (Turnhout: Brepols, forthcoming 2019).

44. On the *familia*, see Stanford *Book of Donors* 256.

Yet the Obituary is also a changing object through time, as the multiple hands on many of its pages, in some cases spanning centuries, attest: it both is and is not a 'medieval' book. It bears witness to particular, chronologically definable moments, such as the passing of X on Y date, even as it unites the whole community into one bibliographic and conceptual space and links the *familia* together through repeated vocabulary and formulae as well as through the repetition of anniversary commemorations.

Commemoration of the dead is effected rhetorically or performatively by, in the evocative words of David Carrillo-Rangel, 'praying them back' into the community through anniversary celebrations and prayers for the dead.[45] Carrillo-Rangel here refers particularly to the accretive addition of personal rubrics and prayers to prayer books passed among members of a Birgittine community over time, constructing collective, communal memory.[46] Yet the image of a 'pray-back' might also describe the repeated practices of commemoration tied to more structured, cyclical, liturgical celebrations which the Huy Obituary facilitates. Furthermore, many of the Obituary's entries remind the community of the 'presence' of the dead all around them through association with the everyday objects and buildings which surround the sisters. This is done by the common practice of using an individual's obit not just to record for future use the date of their anniversary, but also to list in close detail pre- and post-mortem donations to the house. Some of these gifts take the form of money, land, or comestible goods; but many are, of course, *things*, such as textiles, vestments, and other costume, works of art, relics, objects for ceremonial use within the convent and its church. These are objects which may on occasions have been repurposed for theatrical activities within the convent (and possibly even outside it): sisters may have deployed various kinds of donated object bearing commemorative resonance

45. 'Elizabeth Edward's Devotional Book: Uses of Liturgical Books for Private Reading in Syon Abbey', paper delivered at the *Women's Literary Culture and the Medieval Canon* conference in Bergen, June 2017. We are very grateful to David for his helpful and constructive feedback on an early draft of this article, and for his generosity in sharing his unpublished paper and forthcoming work with us.

46. See also: David Carrillo-Rangel 'Textual Mirrors and Spiritual Reality: Exempla, Mnemonic Devices and Performance in the Birgittine Order' in *Continuity and Change: Papers from the Birgitta Conference at Dartington 2015* edited Elin Anderson, Claes Gejort, E.A. Jones, and Mia Åkestam (Stockholm: Kungl. Vitterhetsakademien, 2017) 160–83, at 173–4.

within their theatrical work, both in the fifteenth century and later.[47] Even if this did not happen and such bequeathed items were *not* used 'onstage', they would still have possessed multiple significations: they embodied a recorded connection to the person who gave them, traceable through that person's obit, while being reused over time within the convent by different sisters in new contexts.

The *Huy Nativity* seems, to us, to take part in a much wider culture within the convent in which it was composed and performed, involving the reiterative commemoration and celebration of the house's history and heritage by a variety of cultural, performative, and liturgical means. The reworking of a pre-existing medieval play, we suggest, participates in the processes of shaping the nuns' identity as members of a specific community, with a well-defined past.[48] The seventeenth-century sisters' translation, adaptation, and likely performance of the medieval play produced in their own convent might, therefore, be read as a powerful method of aligning themselves with their predecessors and bringing the creative work of those predecessors into the present, uniting the sisters in one devotional community.

Université de Fribourg

47. James Stokes gives an example of an English monastic house utilising its sacred textiles in performative activities: in 1440, the visitation records of Thornton Abbey (Augustinian, male) record that: *sacrista accomodat vestamenta Meliora Monasterij ludentibus ludos noxios in partibus inter laicos per quod deteriorantur et scandalum generator Monasterio petit* ('the sacrist is lending the monastery's better sets of vestments to those playing harmful pastimes/games in parts among the laypeople. On this account they are damaged and a scandal arises concerning the monastery'). *REED: Lincolnshire* edited James Stokes (London: British Library; Toronto and Buffalo, NY: University of Toronto Press, 2009).

48. If, as Delbouille suggests, the play was perhaps played before royalty as well as internally within the convent, it would additionally have formed a way of communicating that identity to those outside of the cloister.

APPENDIX: SYNOPSIS OF THE *HUY NATIVITY*

The *Anoncemant*: a prologue, not attributed to any character.

Joseph and Mary look for lodgings; they rest in an old stable; Jesus is born; Joseph and Mary worship Jesus; Joseph worries about the well-being of Jesus in the cold but Mary reassures him and prays to God.

The Angel appears to the shepherds; they rejoice and make their way to the stable; the shepherdesses Mahai and Eylison follow them; the Shepherds and Shepherdesses arrive at the stable and adore Jesus; they rejoice and sing a song to Mary, which draws the attention of two more Shepherds who join them to worship at the crib, before leaving.

Jaspar, Melchior, and Balthazar meet, introduce themselves and state their intent.

A Duke tells Herod that three Kings have come to worship Jesus the King of the Jews; on the advice of the Duke, Herod asks his messenger to bring him a clerk; Herod asks the clerk to tell him the place of Jesus' birth; Herod addresses the people and tells them the news; the people claim they will never have another king; Herod orders his messenger to find the Sybil; he asks her if there is anyone in the world higher than him in power; the Sybil answers, following her vision, that Jesus is.

Herod orders the messenger to bring him the Kings; Herod welcomes the Kings and asks them about Jesus; Herod's Knight and Duke talk of the Kings; the Fool tells the Kings Herod's real intentions are not friendly; the Kings take their leave, suspicious of Herod and his court.

Jaspar prays to God; the Kings find the stable and offer Jesus their gifts in turn; as they are about to leave, the Angel warns them not to return to Herod.

Herod is angry because the Kings have not returned and argues with his Fool; Herod orders the Seneschal to bring him the Three Kings and vows vengeance.

(*unfinished*)

A 'GLADNES' OF ROBIN HOOD'S MEN:
Henry VIII Entertains Queen Katherine

John Marshall

The Prologue

It may seem bizarrely contentious to begin an article by invoking an early-twentieth-century advertising maxim that 'a picture is worth a thousand words'.[1] But in the case of Henry VIII, two portraits, nearly thirty years apart, graphically encapsulate the extent of the king's physical decline and, paradoxically, the increasing use of his gargantuan appearance and imposing stance to self-publicise his formidable and imperious rule. The most familiar of the portraits, and the progenitor of the iconic image of Henry, is the Holbein workshop painting of the king presenting the Charter of the Incorporation of the Company of Barber-Surgeons that took place in 1540.[2] The picture clearly draws on an earlier piece of Tudor propaganda that depicts Henry as a supreme and grandiose example of kingship as red in tooth and claw contrasted with his financially shrewd and publicly cautious father who stands behind him. This wall painting in the Privy Chamber of Whitehall Palace was destroyed by fire in 1698. Fortunately, a copy by Remigius van Leemput made in 1667 survives in the Royal Collection.[3] The Barber-Surgeons' portrait positions Henry seated in a Godlike pose towering above the kneeling and dourly liveried guild members and the royal physicians. He exudes pomp in his rich ermine-lined robes with crown and sword as symbols of divine power and authority. He strikes a Falstaffian figure: bloated, bearded, and fat-in-face with podgy fingers. The size of his codpiece as an emblem of potency and sexual

1. *OED* sv *picture*, phrases P2.
2. The painting is regularly reproduced in works on Holbein and Henry VIII. For convenience of access see *Henry VIII: Man and Monarch* edited Susan Doran (London: The British Library, 2009) 252, or see <https://commons.wikimedia.org/wiki/File:Henry_VIII_and_the_Barber_Surgeons,_by_Hans_Holbein_the_Younger,_Richard_Greenbury,_and_others.jpg>. More detail on the composition and Holbein's workshop involvement in Susan Foister *Holbein and England* (New Haven and London: Yale UP, 2004) 65–7.
3. Foister *Holbein and England* 175–8.

vigour was, as rumour would have it, in disproportion to his performance. By the time of the painting he had ceased to joust or even participate in revels and dances. He was seriously disabled by injury and illness, but his response to ailment and changing circumstances was to be tyrannical to friends and foes alike.

What a contrast to the lesser known portrait, by an unknown artist, of Henry shortly after his marriage and coronation. The figure is lithe, contemplative and sensitive. Bejewelled but not extravagantly so, clean-shaven, and with long artistic fingers. Placed next to Michael Sittow's painting of the young Katherine of Aragon, when she was only a few years older than Henry in his portrait, they look as though, in another age, they might audition for *Romeo and Juliet*.[4]

Not surprisingly, the popular opinion of Henry as a self-indulgent womaniser, tyrant, and relentless pursuer of power is retrospectively evident in the later painting. This article concentrates on the Henry of the earlier portrait when, released from the constraints of a stern father, he embraced love for Katherine with a youthful delight and prowess in jousting, disguising, and dancing. This article is a celebration of a king who initially made a major contribution to a diversity of entertainment, some of it adopted from Burgundy and Italy, that is unparalleled by any other monarch in this country.

Here my purpose is to explore a single, but highly significant, event early in Henry's reign. A private entertainment that has often been referred to, frequently inaccurately, but rarely, if ever, analysed.

The Historical Record: Hall's Chronicle

Since its publication in 1548, the first source of reference to Henry VIII's entertainments has been Edward Hall's *Chronicle*.[5] There are inevitably

4. Both portraits are adjacently reproduced in *Henry VIII Man and Monarch* 58–9. The dating of the king's portrait to c.1513 is based on tree-ring research; J.M. Fletcher 'A Group of English Royal Portraits Painted Soon After 1513: A Dendrochronological Study' *Studies in Conservation 21* (1976) 171–8. The painting of Henry is in The Berger Collection of Denver Art Museum <https://denverartmuseum.org/object/TL-17964> and the young Katherine portrait (c.1504–05) is in the Kunsthistorisches Museum, Vienna; see <https://www.khm.at/objektdb/detail/1788>.

5. Hall's *Chronicle* was originally published in 1548, a year after Hall's death. The edition mostly referred to is *Hall's Chronicle; Containing the History of England, During the Reign*

caveats attached to what he records, especially in the early entries. Hall was born in Poultry, London in 1497. He attended Eton College and progressed to King's College, Cambridge in 1514 where he graduated in 1518. He entered Gray's Inn in 1521.[6] It is impossible he was a witness to the event in 1510, quoted below, or indeed, subsequently to any but the most public of entertainments. Instead he relied on contemporary accounts drawn from Polydore Vergil, the London Chronicles and, as in this case, the accounts of the court Revels. In many instances Hall copied directly from these sources, even for some of the events that he had witnessed.

> The king sone after, came to Westminster with the Quene, and all their train: And on a tyme beyng there, his grace, therles of Essex, Wilshire, and other noble menne, to the numbre of twelve, came sodainly in a mornyng, into the Quenes Chambre, all appareled in shorte cotes, of Kentishe Kendal, with hodes on their heddes, and hosen of thesame, every one of theim, his bowe and arrowes, and a sworde and a bucklar, like out lawes, or Robyn Hodes men, wherof the Quene, the Ladies, and al other, there were abashed, aswell for the straunge sight, as also for their sodain commyng, and after certain daunces, and pastime made, thei departed.[7]

The Revels Account: Richard Gibson

National Archives E36/217 fols. 2 and 15[8]

Jenever the xviij day the furst yere	Inprimis the xviijth day of Jenever the furst yere of our soueraigne lordys Raygne at westmynster in the queenys chambere for a gladnes to the queenys grace ther wer xij parsons dysgysyd that ys to weete xj yn mens Apparel

of Henry the Fourth And The Succeeding Monarchs, To The End Of The Reign of Henry The Eighth etc. edited Henry Ellis (London: J. Johnson and others, 1809). I have chosen to use the more accessible and annotated selection of Janette Dillon *Performance and Spectacle in Hall's Chronicle* (London: Society for Theatre Research, 2002).

6. *Oxford Dictionary of National Biography* sv *Edward Hall.*
7. Dillon *Hall's Chronicle* 31.
8. The original Gibson account appears on fol. 2 but it is severely damaged with much content missing. A fair copy in a different but contemporary hand on fol. 15^{r} is transcribed here. Contractions have been silently expanded. I am very grateful to Peter Meredith for checking and improving my transcription. I am also indebted to Meg

> & oon yn womans apparell the kyngys grase the lord harry stafforth the erll of essex / lord hastyngys / lord fewater / syr edward haward / master thomas a par / syr thomas bollyn / master edward nevell / master edward gyllforth / master syr harry gyllforth / master wyllyam a par / the xj yn grene cottys & grene hosyn of kentyshe kendall the facyon lyke Robyn hodes men the woman lyke mayd maryan thys stuff was dellyuerd by master edward gyllforth to Rychard gybson & the sayd Rychard gybson when yt was wrought / brought the sayd stuff to westmynster & ther dellyuerd yt to master edward gyllforth wher yt was spent / for euery parson had hys ymparell but as for the kyngys ymparell was gevyn to Jamys bell or basset

Richard Gibson, who drew up this account, produced most of the revels at the court of Henry VIII from the beginning in 1510 to Gibson's death in 1534. During this period, he held the office of Yeoman of the Revels. He was also Sergeant of the Tents from about 1518 to 1534 having previously been Yeoman of the Tents between 1513 and 1518.[9]

Comparison between Gibson's account and Hall's *Chronicle* entry clearly shows the debt of the latter to the former. There is the obvious overlap of essential information. Both identify the place and the content of the occasion. Hall's description of the costume, especially the material of 'Kentishe Kendal', is almost identical to Gibson's. And, significantly, the fictive context of 'Robyn hodes men' is repeated. There are also some differences created by the contrasting purpose of the two documents. Gibson identifies the event as a 'gladnes' which Hall does not. This is, perhaps, because in his capacity as Yeoman of the Revels it was important that Gibson distinguished between the activities of tournament, joust, mumming, mask, dance, and disguising. The word *gladnes* is, to my knowledge, only used this once in the Revels' accounts

Twycross for her editorial help in checking my transcript with hers that appeared in her 'Two Maid Marians and a Jewess' *METh 9: 1* (1978) 6–7.

9. For details of Gibson's career and his responsibilities in office see W.R. Streitberger *Court Revels, 1485–1559* (Toronto, Buffalo, London: University of Toronto Press, 1994) 71–4, 430–2 especially, but also throughout chapters 3–5.

and seems to be employed here either, as Streitberger suggests,[10] as a synonym for an 'informal disguising', or, perhaps more simply, as an alternative term for the more general *pastime*. Both the *Middle English Dictionary* (*gladnes(se)* n. 1) and the *Oxford English Dictionary* (*gladness* n.) give similar definitions of 'joy', 'rejoicing', and 'cheerfulness'. Hall might have chosen not to repeat the expression in his *Chronicle* for concern that outside the Revels' fraternity it would not have been understood. Instead, he emphasised the element of dancing. Similar reasons may lie behind his shortened list of participants. Gibson names, or identifies by title, all the men who took part, whereas Hall prioritises only the first three in Gibson's list: the King, the Earl of Essex (Henry Bourchier), and the Earl of Wiltshire (Henry Stafford). The rest are, anonymously, 'noble menne'. He provides no more information than was necessary to convey the eminence of those performing.

To a Robin Hood enthusiast, the most glaring of Hall's omissions is his failure to mention 'mayd maryan'. And yet he may have had a very good reason. Maid Marian's romantic relationship with Robin Hood is a late development in the shaping of the myth and does not make a significant impact until Anthony Munday's two Robin Hood plays at the end of the sixteenth century. Although there are some early references to her in possible connection with Robin Hood, notably at Kingston upon Thames in 1509, her involvement with Robin Hood's men in Queen Katherine's chamber in 1510 is the first unequivocal association.[11] Although Hall wrote his entries from contemporary records and accounts after the events, he might not have been aware of who Maid Marian was, and assumed a similar lack of familiarity among his readers.

An omission that travels in the opposite direction is Gibson's lack of reference to Hall's information that Robin Hood's men were equipped with bows and arrows and swords and bucklers. If, as seems feasible in the context, this was accurate reporting, the explanation for the discrepancy is one of job

10. Streitberger *Court Revels* 255.
11. The churchwardens' accounts for Kingston upon Thames are held in the Surrey Record Office at KG2/2/1. The accounts for 1509 include a payment for gloves for Robin Hood and Maid Marian but it is not clear whether it is the characters that are connected or the gift of gloves in common that unites them for accounting purposes. Although the Revels account is the first surviving record of a clear association of Robin Hood with Maid Marian, it is unlikely to have been their earliest encounter. Gibson appears to be unfazed by the request to make a costume for Maid Marian, suggesting that he had prior knowledge of what was required.

demarcation. Richard Gibson dealt with the making of costumes and the overseeing of set-building. Weapons would have been the responsibility of the Master of the Royal Armoury. From 1493 to 1506 Sir Edward Guildford shared the office with his father. From 1506 to 1534 he was sole master. During these dates he supervised the preparations for most of the international jousts and tournaments. This explains why Gibson had no need to record an aspect of planning that was not his responsibility. It also makes clear that the toing and froing between himself and Guildford, recorded in the account, indicates that, apart from costumes, Guildford was the man who organised this semi-military 'gladnes'. In other words, it fell within the management of entertainment that stemmed from the joust and tourney where participants were often *disguised.* Put simply, Gibson was recording the administration of production for court officials while Hall was chronicling an event for historians. To create the illusion of a first-hand report, Hall goes beyond a description of the players' appearance and accoutrements to include the reaction of an 'abashed' audience. A consequence of no concern to Gibson.

The Cast

Brief biographies of the participants listed by Gibson follow.[12] Names are succeeded by dates of birth and death, and the approximate age at the time of the 'gladnes' on 18 January 1510.

King Henry VIII (1491–1547) 18.

Henry Stafford (c.1479–1523) c.30: Earl of Wiltshire; nobleman and courtier. Stafford was created Knight of the Garter in April 1505. He was a part of the court of Henry VII, and may have accompanied the king to the meeting with Archduke Philip of Castile at Windsor in January 1506. Stafford was imprisoned in the Tower on the suspicion of treason shortly after Henry VIII's accession. It is likely that this was a consequence of his brother's claim to the throne as a descendant of Edward III. Henry Stafford was released without charge in January 1510. It is possible that his participation in the 'gladnes' was his first semi-public engagement following his release. Ten days after dancing with the king he was made Earl of Wiltshire. Stafford became a select member of the group of courtiers that were particularly favoured by the new king, not

12. The information here is drawn from the online *ODNB* in entries under the names given above.

least because they shared a love of tournaments and hunting. As captain of 651 men, he sailed with Henry VIII to Calais in June 1513.

Henry Bourchier (1472–1540) 37: second Earl of Essex; magnate.
Bourchier was a man well-connected. His grandfather was a leading Yorkist councillor, and his great-uncle the Archbishop of Canterbury and first cousin to Elizabeth, Henry VII's queen. As a young man in the 1490s he was a prominent participant in the courtly jousts and revels. He advanced further in the court of Henry VIII where he was elevated to the position of Captain of the King's Spears and Constable of Windsor Castle. He was sufficiently favoured by Henry VIII for his ability to dance and joust, which he did regularly with the king in the first two years of his reign. By 1517 his participation in such events had ceased.

George Hastings (1486/7–1544) 23: first Earl of Huntingdon; magnate.
Hastings was created a Knight of the Bath on the occasion of the marriage of Prince Arthur and Katherine of Aragon in November 1501, when he was only fourteen. He was an active participant in court celebrations from 1509 at the latest.

Robert Radcliffe (1482–1542) 27: first Earl of Sussex; soldier and courtier.
Radcliffe's right to the title of Baron Fitzwalter (hence Gibson naming him 'lord fewater'), following the execution of his father in 1496 for involvement in the Perkin Warbeck conspiracy, was confirmed by an act of parliament in 1509. He was made Knight of the Bath to coincide with his appointment as Lord Sewer at the coronation of Henry VIII. From the beginning of the king's reign, Radcliffe was a close and loyal friend, and was rewarded with many appointments and military campaigns. He supported the king's decision to divorce Katherine. Benefiting from the king's patronage, he rose to become Lord Chamberlain of England for life in 1540.

Edward Howard (1476/7–1513) 33: naval commander.
Howard was not a distinguished soldier but seems to have impressed Henry VII with his prowess as a jouster. Recognition of his achievements may have been the reason for making him a standard-bearer to Prince Henry in May 1509. He also made a major contribution to the coronation tournaments in the same year. In 1512 Henry VIII appointed him Admiral of the Fleet in command of eighteen ships to protect the waters between the Thames estuary and Brest.

Sir Thomas Parr (1478–1517) 31.
Half brother to William Parr (see below). Both brothers grew up within the Tudor court. Thomas Parr enjoyed a particularly close relationship with Henry VIII that was curtailed by his relatively short life. If he had lived longer he would have become the king's father-in-law on the marriage of his daughter Katherine (1512–48) to Henry.

Thomas Boleyn (1476/7–1539) 33: Earl of Wiltshire and Earl Ormond; courtier and nobleman.
Boleyn was the second dancing companion of the king to qualify, in the future, for the title of his father-in-law through his daughter, Anne (c.1500–36). Thomas Boleyn was Henry VIII's Squire of the Body before being made a Knight of the Bath on 23 June 1509 to coincide with the coronation. In many respects, Boleyn was the complete courtier. He took on major diplomatic roles in government and encouraged the king to embrace his warlike sympathies and reject his father's caution. Adding to his appeal was the fact that he was a much-appreciated participant in tournaments and revels.

Sir Edward Neville (c.1482–1538) 27: courtier.
Neville, like most of the 'gladnes' dancers, was admired for his military successes and his passion for jousting and hunting. He entered royal service as early as 1509 when he was appointed Squire of the Body: a role that required his attendance at the funeral of Henry VII. After the coronation of Henry VIII, he became a Gentleman of the Privy Chamber which brought him into close contact with the king. According to George Cavendish, a gentleman-usher in Wolsey's household, who reports on maskers interrupting a banquet given by his master, Neville entered in disguise as the king to a degree that he 'mych resembled the Kynges person'. So convincing was this impersonation that it subsequently prompted speculation that Neville was Henry VII's illegitimate child.

Sir Edward Guildford (c.1479–1534) 30: administrator.
From the early age of fourteen to the end of his life, Edward Guildford was involved with the Royal Armoury. From 1493 to 1506 he was joint Master with his father and from 1506 to 1534 sole Master. As a squire of the body he attended the funeral of Henry VII and joined his brother, Henry, in the celebrations of the marriage and coronation of Henry VIII. He oversaw royal matters in France, negotiated with heads of state, and organised international jousts. In common with several of his fellow dancers, he attended the Field of the Cloth of Gold in 1520.

Sir Henry Guildford (1489–1532) 20: courtier.
A career courtier and friend of Henry even before he succeeded to the throne. Of all the dancers, Henry Guildford was nearest in age to the king with only two years between them. Both men enjoyed and excelled at jousting and other revels. Appointed a squire of the body at a young age, he became Master of the Revels in 1513, and given his involvement with many entertainments that required extensive staging and morris dancing, it is not unlikely that he could have been, with his brother, involved in shaping the 'gladnes'.[13]

William Parr (c.1480–1547) 29: Baron Parr of Horton; soldier and courtier.
Half brother to Thomas Parr. He was a courtier in Henry VII's household as a King's Spear and Squire of the Body. He carried these duties into the reign of Henry VIII. He was not alone in this group of dancers to be part of the contingent that invaded France in 1513. An accomplished soldier, he fought in skirmishes in Scotland and Lincolnshire. More of a warrior than a diplomat, he seems to have preferred to engage in battle rather than the regulated control of tournaments and jousts. One wonders what his reaction was to a request from the king to dress-up and dance.

By any reckoning, this is an impressive list of men in their prime. Not including the youthful king, the average age of the dancers was twenty-nine with the youngest twenty and the oldest thirty-seven. Henry inherited some of the older members from his father's court providing a necessary and secure succession. He also inherited and sought to extend his father's belief in a meritocracy.[14] In addition to the men's administrative credentials, reflected in their key appointments, they shared other attributes. They all seem to have been highly proficient jousters, enthusiastic participants of revels, and leading military campaigners. In many cases their loyalty to the king brought close friendship. Most participated in the invasion of France in the summer of 1513 and attended the Field of Cloth of Gold in 1520. It hardly needs saying but they were also doubtless the best male dancers at court.

13. As a typical example of his involvement see Streitberger *Court Revels* 69–70.

14. For a thorough exploration of the impact of Henry VII's promotion of 'new men' see Stephen Gunn *Henry VII's New Men and the Making of Tudor England* (Oxford UP, 2016).

The Audience

Gibson and Hall make clear that the presentation was aimed at the 24-year-old Queen Katherine. Hall reassures his readers that she was not alone but accompanied by her 'Ladies'. They were her ladies-in-waiting, certainly, and maids of honour, probably. As the title suggests, maids of honour were unmarried and about sixteen years of age when appointed. Ladies-in-waiting were generally married and often chosen from maids of honour once they had become wives. Other women may have entered the queen's household because their husbands, brothers, or fathers were members of the king's court.[15] From the beginning of Katherine's reign her household consisted of thirty-three women of whom eighteen were wives or daughters of men in Henry's court.[16] How many of them witnessed the 'gladnes' is not known. Some of this nepotistic, family privileged, arrangement can be seen in the following examples.

Elizabeth Stafford (c.1479–1532) was lady-in-waiting to Katherine and sister to Henry Stafford who participated in the 'gladnes'. She married, before 1507, Robert Radcliffe, another of the king's dancers.[17] Her sister, Anne Stafford (c.1483–1544), married, in December 1509, George Hastings who also danced. His experience must have been an intensely family affair as another lady-in-waiting likely to have attended was his aunt, Anne Hastings (c.1471–c.1512). Mary Say (1485–c.1535) married, in around 1497, Henry Bourchier, yet another performer. The dancers' disguise as Robin Hood's men must have been spectacularly convincing if the intention was to fool these women. Rather like the game of hide and seek, it is possible that there exists an unspoken acknowledgement of the nature of the game between the hider/performer and the seeker/audience. There is a pretence that costume and masking are sufficient devices to dissemble appearance to a point where a leading participant is unrecognised.[18] The performers' access to the Queen's Chamber, though, might have given the game away.

15. Barbara J. Harris *English Aristocratic Women, 1450–1550: Marriage and Family, Property and Careers* (Oxford UP, 2002) 210.
16. Harris *Aristocratic Women* 216.
17. Harris *Aristocratic Women* 218 and online at <http://www.tudorsdynasty.com/katherine-aragons-ladies-beginning/>.
18. For an exploration of this type of disguise see Meg Twycross and Sarah Carpenter *Masks and Masking in Medieval and Early Tudor England* (Aldershot: Ashgate, 2002) 148–50 and 166–8.

The Place and Space[19]

The place chosen for the performance was Westminster Palace, the principal royal residence from the reign of Henry III to 1512 when fire destroyed much of the privy quarters. Situated on the west bank of the Thames, adjacent to Westminster Abbey, it increasingly became the centre of governmental power and administration.[20] The magnificence of the building and the grandeur of its contents of secular and religious artefacts glorified beliefs in divine right and temporal legitimacy of successive monarchs. The choice of venue for this presentation carried elevated connotations beyond those possible in any other royal environment.

More meaningful still was the space in which the men performed their disguising; the Queen's Chamber. Gibson and Hall both consider the location noteworthy. Not least, one imagines, because of its all-female intimate privacy. The privy rooms of the queen were barred to anyone not a servant of hers granted the right of admission, or the king and those invited to accompany him.[21] One of the reasons for the choice of this space was the opportunity it plainly provided for the king and his all-male company to act out surprise in disguise. In fact, the elements of concealment, intrusion, and disruption were devices progressively favoured by the king in his revels.

The Queen's Chamber was located at the southern end of Westminster Palace lying in a north/south direction not far from the king's quarters.[22] Between 1238 and 1242 much work was undertaken in the Queen's Chamber and Chapel that included paintings of the Evangelists and God with his angels.

19. For discussion of these terms in the context of court performance see Janette Dillon *The Language of Space in Court Performance, 1400–1625* (Cambridge UP, 2010) 6–9.
20. For details of Westminster Palace and royal residency see Simon Thurley *The Royal Palaces of Tudor England: Architecture and Court Life 1460–1547* (New Haven and London: Yale UP, 1993); Simon Thurley *Houses of Power: The Places that Shaped the Tudor World* (London: Bantam Press, 2017) 15–20; David Souden *The Royal Palaces of London* (London and New York: Merrell, 2008) 25–39.
21. Harris *Aristocratic Women* 21.
22. For a general historical plan see Thurley *Royal Palaces* Plan 12; a Victorian pen and ink drawing by Henry William Brewer of a 'perspective view of the Old Palace of Westminster in the reign of Henry VIII' is available at <https://www.parliament.uk/worksofart/artwork/henry-william-brewer-and-/no-title--perspective-view-of-the-old-palace-of-westminster-in-the-reign-of-henry-viii-/82>. The Queen's Chamber is shown in the left-hand corner running from left to right and above the immediate bankside buildings.

And, with a nod to the secular, a painting of Winter next to the fireplace.[23] Some, or all, of this may have survived into Katherine's occupancy. What neither Gibson nor Hall identify, or possibly even knew, is where the King and his courtiers apparelled themselves and how they entered the Queen's Chamber. Not much detective work is needed here. Neighbouring and at a right angle to the Queen's Chamber was the king's Painted Chamber, renowned and highly regarded throughout Europe. A chamber for the king had existed on the site from the twelfth century. Major alterations were made to the fabric and decoration during the reign of Henry III. It was, largely, these modifications that Henry VIII inherited. Internally, the chamber measured 24.5 by 7.9 metres with a height of 9.7 metres.[24] At the south-east corner of the king's chamber was a door which led to a newel staircase and vestibule that accessed the ground floor and the Queen's Chamber.[25] Built on a west-to-east axis, the two-storey Painted Chamber faced the Thames and was magnificently decorated. Even though the chamber was gutted by fire in 1834, images of the building and its murals were made as part of a conservation survey undertaken from the end of the eighteenth century to 1820. The sketches preserve, at the time, what remained of the damaged medieval murals. Paul Binski valuably catalogued the known copies of the murals and described them fully as well as reproducing several of them.[26] The murals are categorised by subject: the Old Testament, the Virtues, and the Coronation of St Edward the Confessor. The coronation mural occupied a particularly propitious position. It was situated at the heart of the chamber on the north wall towards the east end where the king's bed was placed. The head of the bed was against the wall with the image of the royal cult figure, epitomising good kingship, guarding, guiding, and authenticating the resting monarch below.[27] This must have focused the newly crowned king's mind on the momentous responsibility he inherited following the death of his elder

23. Paul Binski *The Painted Chamber at Westminster* (London: The Society of Antiquaries of London, 1986) 17.

24. Binski *Painted Chamber* 9 and 11.

25. Binski *Painted Chamber* 11.

26. Binski *Painted Chamber* 113–23 for the catalogue. The 74 Plates are found at the end of the book after the index.

27. For Henry III's idealisation of Edward, see D.A. Carpenter 'King Henry III and Saint Edward the Confessor: the Origins of the Cult' *English Historical Review 122* (2007) 865–91.

brother. For the first ten years of his life he had no expectation of becoming king. He was given no responsibility for state affairs during his father's lifetime nor allowed any independence.[28] His secondary status was reflected in his early education with his sisters. When in residence at Westminster, Henry, like the kings before him since Henry III, would have had a constant and onerous reminder of what it meant to be a king. As Paul Binski has noted in the context of the history of the Painted Chamber, the end of Edward I's reign was associated with a new royal ideology that emphasised an increasingly secularised court culture. The impetus for this change was 'the understanding that the authority of kingship lay as much in its historical as in its spiritual claims'.[29] Both were necessary reassurances, not only for Henry VIII's belief in his legitimate right to reign, but for those loyal courtiers who fought and danced with him. Within his place in the space of the Painted Chamber the iconography that surrounded the king brought, internally, confirmation, justification, and dedication. Externally, for privileged visitors, it was a reminder of the rightful obeisance due to the man who occupied this special place and its exalted space. The Painted Chamber and the Queen's Chamber were not only physically contiguous, with a private connection, but both shared the status of enshrined intimate spaces within a p(a)lace of public majesty. The two spaces constructed the meaning of the performance.

The Performance

Richard Gibson, in his Revels account, gives no clear indication of the active ingredient in the 'gladnes'. Hall offers only a little more clarity in reporting that after 'their sodain commyng, and after certain daunces, and pastime made, thei departed'.[30] It seems that if this revel was a genuine surprise, although with the number of relatives on both sides it could have been a secret difficult to keep, there was no opportunity to rehearse dances between the women and the men: unless, of course, the dances were already well known in court circles. The syntax of the sentence, however, suggests that the sudden coming, the dances and pastimes, and the departure all pertain to the king's men. There is another piece of evidence that implies that the queen and her 'Ladies' did not dance. On the day of Epiphany in 1512 the

28. J.J. Scarisbrick *Henry VIII* (New Haven and London: Yale UP, new edition, 1997) 6.

29. Binski *Painted Chamber* 111.

30. Dillon *Hall's Chronicle* 31.

king with eleven others (same number as in the 'gladnes') were disguised 'after the maner of Italie, called a maske, a thing not seen afore in Englande ... sixe gentlemen disguised ... desired the ladies to daunce, some were content, and some that knewe the fashion of it refused, because it was not a thing commonly seen'.[31] If it was not 'commonly seen' in 1512 how much more unfamiliar was it in 1510? Given that Hall had reason to believe that the female audience of the 'gladnes' were 'abashed' by what they had witnessed, it seems doubtful that they participated any further than their role as spectators. There was no dancing queen. Indeed, Katherine was pregnant at the time and miscarried the child only thirteen days later.[32]

If the women's function was to be amazed and manifestly discomfited by what they witnessed, what of the men? Gibson records that all twelve who invaded the Queen's Chamber were 'dysgysyd'. There is a problem here in the definition of his choice of word. His description need not necessarily be an indication of the intention to conceal a performers' identity. It can simply mean that a person is dressed in a fashion that is either different from customary wear or considered inappropriate to position (*OED* sv *disguise* v. 1). Alternatively, it can refer to the more common usage today: 'to hide a person's identity' (*OED* sv *disguise* v. 4). Which of these meanings did Gibson intend? Did he write *dysgysyd* to identify the entertainment as a *disguising* or to signal a disjunction between player and role as in the king dressed as a follower of Robin Hood? Or was Gibson simply drawing attention to the fact that the costumes not only served the purpose of fictionalising the dancers' domain but also of obscuring their identity by using hoods to partially cover their faces? Of course, the costumes could have served both purposes and the conceit of Robin Hood's men been partly chosen because the wearing of hoods not only helped define the milieu of the dancers but also provided the means of concealment.[33]

Some support for the meaning of *disguise* as a way of hiding identity is found in what seems to be Henry VIII's first public jousting after his father's protectionist embargo on his son's participation. Six days before the 'gladnes' on 12 January 1510, Henry and William Compton, a Privy Councillor,

31. Dillon *Hall's Chronicle* 43.

32. Giles Tremlett *Catherine of Aragon: Henry's Spanish Queen* (London: Faber and Faber, 2010) 168.

33. For a thorough exploration of the meaning and implications of the terms *disguised* and *disguising* see Twycross and Carpenter *Masks and Masking* 128–33.

jousted against Sir Edward Neville and others. The king had, apparently, not previously been informed of this event. When, as Hall notes, he was 'secretely informed' he decided to enter the joust with Compton 'secretly armed'.[34] They came into the joust 'unknowen to all persones, and unloked for'. After breaking many staves, the strangers received much praise from the crowd. Compton then rode against Neville who 'hurte hym sore, and was likely to dye'. Someone in attendance suspected that the injured jouster might be the king and 'cried, God save the kyng' at which point Henry 'discovered himself', presumably by removing his helmet, to the relief and joy of all.

The next court event after this joust and the dancing Robin Hood's men was an entertainment for ambassadors on 28 February 1510. After the niceties of introductions and the guidance of them to their places, the King disappeared only to reappear with the Earl of Essex 'appareled after Turkey fashion'.[35] More nobles then appeared in the guise of other nationalities. Whether this fooled anyone or, indeed, was intended to do so is not clear but it does illustrate the King's fondness for dressing-up as a distinct 'other' for jousts and revels alike.

Between them, all that Hall and Gibson tell us about the 'gladnes' is who was involved, what they wore, what they carried, and where they performed before whom. The rest can only be determined by the nature of similar events and a degree of speculation. Everything points to the display being a dance; the sudden irruption and the equally speedy departure do not support a play-like linear narrative. This was an explosive experience where the fiction was used metaphorically. The initial purpose seems to have been to surprise and astound. Only then were issues of kingship and masculinity raised. This invites the question of what kind of dance this was.

The first indication is the numbers involved. There were eleven performers dressed as Robin Hood's men, and one dressed as 'mayd maryan'. This replicates the number frequently recorded in costume lists for disguisings and other entertainments that accounted for sets of two, eight, ten, and most often, twelve.[36] The uniformity of costume, as far as the eleven men were

34. Dillon *Hall's Chronicle* 31.

35. Dillon *Hall's Chronicle* 32.

36. Maria Hayward 'Temporary Magnificence: The Offices of the Tents and Revels in the 1547 Inventory' in *The Inventory of King Henry VIII: Textiles and Dress* edited Maria Hayward and Philip Ward 4 vols (Turnhout: Harvey Miller, 2012) 2 109–30, especially 123.

concerned, is significant because it emphasises a commonality rather than a hierarchy. This is a band of equal brothers, not a representation of social order. If Robin Hood is their leader, as future ballads, games, and plays would emphasise, then here he is physically absent. There is no indication in the wording of the accounts by Hall and Gibson, or the costume they describe, that he was conspicuously present. It has been suggested that Henry himself took the role. This seems unlikely. It was the first 'disguising' in which Henry played a part since becoming king. He was only eighteen and recently married. He appears to have used the medium of dance to convey to court and wife his precepts of kingship and marriage. As much as anything, he was distancing himself from his socially withdrawn father and his somewhat insipid brother. The dance gave him the opportunity to set out his stall and celebrate the virtues of comradeship and good fellowship. As he put it himself in a song written soon after this episode, 'Pastyme with good companye | I love and shall untyll I dye'.[37] He then lists the sports on which his heart is set as 'hunt, synge and daunce'. Whether consciously or not, in the 'gladnes', he elides form and content to express a revisionist philosophy.

The inclusion of Maid Marian is the biggest clue to the type of dance performed. The earliest reference to her, from the Kingston upon Thames churchwardens' accounts for 1509, long before she becomes Robin's love interest, links her with the popular or urban morris dance.[38] And this association may account for her name. It was not uncommon, in England at least, for the dance to include a friar and a man dressed as a woman. The dance style is often associated with the Moors, and Moorish characters were often referred to in records as *moryans* and the female role as the 'woman morian'.[39] It's not much of a step to call her/him the 'maid morian'.[40] The

37. British Library Additional MS 31922 folios 14^{v} – 15^{r}.

38. John Forrest *The History of Morris Dancing 1458–1750* (Toronto and Buffalo: University of Toronto Press, 1999) 161.

39. *REED: Civic London to 1558* edited Anne Lancashire, 3 vols (Cambridge: D.S. Brewer, 2015) *1* 382.

40. Obviously, this is mere speculation and maybe no more than coincidence. It should also be noted that there is a long tradition of entertainments involving lovers called Robin and Marian without the outlaw context. See the thirteenth-century *Adam de La Halle: Le Jeu de Robin et Marion* edited and translated Shira I. Schwam-Baird music edited by Milton G. Scheuermann Jr (New York and London: Garland, 1994).

most likely candidate for the Marian role here is Henry Guildford.[41] Apart from the king, he was the youngest of the group. He participated as organiser, singer, dancer, and player in many of the revels, including morris dances, becoming Master of the Revels in 1513 at the age of twenty-three. And as a possibly static individual in the dance around which Robin Hood's men swirled he was in a perfect position to choreograph the action. At this time, this should not conjure up modern visions of village greens and a group of, usually, men waving handkerchiefs above their heads, although the bells do have historical credence.[42] In the early sixteenth century the dance appears to have been an exotic and grotesque expression of martial athleticism.

The morris dance, or *morisk* as it is sometimes described, was a favoured entertainment at the royal courts of Henry VII and Henry VIII. It was either performed as a stand-alone entertainment by visiting or court dancers or played as an integral part of the broader *disguising*. In John Forrest's absorbing history of morris dancing, he convincingly makes a case for the diffusion theory of England's and Scotland's introduction to European dances in the late fifteenth century, and the transformation of those dances through exposure to national cultural differences. Through seriation graphs he plots a chronological movement of morris dancing by venue. Beginning in 1480, the migration is shown to be geographic and social. Earliest is the Royal Court followed by moves through Urban, Church and Stage, Village (including Public House and Open Country), and Special Group's Premises, to Private House, ending at 1750, the *terminus ad quem* of the study. The written evidence that survives points to the royal court as the venue that introduced the morris dance to England and Scotland. References to morris dances in the English royal court are primarily for accounting expenses either paid directly to dancers or incurred for costume making. Useful as these insights are they give almost no indication of what type of movement distinguished a morris from other forms of court dance. It is for this reason that Forrest turns to the more

41. My casting of Henry Guildford as Maid Marian is influenced by later Elizabethan theatre practice of boys playing women. Meg Twycross, on the other hand, chooses William Parr for the role, on the grounds that he is the last listed in Gibson's order of participants: Twycross 'Two Maid Marians' 6. This brings into play a different future theatre genre: the pantomime. William Parr was 29 (11 years older than the king) and by all accounts a bluff soldier preferring the uncertainty of battle to the regulated tournament and joust. The choice is between youthful good looks and gnarled masculinity.

42. See Forrest's list of 'prototypical characteristics' of morris dances below on page 115.

effusive documents from France, Spain, and Italy. With this information he tentatively identifies 'a few prototypical characteristics' of European *morisks*:

> High leaping, fighting, mimed action, individual rather than concerted or figured action, dancing in a circle or around the room, rhythmic stepping, beating time with implements, and the use of dancing bells.[43]

Other features of the *morisk*, noted by Forrest, are the role of swordplay, the frequency of dancers entering the space one-by-one, and the emphasis in the dance on individual movement rather than synchronised group action.[44] All of the above, with the possible exception of the bells, could easily be accommodated by the little that is known of the 'gladnes'. Another factor supporting the theory that this was a *morisk* is the date. The performance took place on the morning of Friday, 18 January 1510. Of the eight morris dances recorded by that name in the Revels accounts between 1494 and 1514, five took place in January mostly on or before Epiphany, with only one falling outside of the Christmas revels on 25 January 1502. The reason for this was that the dance was part of the celebration for the proxy wedding of Princess Margaret with James IV of Scotland.[45] The event under discussion here also falls outside the festive period. If it was a type of morris dance straying beyond what appear to be its usual calendar confines it is not easy to see why. It could be because the Lord of Misrule that year received for 'business at Christmas' two quite large payments of 100s and 66s 8d that may possibly reflect a busy time. The Gentlemen of the Chapel certainly played on the evening of Twelfth Night.[46] Perhaps the king waited until the court had removed to Westminster before springing his seasonal surprise.

Maid Marian's presence suggests another dimension to the nature of the dance. She is demonstrably central to the fictive context by her gendered difference and individual costume. Like the role of actual women in the tournament and joust prize-giving, Marian is there to be wooed and won. It could be the best individual athletic performance that won her – a kind

43. Forrest *Morris Dancing* 74.
44. Forrest *Morris Dancing* 76–9.
45. *Joannis Lelandi antiquarii De rebus Britannicis collectanea* 6 vols (London: Benjamin White, 1774) *4* 263. I am most grateful to Meg Twycross for drawing my attention to this reference.
46. Streitberger *Court Revels* 255.

of 'strictly come morris dancing' – or the last man standing after a series of swordplay contests. In some examples of such dances the winner was the fool and his reward a ring or other prize that she held in view throughout the dance. This was not the case here. There is no evidence of the distinctive fool's costume or accoutrements and such a presence would be out of place in the context and apparent purpose of the dance. With or without a fool, the motif of rewarding a champion with a ring has been taken as giving the activity the title of 'ring dance'. Of course, it also aptly describes the dance's circular configuration of men surrounding a 'woman'.[47] The Westminster dance sounds like a conflation of a morris dance with a ring dance, a hybrid that Forrest describes as a 'ring *morisk*'.[48]

With a degree of licence and the evidence available, it is now possible to reconstruct, cautiously, what happened that day in January.

Early on a cold winter morning in Westminster Palace, Henry VIII, an ebullient eighteen-year-old novice king, gathered in the Painted Chamber with eleven of his loyal and trusted courtiers. Surrounded by religious and secular imagery, all but one of the men changed from day clothes into costumes of short coats, hoods, and hose of Kentish Kendal and the other into the guise of a young woman who held a ring. Across the shoulders of Robin Hood's men were slung their bows. Into their belts they strapped the arrows. In their hands they each held a sword and buckler. A short distance away, the Queen and her female attendants were preparing for the day ahead. Unbeknown to them, the king and men of the court were gathering at the top of the stairwell that led to the Queen's chamber. At a signal from Edward or Henry Guildford, the men, suppressing an almost uncontrollable desire to laugh, crept down the stairs. This is why I doubt they were wearing bells. On arrival at the queen's private door, two alternative entrance strategies are possible. Either the Queen and her retinue were shocked by a sudden cacophony of eleven men rhythmically crashing their swords against the bucklers – there

47. See the engraving by Israel van Meckenem c.1475 illustrating a rigorous and contorted ring dance in Forrest *Morris Dancing* 78. A copy is held by the Staatliche Museen, Berlin. The engraving can be seen online at <https://www.wga.hu/html/m/meckenem/index.html>; scroll down to 'Morris Dance'. I am aware that the case for the ring dance as a type of morris is more contentious than I am allowing for here. For a more cautious view that warns against using images as 'accurate renderings of actual morisks' see Forrest *Morris Dancing* 81–2.

48. For reference to the 'ring morisk' see the index entries in Forrest *Morris Dancing* 435. The term 'ring morisk' appears to be Forrest's own.

is no evidence of minstrels being present – who burst one at a time into her chamber, or the men entered the chamber silently to create the ear-shattering noise once they were in place. Hall's reference to the 'sodain commyng' of the dance favours the first alternative. What follows is more conjectural.

It is tempting to believe that the men entered one at a time in the order that Gibson listed them in his account with the king being first.[49] Such an order would mean that Henry Guildford was the last but one to enter just before William Parr. Such a position seems to disqualify him and his youthful good looks from the role of Maid Marian. As the only 'woman' dancer, who takes centre stage, it could be thought that he/she should come in first or probably last. Who ever played Maid Marian and wherever he came in the queue at the door, it is a fair assumption that he took up a central position in the dancing space to allow the eleven Robin Hood's men to encircle him. Other than observing that each of the 'prototypical characteristics' catalogued by Forrest would fit very well into a ring-morris dance with a martial aspect and weapons as accoutrements, it is not possible to go much further. This is especially so in the context of individual movements involving high leaping and extreme gestures rotating around Maid Marian. What is reasonably certain is that the entertainment included an episode of fighting with sword and buckler. This form of swordplay frequently appears in early Robin Hood material and was used in military training and often featured in tournaments. Each of the dancers would have been familiar with and expert in this style of combat. It is unlikely to have been a free-for-all as in the mêlée of a tournament. In the framework of a dance, some element of choreography would have been essential. A clue to its nature lies in the number of dancers. With an odd number of participants ruling out one-to-one contests, there is only one realistic solution. The eleven men form a circle around Marian, a number that must have been a deliberate choice in the planning stage. This implies that in the mind of the organiser, the number required met the demands of the entertainment and not the other way around. Robin Hood's men could have danced something no more complicated than linking-up by holding their own sword in one hand and, depending on sharpness, the tip end of the sword behind them in the other hand and moving around in the manner of a sword dance.[50] As a preliminary

49. Forrest *Morris Dancing* 274 observes that the entry of dancers in single file was 'normal for the performers of the ring morisk'.

50. For a history of linked sword dancing see Stephen D. Corrsin *Sword Dancing in Europe: A History* (London: Hisarlik Press, 1997).

to something livelier, this was, no doubt, an acceptable start but it does rather beg the question of what they did with their bucklers. If a more active display of weaponry skills was planned then certain constraints would apply. The men could not simply pair up because that would leave one person left over with no one to fight. However, if each contestant fights in turn the person to either side of him in the circle, left for one, right for the other, with each pair matching the same number of strokes as the others before turning to his partner on the other side, a spectacular and noisy display of military precision would materialise.

How this series of dancing and stylised combats was concluded is not known. Hall only records that the dancers departed.

In the writing of this article I have been struck by the sexual symbolism of the event. A group of macho and virile men meet in a predominantly male enclave for an early morning surprise and sudden penetration of a female sanctum. They play with weapons and make a lot of noise throwing their bodies about with conspicuous masculine skill. After a thunderous climax they withdraw as quickly as they had come. What was Henry trying to prove? I think we know.

The Epilogue

It is not always fully appreciated by all historians and Robin Hood scholars how broad the extent of familiarity with the myth of Robin Hood was in the fifteenth and sixteenth centuries. In terms of social standing, it encompassed yeomen, the middling sort, the gentry, and royalty. In terms of educational levels, too, the tales disseminated through manuscript, print, and oral performance probably reached a similarly wide audience. Not only is Robin Hood the subject matter of Henry's first disguising as king but he must have felt confident that his court performers and the queen and her ladies shared his awareness of the myth. Moreover, Hall and Gibson speak of 'Robyn hodes men' as though he and his adventures were common knowledge.

Henry's introduction to the early poems and ballads may have come from his tutor, John Skelton. How much Skelton knew or read of Robin Hood is debatable. What is indisputable is that he possessed enough acquaintance to reference, in his writings, Friar Tuck once and Robin Hood twice.[51] There is

51. John Skelton *The Complete English Poems: Revised Edition* edited John Scattergood (Liverpool: Liverpool UP, 2015); Friar Tuck is mentioned in *Magnyfycence* 132 line 357; Robin Hood in *Speke Parott* 209 line 341 and *Why Come Ye Nat to Courte* 248 line 197.

also some circumstantial evidence. In Alexander Barclay's translation of and extension to Sebastian Brant's *The Ship of Fools* he excoriates Skelton for his religious views and his works. At one point he appears to imply that Skelton wrote Robin Hood tales. In the last stanza to his 'brefe addicion', Barclay concludes with the statement that 'It longeth nat to my science nor cunnynge | For Phylyp the Sparowe the (Dirige) to synge'. At the beginning of the stanza Barclay proclaims that his will is to induce good men to virtue and goodness followed by the exemplification, 'I wryte no Iest ne tale of Robyn hode'.[52] Is this simply a stark condemnation of popular literature, or are readers encouraged to connect the author of *Phyllyp Sparowe* with an idle tale or two of Robin Hood?

More tenuous is Anthony Munday's decision to frame his late-sixteenth-century play, *The Downfall of Robert Earl of Huntingdon*, in the circumstance of a performance composed and rehearsed by John Skelton, who also played Friar Tuck, for performance before Henry VIII. It is difficult to see much point in this precise construction if it did not carry a grain of historical truth or rumour.

An altogether different exposure of Prince Henry to Robin Hood activity is hinted at in accounts made by John Heron, Treasurer of the Chamber, during the reign of Henry VII. On 31 May 1505 Heron records, 'Item to the players at Kingeston towarde the building of the churche stiple in almns iij^{s} iiij^{d}'.[53] This almost certainly refers to the town's King Game of which the Robin Hood game was an integral part. The All Saints' churchwardens' accounts now begin at 1503, although they once started at 1496, and stop, with some years missing, at 1538.[54] For most years between 1504 and 1538, expenses and receipts are recorded for both types of game, initially for the King Game alone, followed by the two together, and from 1511, predominantly, for just Robin Hood.[55] Whether this is an accurate reflection of format changes over time or simply the result of inconsistent accounting is uncertain.

52. Alexander Barclay and Sebastian Brant *The Ship of Fools* 2 volumes (Edinburgh: William Paterson, 1874) 2 331.
53. Sydney Anglo *The Court Festivals of Henry VII: A Study Based Upon the Account Books of John Heron. Treasurer of the Chamber* (Manchester: John Rylands Library and Manchester UP, 1960) 39.
54. W.E. St Lawrence Finney 'Mediaeval Games and Gaderyngs at Kingston-Upon-Thames' *Surrey Archaeological Collections 44* (1934) 102–36 at 102.
55. Sally-Beth MacLean 'King Games and Robin Hood: Play and Profit at Kingston upon Thames' *RORD 29* (1986–87) 85–94.

The games, morris dances, and probably plays, happened during the week of Whitsun. In 1505 this fell between 11 May and 17 May: calendrically, the second earliest possible. The payment on behalf of the king was made or registered fourteen days later. On the evidence of a separate account made at the same time, it is possible that the king was in residence at Richmond, a short distance by river from Kingston.[56] For reasons of safety and security he probably did not attend in person, but it would have been in keeping for the players to visit the king and his retinue for a private viewing in Richmond. Was Robin Hood part of the show that year? Was an excited and enthralled thirteen-year-old prince in attendance? Far less thrilling for me and the future king is the very real possibility that his father was merely arranging a donation to the steeple fund.

The appeal of Robin Hood to Henry VIII was no doubt enhanced by his legendary prowess in archery, a quality shared by Henry. During his first campaign at Calais in July 1513 the king practised archery in a garden with archers of his guard while waiting for a visit from three ambassadors. In the diary of John Taylor, Clerk of the Parliaments, the king 'cleft the mark in the middle, and surpassed them all'.[57] An achievement of remarkable accuracy for which Robin Hood was renowned. I imagine, as a form of flattery, it was a comparison frequently made. In choosing a Robin Hood theme for his first disguising, Henry may also have been partially influenced by the fact that Katherine's two identifying badges were the pomegranate and a sheaf of arrows.

It may be coincidental rather than deliberate but a possible additional indication of an interest in tales of Robin Hood is the names Henry gave to his two pet dogs: Cut and Ball. In the May-game play of *Robin Hood and the Friar*, published in the early 1560s by William Copland, Friar Tuck calls up, in response to Robin bringing on his men to fight the friar, two characters called Cut and Bause.[58] In the corresponding ballads of *Robin Hood and the*

56. An organist was engaged to play in the 'galery at Richemount'; Anglo *Court Festivals* 39.

57. *Letters and Papers, Foreign and Domestic, Henry VIII, Volume 1, 1509–1514* edited J.S. Brewer (London: HMSO, 1920) item 2391.

58. 'Ball' and 'Bause' share the same meaning of a white streak or spot on the face; *OED* sv *ball* n.2 and sv *bauson* n. and adj. 'Cut' refers, of course, to the docking of a dog's tail. This was originally done to prevent hunting dogs snagging their tails in briars. Henry's dogs were prone to getting lost and he paid out considerable sums to those

Curtal Friar, the names are not used, and the friar's militia are fifty band dogs instead. In the Garland version from the 1660s they are 'curtal dogs'. The surviving ballads of this tale are later than Copland's play, but this means relatively little in trying to establish a point of origin. And in the case of the May-game play its creation must have preceded the publication, possibly by some years. It is surely significant that the names Henry chose for his pet spaniels are identical in meaning to those in a Robin Hood play that was possibly the one performed at Kingston upon Thames.[59]

For Henry VIII the 'gladnes' of Robin Hood's men in the Queen's Chamber was not a one-morning-wonder. Five years later when plans for a major court entertainment at Greenwich in May had to be scrapped for political reasons, Henry instructed Richard Gibson to substitute it with a festival of Robin Hood at Shooters Hill.[60] This time, Robin Hood's men were represented by 121 of the Yeomen of the Guard. The king, now almost six years into his reign, no longer needed the reassurance of a brotherhood, nor did he wish to take on the role of leader of outlaws: at nearly twenty-four he was ready and fit to play the king.

University of Bristol

servants who found them. On 11 May 1530 one of the Queen's servants was rewarded 10s for returning Cut 'again', and on 14 May 1530 Ball, who was lost in Waltham Forest, was brought home. The reward this time was 5s; *Letters and Papers, Foreign and Domestic, Henry VIII, Volume 5, 1531–1532* edited James Gairdner (London: HMSO, 1880) 749–50.

59. For speculation that Robin Hood and the Friar was one of the plays performed at Kingston upon Thames see John Marshall 'Show or Tell? Priority and Interplay in the Early Robin Hood Play/Games and Poems' in *Telling Tales and Crafting Books: Essays in Honor of Thomas H. Ohlgren* edited Alexander L. Kaufman, Shaun F.D. Hughes, and Dorsey Armstrong (Kalamazoo: Medieval Institute Publications, 2016) 177–202.

60. Reasons for the cancellation and a description of the replacement entertainment are given in John Marshall 'Revisiting and revising Robin Hood in sixteenth-century London' in *Robin Hood in Outlaw/ed Spaces: Media, Performance, and Other New Directions* edited Lesley Coote and Valerie B. Johnson (London and New York: Routledge, 2017) 111–31.

READING *MANKIND* IN A CULTURE OF DEFAMATION

Clare Egan

> MERCY: Wyrschepyll sofereyns, I have do my propirté:
> Mankynd ys deliveryd by my faverall patrocynye.
> God preserve hym fro all wyckyd captivité
> And send hym grace hys sensuall condicions to mortifye!
>
> Now for Hys love that for us receyvyd hys humanité,
> Serge your condicyons wyth dew examinacion.
> Thynke and remembyr the world ys but a vanité.
>
> *Mankind* 903–9[1]

At the close of the play *Mankind*, performed during the Shrovetide of 1471, the character Mercy explicitly conflated the play world and the real world by entreating the provincial audience, with the lines above, to examine their personal moralities. Since the performance had come to its end and Mercy had completed his task of delivering the play's eponymous protagonist, Mankind, from eternal damnation, all that was left to do was to remind the audience that they needed to apply this exemplar to their own moral 'condicyons' (*Mankind* 908). They must search and examine themselves, think and remember that the world they lived in was as full of 'vanité' (*Mankind* 909) as the allegorical play world in which they had just been immersed. Scholars have suggested that the play was performed either in a guildhall or in a church; certainly this performance took place somewhere in East Anglia close to either Bishop's Lynn or Cambridge, and it was thus to this real-world context that Mercy gestured when, with his final lines, he elided drama and reality.[2]

1. *Mankind* edited Kathleen M. Ashley and Gerard NeCastro (TEAMS Middle English Texts Series; Kalamazoo: Medieval Institute Publications, 2010); online at <http://d.lib.rochester.edu/teams/publication/ashley-and-necastro-mankind>. Subsequent references are to this edition.
2. For the most detailed and convincing narrative of *Mankind*'s dramatic context see John Marshall '"O ye Souerens that Sytt and ye Brothern that stonde ryght wppe": Addressing the Audience of *Mankind*' *European Medieval Drama 1* (1997) 105–19. See also Kathleen M. Ashley 'Introduction' in *Mankind* edited Ashley and NeCastro;

The epilogue above is just one example of the play's distinctive ability to make its audience complicit in the action of the drama by bridging the divide between the play world and the real world; other well-known examples include the Christmas song and the request for payment from the audience for the devil, Titivillus, to appear.[3] However, Mercy's closing remarks, like so many other moments in the play, reward closer inspection, for they may be making a more pointed accusation than at first appears. If, as many scholars have noted, the play's often-quoted line 'O ye soverens that sytt and ye brothern that stonde ryght uppe' (*Mankind* 29) distinguishes between the different social statuses of groups in the audience based on their locations in the playing space,[4] then it is significant that Mercy's final speech is addressed solely to the 'wyrschepyll sofereyns' (*Mankind* 903). Of course, the whole audience was expected to take away a moral lesson from this kind of play and conventional social deference dictated that only superiors be directly addressed.[5] It is also true that the play uses the term 'sovereigns' more frequently as its default address to the audience as a collective. However, in addition to line 29's distinction between the 'soverens' who were seated and the 'brothern' who stood at performances, a later reference to the audience as 'brother[s]' (*Mankind* 631) occurs when Nowadays pushes through some audience members as he re-enters the stage. The audience members that the vices would need to push through on re-entry were those same standing spectators distinguished previously as 'brothern'. Moreover, in the play world, Mercy addresses Mankind as 'brother' and Mankind significantly is not an elite figure but is a farmer who tills his own

Jessica Brantley and Thomas Fulton '*Mankind* in a Year without Kings' *Journal of Medieval and Early Modern Studies* 36: 2 (2006) 321–54; Lawrence M. Clopper '*Mankind* and Its Audience' *Comparative Drama* 8 (1974) 347–55; John A. Geck '"On Yestern Day, in Feverere, the Yere Passeth Fully": On the Dating and Prosopography of *Mankind*' *Early Theatre* 12: 2 (2009) 33–56; W.K. Smart 'Some Notes on *Mankind* (Continued)' and 'Some Notes on *Mankind* (Concluded)' *Modern Philology* 14: 1 and 14: 5 (1916–17) 45–58 and 293–313.

3. Pamela King 'Morality Plays' in *The Cambridge Companion to Medieval English Theatre* edited Richard Beadle and Alan J. Fletcher (Cambridge UP, 2008) 235–62, at 246–7; Meg Twycross and Sarah Carpenter *Masks and Masking in Medieval and Early Tudor England* (Aldershot: Ashgate, 2002) 251.
4. Marshall 'Addressing the Audience'; Clopper '*Mankind* and Its Audience'; John J. McGavin and Greg Walker *Imagining Spectatorship: From Mysteries to the Shakespearean Stage* (Oxford UP, 2016) 18; Ashley *Mankind* note 29.
5. Marshall 'Addressing the Audience' 191.

lands, he is explicitly a representative of the rural labouring poor.[6] Therefore, if the epilogue's epithet 'sofereyns' distinguishes the upper classes from the 'brothern', then this closing address acts less as a plea for the general condition of mankind and more as a veiled accusation that those who sit, the nobles and their guests, in particular needed to beware of the vanities of their worldly conditions. Were these audience members, more than the others watching the play, those whose 'sensuall condicions' (*Mankind* 906) particularly required 'dew examinacion' (*Mankind* 908)? This reading of the play's epilogue relies on its performance context – it only functions as a coded accusation of the need for moral reform in certain people *if* it is directed only at one identifiable group among a larger, socially diverse body of spectators.

This article argues that another section of the play, lines 490–520, makes a similarly allusive accusation of vice in socially superior members of the local society (although not necessarily those present in the audience), which relies on performance context, the bridging of the play world and the real world, and the drawing of distinctions between identifiable groups of people. In lines 490–520 the three 'distraction' vices, New Guise, Nowadays, and Nought, name a group of real, local men whom they claim they will visit when the devil, Titivillus, asks them to go abroad and steal horses or whatever else they can. In this article, I argue that this section of the play aims allusively to slander the men that it names while deliberately and carefully engaging with late medieval practices surrounding the offence of defamation. Being dependent upon allusive, non-literal readings of this scene based on the making of connections between the play and a defamatory tradition, some of my interpretations in this article are necessarily speculative; however, this approach to the naming episode in the play is not without scholarly precedent and I endeavour to advance a convincing argument as to the plausibility of such interpretations.[7] This episode in the play, I argue, demonstrates familiarity with the existence of two separate legal contexts for defamation: the moral offence tried in ecclesiastical courts and the criminal offence of *scandalum magnatum* (defamation of the monarch or magnates) tried in secular, royal courts. The play deploys its own, and

6. Ashley 'Introduction'.

7. For equally metaphorical readings of the episode see Eleanor Johnson *Staging Contemplation: Participatory Theology in Middle English Prose, Verse, and Drama* (Chicago: University of Chicago Press, 2018) 169–90; Paula Neuss 'Active and Idle Language: Dramatic Images in *Mankind*' in *Medieval Drama* edited Neville Denny (London: Edward Arnold, 1973) 41–67.

presumably its audience members', familiarity with these legal contexts in order to distinguish between those men whom it is safe to accuse publicly of vice and those whose social status and official roles would make the three N's dub them '*noli me tangere*' ('Touch me not', John: 20: 17; *Mankind* 512).

It has been convincingly argued that the play was performed during the politically unsettled seven months of the Lancastrian Readeption when Henry VI temporarily reclaimed the throne from Edward IV.[8] It has also been suggested, therefore, that the official roles and political allegiances of those high-profile men named in the play would recently have been temporarily changed, making their position in the context of national politics perhaps more prominent than usual in local consciousness at the time of performance.[9] Bearing this in mind, the naming section of the play, just like the mock court record in lines 686–93, deliberately exploits the political disruption of the real world context in which it was performed. In light of the analysis of this section of the play in a context of defamation, however, I would argue that its opportunistic use of national disruption in official governmental roles is aimed more at influencing local, provincial, communal relations than it is at satirising political allegiances at a national level. As well as rereading the naming section of the play and contextualising it in the late medieval culture of defamation as a legal offence, this article considers the impact of the section on the individual identities and communal relationships of its spectators.

In addition to the real-world implications of the naming section, in engaging with slander the episode also contributes to what has been seen as the play's wider allegorical concern with the danger of words, and especially idle words, in the *psychomachic* battle for mankind's soul;[10] the section plays with the supreme sinful and criminal use of words: defamation. This article will place the defamation episode within the play's broader thematic concern over the importance of the battle of words in mankind's fight between good and evil, especially considering the significance of the play's horse-stealing metaphor. The naming section functions as an accusation of vice in local people where socially superior men in official roles are designated morally suspect

8. Brantley and Fulton 'A Year without Kings'.

9. Geck 'Dating and Prosopography' 49. Geck reads the play as 'overtly political to its original audience'.

10. For the play as particularly concerned with good and evil words see Kathleen M. Ashley 'Titivillus and the Battle of Words in *Mankind*' *Annuale Mediaevale* 16 (1975) 128–50; Neuss 'Active and Idle Language'.

but untouchable in terms of reputation on pain of hanging for defamation. Understanding the naming section in this way allows a reinterpretation of the direction of the play's final lines only to the 'wyrschepyll sofereyns'; a final allusive suggestion of worldly vanity in the upper echelons of local society then appears as the ultimate expression of the naming section's accusations of vice under the guise of a socially reverent epilogue.

The play *Mankind*, preserved in the Macro manuscript alongside the moralities *Wisdom* and the *Castle of Perseverance*, offers tantalising if inconclusive evidence of early dramatic conditions.[11] One of the most intriguing sections of the text, both in this regard and for the purposes of this article, is contained in lines 490–520; here the three distraction vices, New Guise, Nowadays, and Nought, name a group of real, local men, historically identified by W.K. Smart, and their places of residence in the region.[12] Before this point in the play, the character Mischief, who is the play's principal Vice, disrupts the conventional relationship established between Mankind and Mercy and is aided by New Guise, Nowadays, and Nought to tempt Mankind away from his life of diligent labour. New Guise, Nowadays, and Nought, however, fail in their first attempt at corrupting Mankind and instead receive a beating from his trusty spade for their endeavours. In reaction to this beating, the three Worldlings summon a new devil, Titivillus, traditionally the devil of idle words who waits in the church to collect linguistic transgressions in his bag or in written form on his scroll ready for the Last Judgement, to aid them in their mischief.[13] At

11. See scholarship in note 2, plus Richard Beadle 'Monk Thomas Hyngham's Hand in the Macro Manuscript' in *New Science Out of Old Books: Studies in Manuscripts and Early Printed Books in Honour of A.I. Doyle* edited Richard Beadle and A.J. Piper (Aldershot: Scolar Press, 1995) 315–41; Richard Axton *European Drama of the Early Middle Ages* (London: Hutchinson University Library, 1974); Gail McMurray Gibson 'The Play of *Wisdom* and the Abbey of St Edmund' *Comparative Drama 19* (1985) 117–35 and *The Theater of Devotion: East Anglian Drama and Society in the Late Middle Ages* (Chicago: University of Chicago Press, 1989); and Peter Happé 'The Macro Plays Revisited' *European Medieval Drama 11* (2008) 37–57.
12. Smart 'Notes (Continued)' and 'Notes (Concluded)'.
13. For an account of Titivillus, or Tutivillus, and his tradition, see Lorna Hutson *The Invention of Suspicion: Law and Mimesis in Shakespeare and Renaissance Drama* (Oxford UP, 2007) 23–31.

this point, the three vices directly call upon the audience to pay for Titivillus to appear and presumably collect funds from audience members.[14] Titivillus then appears and warns the audience to beware of his 'abyll felyschyppe' (*Mankind* 477) who are ready to steal their horses. Having heard the three vices' complaints at their prior beating from Mankind, Titivillus speaks these lines:

> TITIVILLUS [*to the audience*]: Now I say yet ageyn, *caveatis*!
> Her ys an abyll felyschyppe to tryse hem out
> of yowr gatys. [*steal them (your horses)*]
> Now I sey, New Gyse, Nowadays, and Nought,
> Go and serche the contré, anon yt be sowghte,
> Summe here, summe ther, what yf ye may cache owghte.
> Yf ye fayll of hors, take what ye may ellys ...
> Forth, and espye were ye may do harme.
> Take William Fyde, yf ye wyll have ony mo.
> I sey, New Gyse, wethere art thou avysyde to go?
> *Mankind* 490–5 and 502–4

To which the vices reply:

> NEW GYSE: Fyrst I shall begyn at Master Huntyngton of Sauston,
> Fro thens I shall go to Wylliam Thurlay of Hauston,
> Ande so forth to Pycharde of Trumpyngton.
> I wyll kepe me to thes thre.
>
> NOWADAYS: I shall goo to Wyllyham Baker of Waltom,
> To Rycherde Bollman of Gayton;
> I shall spare Master Woode of Fullburn,
> He ys a *noli me tangere*. *'Touch me not'* (John: 20: 17)
>
> NOUGHT: I shall goo to Wyllyam Patryke of Massyngham,
> I shall spare Master Alyngton of Botysam
> Ande Hamonde of Soffeham,
> For drede of *in manus tuas* – qweke. *'into Thy hands'* (Luke 23: 46)
> Felous, cum forth, and go we hens togethyr.
> *Mankind* 505–17

14. Clopper '*Mankind* and Its Audience' 347.

Smart and other scholars have since uncovered a great deal of prosopographical detail to identify those named in this passage.[15] Some of those named were prominent, wealthy residents who had held official positions associated with local and national courts, and all were from clusters of locations to the east of Cambridge (Fulbourn, Bottisham, and Swaffham Bulbeck), to the south of Cambridge (Sauston, Hauxton, and Trumpington) and Norfolk (Walton, Gayton, and Massingham). In summary, Alyngton of Botysam is known to have been a Justice of the Peace frequently between 1461 and 1470 and again in 1473. Alyngton was also MP for Cambridgeshire and speaker of the House of Commons in 1472 and 1478. In 1479, he was a member of the Privy Council. Woode of Fullburn was a Justice of the Peace from November 1471 until 1479 and was associated with Alyngton and others in positions of authority via joint commissions before 1471. Hamonde of Soffeham was escheator for Cambridgeshire and Huntingdonshire from 1468 to 1469 and also closely associated with other authority figures in the locality. Significantly, these three men, Alyngton, Woode, and Hamonde, are those that the vices say they will 'spare'. For the other men, the records are less extensive but Wyllyham Baker of Waltom was certainly of a landed family by evidence from 1495 and Huntyngton of Sauston was sheriff for Cambridgeshire and Huntingdonshire later in the century from 1479 to 1480. Pycharde of Trumpyngton was probably a member of a Cambridgeshire gentry family, but Wylliam Thurlay of Hauston and Wyllyam Patryke of Massyngham appear only once in extant records with little telling information. No extant information has yet been discovered for Rycherde Bollman of Gayton and William Fyde has only tentatively been linked with the location of Waterbeach, Cambridgeshire.[16]

This information has been crucial to our knowledge of the play's context; at first, it was used by Smart to locate the play's performance geographically and by Bevington to suggest that it may have been a touring production moving between the clusters of locations named.[17] The biographical information has also been used to corroborate the dating of the play. Most recently, the passage has been viewed, by scholars tracing the extended court connections of those that the vices avoid, as implying political support for the exiled king,

15. Smart 'Notes (Continued)' and 'Notes (Concluded)'; Geck 'Dating and Prosopography'; Marshall 'Addressing the Audience'.

16. Geck 'Dating and Prosopography' and Smart 'Notes (Continued)'.

17. Smart 'Notes (Concluded)'; David Bevington *From Mankind to Marlowe: Growth of Structure in the Popular Drama of Tudor England* (Cambridge MA: Harvard UP, 1962) 15.

Edward IV, and, more broadly, it has been seen as a marker of the legal landscape for the play's contemporary society expressing a tension between ecclesiastical absolution and secular legal systems.[18] But what if we were to read the naming episode as an early example of performed libel, or slander, in the legal context of defamation?[19] What if the passage seeks to ruin the good reputations of the men it names by accusing them of vice through allusive association with each of the Worldlings? And what if its distinctions are based on the technical legalities of defaming different groups of people? In a play that is chiefly concerned with the danger of idle words, this episode appears to have been intentionally designed to function as defamatory verse, to rob the men named of their communal reputations through the performative power

18. For a reading of this section as political satire in support of those connected with Edward IV see Geck 'Dating and Prosopography'. John Marshall makes a similar case for reading aspects of *Wisdom* as political satire of an anti-Lancastrian bent in '"Fortune in the Worldys Worschyppe": The Satirising of the Suffolks in *Wisdom*' *Medieval English Theatre 14* (1992) 37–66. For a reading which locates tensions between common law procedures and ecclesiastical penitence in this episode based on the Worldlings' use of their 'neck verse' to evade secular legal repercussions see Hutson *The Invention of Suspicion* 12–63.

19. I use both of the terms, *libel* and *slander*, deliberately in this instance because I wish to suggest that there is a relationship between early modern performed libels and this earlier instance of performed defamation. Although during both the medieval and early modern periods the terms *libel* and *slander* were not legally separated into written or spoken attacks as in our modern understanding, the term *slander* is more appropriate for the spoken *Mankind* instance because the early modern understanding of the term *libel* is a much more specific and precisely defined one. Scholars have argued that although it was not statutory, the distinction between spoken and written attacks as those labelled *slander* and *libel* respectively appears to have been widely observed from an early stage. On the evidence of Star Chamber records for libel cases during the reign of James I, I do not believe such a clear distinction to have been widely observed in practice. However, hereafter the terms *slander* or *defamation* will be used in reference to the *Mankind* instance, whereas the term *libel* will be used to refer to early modern examples. For further work on these later examples of libel see Adam Fox 'Ballads, Libels and Popular Ridicule in Jacobean England' *Past and Present 145* (1994) 47–83 and *Oral and Literate Culture in England 1500–1700* (New York: Oxford UP, 2000), especially 299–334; for their performance qualities see Clare Egan '"Now fearing neither friend nor foe, To the worldes viewe these verses goe": Mapping Libel Performance in Early-Modern Devon' *Medieval English Theatre 36* (2014) 70–103. For a concise explanation of the early modern legal definition of libels see David Ibbetson 'Edward Coke, Roman Law, and the Law of Libel' in *The Oxford Handbook of English Law and Literature, 1500–1700* edited Lorna Hutson (Oxford UP, 2017) 487–506.

of words. It also appears to act as a commentary upon the legal punishment of such offences, which distinguished between the slander of those in public office and that of private individuals. The explicit association of defamation with the performance of communal morality in *Mankind* sheds new light on the ways in which the early dramatic tradition engaged with its socio-legal context. Furthermore, this reading of *Mankind* establishes a historical precedent for the early modern trend of performed libels and furthers our understanding of how such libels might have functioned in provincial communities.

Ostensibly, Titivillus initially talks of the 'abyll felyschyppe' (*Mankind* 477) going abroad to steal men's horses, but his command in lines 492–5 is actually rather vaguer: 'Go and serche the contré ... what yf ye may cache owghte. Yf ye fayll of hors, take what ye may ellys'. And again a few lines later: 'Forth, and espye were ye may do harme' (*Mankind* 502). While the satirical potential of this episode has been highlighted, scholars have tended to read this naming joke straightforwardly as indicating those who will be the targets of theft.[20] They read the distinction between those in positions of authority (Master Woode, Master Alyngton, and Hamonde) who the vices claim they will not visit, and the others (Master Huntyngton, Wylliam Thurlay, Pycharde, Wyllyham Baker, Rycherde Bollman, and Wyllyam Patrycke) that they will thieve from, as an indication that one would not wish to steal from the former group for fear that their authority and social standing might result in the culprits being hanged for theft.[21] This is an adequate explanation for the episode; its local circumstantiality and reference to individuals in positions of authority as those to be afraid of stealing from provides a coherent, sufficient explanation for the scene. However, this need not stop us from positing alternative possible explanations and contexts. If we read this section as slandering the men, then rather than planning actual theft of property, the implication is that Titivillus invites the vices, via their subsequent words, to plunder the good reputations of these men by associating them with the particular vices that name them. What follows here is a thorough consideration of another possible socio-legal discourse in which the episode may participate: the defamatory tradition.

By allusion, then, Master Huntyngton, Wylliam Thurlay, and Pycharde are accused of overindulgence in the latest guise (or fashion), Wyllyham

20. Geck 'Dating and Prosopography' 48 and 52.

21. Geck 'Dating and Prosopography' 41 and 48. Marshall describes those who are avoided as being '"spared" for reasons of judicial authority' ('Addressing the Audience' 193).

Baker and Rycherde Bollman live too much by the trends of nowadays, and Wyllyam Patrycke is held to be nought.[22] In other words, if the abstract vices embodied within the play world were actually to be found anywhere at large in the real world surroundings of the play performance, they would be located causing harm in the domestic affairs of Huntyngton, Thurlay, Pycharde, Baker, Bollman, and Patrycke. Because the audience knew these men from their day-to-day lives, the cumulative effect of the whole episode is that the words of Titivillus and the Worldlings function as performative utterances – the 'idle' words of these vices in fact do real damage in the world by robbing local men of their good names. These men may already have been accused of similar faults in the real world, or something about their conditions or reputations may have made them particularly easy targets. Either way, both their inclusion in the play world and their implicit association with vice in the real world could cause laughter in the audience. The men's reputations may then either have been materially damaged by the play or, if they had already been subject to this kind of accusation in the real world, the players' use of easy targets may affirm pre-existing opinions through laughter. If the play triggers laughter at prominent local men being ridiculed then those in the audience who laugh would be inadvertently siding with Titivillus and his vices.[23] I am not suggesting that everybody necessarily would laugh, as no two spectators are the same; however, this in itself might be a means of distinguishing different factions or social classes in the audience from one another based perhaps on who laughs, who frowns in offence, or who fails to react.[24]

Why, then, if the names spoken by the Worldlings allusively connect each man with the vice they represent, would the three N's bother to distinguish between those they will visit and those they will not? After all, those who are

22. Marshall suggests that in places the text of *Wisdom* similarly 'invite[s] the audience to make a connection between the vices portrayed and the Suffolks'; 'The Satirising of the Suffolks' 60.

23. Meg Twycross and Sarah Carpenter argue that Titivillus draws the audience in as his accomplices elsewhere in the play, making them complicit while he tempts Mankind into vice; Twycross and Carpenter *Masks and Masking* 251 (see note 3). Geck supposes that the episode would occasion laughter from an audience; 'Dating and Prosopography' 38.

24. On the 'fluid, corporeal' nature of spectatorship and the resulting cultural power of early drama in this respect see McGavin and Walker *Imagining Spectatorship* 7 (see note 4).

to be 'spared' are still named by the vice of which they are supposed to be guilty. If this section is understood in the legal context of defamation during the fifteenth century, rather than that of theft, there is a pressing reason to make this division of names. The laws of defamation that regulated language through the court systems of England underwent radical and fundamental change during the late sixteenth and early seventeenth centuries.[25] From its thirteenth-century origins in both ecclesiastical canons and royal statutes the medieval offence of defamation was understood in two distinct forms. When the defamatory action related to the ruin of an individual's reputation by accusation of a crime it was considered to be a moral offence, a transgression of religiously instituted communal norms, and so would be tried in a church court where the punishment at its most severe was excommunication, but in its more usual forms was public apology and penance.[26] This moral form of defamation, concerning private individuals, was rooted in the constitution of the English church courts, *Auctoritate Dei Patris*, authorised by the Council of Oxford in 1222, which stated:

> We excommunicate all those who, for the sake of hatred, profit, or favour, or for whatever other cause, maliciously impute a crime to any person who is not of ill fame among good and substantial persons, by reason of which purgation at least is awarded to him or he is harmed in some other manner.[27]

This ruling specifies that a crime must have been maliciously imputed but in ecclesiastical terms this included sins rather than just secular crimes.

Helmholz notes that during the thirteenth century local courts, as well as ecclesiastical courts, exercised jurisdiction over this kind of defamation, but that by 1400 they had lost this jurisdiction almost completely to the ecclesiastical courts.[28] Helmholz then explains that after 1485, defamation cases which would usually all have been heard in church courts were

25. R.H. Helmholz *Select Cases on Defamation to 1600* (London: Selden Society, 1985); W.S. Holdsworth *A History of English Law* 17 vols (London: Methuen, 1903–24) 5 205–12; Debora Shuger *Censorship and Cultural Sensibility: The Regulation of Language in Tudor-Stuart England* (Philadelphia: University of Pennsylvania Press, 2006); Ibbetson 'Coke, Roman Law, and Libel' 487–506.

26. Helmholz *Select Cases* xiv–cxi.

27. Helmholz *Select Cases* xiv.

28. Helmholz *Select Cases* lviii.

beginning to be separated into those which alleged spiritual crimes and those which alleged secular crimes. Around this time, those alleging secular crimes were being moved to secular courts by royal statute so that cases were heard in both ecclesiastical and royal courts during the sixteenth century; this in turn led to a revival of local court defamation cases in the sixteenth century.[29] At the time of *Mankind*'s performance, though, the moral offence was still largely the preserve of the ecclesiastical courts, although some discussion of the separation of secular and spiritual slanders must have been in the early stages of existence.

The other, criminal form of medieval defamation was legally termed *scandalum magnatum*. It related to the slander of the monarch and his magnates and was based on the Statute of Westminster of 1275:

> Whereasmuch as there have been oftentimes found in the country tellers of tales whereby discord or matter of discord hath many times arisen between the King and his People or Great Men of this Realm, for the Damage that hath and may thereof ensue; it is commanded, That from henceforth none be so hardy as to tell or publish any false News or Tales whereby discord or matter of discord or slander may grow between the King and his People or the Great Men of the Realm.[30]

False news or scandalous rumours which targeted the monarch or their magnates were understood as tending to the destruction of the kingdom and so could be tried in the secular royal courts where they were punishable by death as a form of sedition.[31] By the end of the fifteenth century, there is evidence that the category of *scandalum magnatum* in secular courts was being extended to include defaming those in local positions of authority as slandering government.[32] There is also evidence that during the fifteenth century, the only defamation cases tried in secular common law courts were

29. Helmholz *Select Cases* xliii–xlv and lxiv–lxv. See also R.H. Helmholz 'Canonical Defamation in Medieval England' *The American Journal of Legal History 15: 4* (1971) 255–68.

30. Ibbetson 'Coke, Roman Law, and Libel' 490.

31. Ibbetson 'Coke, Roman Law, and Libel' 490; Theodore F.T. Plucknett *A Concise History of the Common Law* (Boston: Little, Brown, fifth edition 1956) 485–8.

32. Helmholz *Select Cases* lxvii–lxviii; John C. Lassiter 'Defamation of Peers: The Rise and Decline of the Action for *Scandalum Magnatum*, 1497–1773' *The American Journal of Legal History 22: 3* (1978) 216–36.

those which constituted a form of contempt against town officials while all other cases of personal individual insult followed the first route to justice in the church courts.[33]

Hence, when New Guise, Nowadays, and Nought label those men who had held, or were very close to holding, public office (as Justices of Peace and an Escheator) as untouchable for fear of being hung and distinguish them from those that they will visit, none of whom held official, local positions of authority or were connected to government office, the legal distinction between an individual moral offence of defamation and that of *scandalum magnatum* provides a very fitting explanation.[34] If trial for the crime of theft was what the three vices feared, in reality they should expect the same legal repercussions whomever it was they were stealing from, albeit perhaps more immediately if they were to steal from a Justice of the Peace who could make sure that trial and punishment were swiftly conducted. However, if the real crime for which the three vices feared hanging was defamation under the Statute of Westminster's offence of *scandalum magnatum*, then they would have very good reason to distinguish between what the law called 'private' persons and those who held positions of governmental authority.

There is sufficient evidence from the period to demonstrate that these defamation offences and their legal distinctions were part of common consciousness. As early as 1418, a dispute between the Mayor, burgesses, and commonality of Cambridge and a group of scholars from the University took a distinctly similar form. The Mayor, burgesses, and commonality complained to the King's council that, on the vigil of St James the Apostle, scholars had terrorised the town overnight and had 'affixed on the mayor's gate a certain schedule, to his great scandal, and so that the mayor and burgesses dared not to preserve the peace'.[35] The schedule that the scholars were alleged to have attached to the Mayor's gate is a thirty-two-line verse which names its targets in turn, ridicules them, and then warns them to expect further violence. The verse opens:

33. Helmholz *Select Cases* lx–lxi.

34. Geck 'Dating and Prosopography', building on Smart 'Notes (Continued)', evidences that those to be avoided held public offices whereas those who were to be visited by the vices did not.

35. G.C. Coulton *Social Life in Britain from the Conquest to the Reformation* (Cambridge UP, 1918) 66.

Looke out here Maire with thie pilled pate,
And see wich a scrowe is set on thie gate; *writing, placard*
Warning thee of hard happes,
For and it lukke thou shalt have swappes....[36]
if it chance you shall have blows

It goes on to ridicule 'the hosteler Bambour, with his goat's beard' and 'that harlot Hierman, with his calves snowte' whom it threatens with equally brutal beatings; the verse prays to 'God Almyth' that 'whatsoever zowe sppare, | That metche sorowe to him bedith, | And evill mote he fare' and ends 'Amen, quoth he, that beshrewed the Mair's very visage'.[37] This case involved a mocking verse that ridiculed its targets by naming them and their associated moral flaws, while also threatening them with violent action – in this case not theft, but bodily harm. It also placed a caveat of evil wishing on those who were spared by God from the night's violence and ridiculing threats. Because the verse and St James' night activities, which were referred to as 'jetting' or night walking in the records, targeted the civic officials of the town, the Mayor and burgesses were entitled to complain to the King's council of the slanders.

A later example, that of William Collyngbourne in 1484, demonstrates quite how seriously the scandal of monarchs and magnates could be taken. For his famous couplet 'The Cat, the Rat, and Lovel our dog | Rule all England under a hog' (which referred to Richard III and three of his counsellors), posted on the doors of St Paul's, Collyngbourne was notoriously

> Put to the moost cruell deth at the Tower Hylle, where for hym were made a newe payer of galowes. Vpon the whiche, after he hadde hangyd a shorte season, he was cutte downe, beygne alyue, & his bowellys rypped out of his bely, and cast into the fyre there by hym, and lyued tyll the bowcher put his hande into the bulke of his body.[38]

36. C.H. Cooper *Annals of Cambridge* 5 vols (Cambridge: Warwick, 1842) *1* 159–63, at 161.
37. Cooper *Annals of Cambridge 1* 161.
38. R.M. Wilson *The Lost Literature of Medieval England* (London: Methuen, 1952) 194. The event was described in 1516 in Fabyan's *New Chronicles of England & France* (VIII fol. 219^{v}): 'The Catte the Ratte And Louell our dogge Rulyth all Englande under a hogge. The whiche was ment that Catisby Ratclyffe And the Lord Louell Ruled the lande under the kynge'. It also featured in Holinshed's *Chronicles* (1586) (*3* 746) '[Richard III executed] a poore gentleman called Collingborne [in 1484], for making a

Although this public display of brutality, a hanging made deliberately visible with a newly made gallows erected high on Tower Hill, was after *Mankind*'s assumed performance date, it demonstrates how seriously the slander of monarch and magnates could be taken in a roughly contemporary period. It also provides evidence for the connection of this offence with the punishment of hanging in public consciousness.

In addition to these instances of defamation relating to the offence of *scandalum magnatum*, Bryan VanGinhoven has recently provided crucial context for our understanding of defamation as a moral offence in his analysis of *The Booke of Margery Kempe*.[39] VanGinhoven, quoting Helmholz, significantly notes that the church canon which was used as the basis for the moral offence of defamation was 'read out to congregations in England's parish churches, regularly warning them of the excommunication they would incur if they slandered their neighbours'.[40] VanGinhoven therefore convincingly argues that defamation laws, and the moral offence tried in church courts especially, as well as their consequences were well known at all social levels during this period.

Moreover, in an even more tantalisingly specific possible context for the *Mankind* episode, John Marshall explains that one of the major concerns for the guild whom he argues were responsible for the performance was the regulation of language:

> In the St Edmund guild statutes the very first regulation that applies to behaviour, rather than organisation, deals with the punishment to be incurred for speaking maliciously or contemptuously of another member in the presence of the alderman or brethren, and is followed by the same fine of vjd for anyone who is 'rebele of his tonge' against the alderman.[41]

small rime of three of his councellors, lord Louell, sir Richard Ratcliffe and sir William Catesbie. The Cat, the Rat, and Louell our dog, Rule all England vnder an hog. Meaning by the hog, the wild boare, which was the Kings cognisance' (as quoted in *The Oxford Dictionary of Proverbs* edited John Simpson and Jennifer Speake (Oxford UP, fifth edition, 2008).

39. Bryan VanGinhoven 'Margery Kempe and the Legal Status of Defamation' *Journal of Medieval Religious Cultures 40: 1* (2014) 20–43.
40. VanGinhoven 'Margery Kempe' 23.
41. Marshall 'Addressing the Audience' 195.

While Marshall connects this ordinance generally to the play's theme of concern over idle words and their consequences, it would seem to me that the guild's regulation of malicious or contemptuous words in front of an audience argues even more strongly for the naming episode as participating in the wider culture of defamation and its legal technicalities.

It is also worth noting that in this reading of the naming episode, besides the separation of the named individuals into men to avoid and men to spare, one man's name is set apart: William Fyde. Titivillus himself recommends William Fyde to the Worldlings as a suitable companion for their ventures if they would have any more men to go with them. The naming by Titivillus, the play's central devil, of a man fit to accompany the vices is, in fact, a more directly defamatory statement than the allusive connection between the men's names and the vices who name them. We should, then, consider whether this section thus labels both the potential perpetrators (the worldlings and Fyde) and the 'victims' of the excursion (the other named men) as the subjects of defamation. Frustratingly, William Fyde, although tentatively connected with a man residing in Waterbeach, Cambridgeshire, has left no further trace of his position or identity. However, if the logic of the association between each specific vice and the men they name is followed, then Titivillus's naming of William Fyde associates Fyde with the sin of evil or idle words, the sin which Titivillus represents. It also then follows that Titivillus would recommend Fyde as a suitable companion for the defamatory activities that the worldlings are about to engage in. If Fyde is guilty of the sin of evil words then he will be of great help to the Worldlings when they steal from or defame other local men.

In this reading of the episode, Fyde is both labelled as a perpetrator of defamation and made a victim of defamation, in that he is defamed for being a defamer. During the medieval period, if somebody brought a case for defamation specifically to an ecclesiastical court and it turned out to be false or malicious then they, initially claiming to be the victim of slander, in fact, became the perpetrators by the false accusation of their would-be opponents. Legally speaking the status of perpetrator and victim in the medieval offence of ecclesiastical defamation were always explicitly and complicatedly tied together; 'in theory, the positions of plaintiff and defendant could be reversed at any time'.[42] This paradox, that the roles of victim or perpetrator in cases of slanderous words were interchangeable dependent on the truth

42. Lindsay Kaplan *The Culture of Slander in Early Modern England* (Cambridge UP, 1997) 14–15, see also chapter 1, 'The Paradox of Slander', 12–33.

or falsity of the words, reveals the fundamental vulnerability of language to misinterpretation and 'debasement'. Indeed, Eleanor Johnson stresses that the naming episode in *Mankind* seeks to reveal this very vulnerability of language to its audiences.[43] Thus, not only does the naming episode distinguish between two separate legal contexts for defamatory acts, the criminal and the moral, it also raises the specific dangers of the ecclesiastical context, which incorporated the reversible and reflexive nature of slander. Again, if the audience knows William Fyde they may be able to judge for themselves whether he is a slanderer or falsely accused by this episode and so a victim of slander; or the episode might sufficiently defame him so as to cause him to be considered a defamer by a local audience. In this reading, the play's naming episode allows for Fyde, a perpetrator of slanders, and the other men, as the subjects of the vices' activities, to be defamed in different ways, and it highlights the fundamental linguistic paradox of offences of the tongue.

Of course, the men labelled as 'to be avoided' are still named in the play and so the audience understands that if they *were* going to be accused of any kind of vice it would be that of 'nowadays' in Woode's case, and 'nought' in the case of Masters Alyngton and Hamonde, even if this was technically qualified by their ostensible exclusion. Indeed, the use of the phrase *noli me tangere* to describe Master Woode (*Mankind* 512) may even have further associations with vice characters: Smart notes that this phrase is applied to Wrath and Arrogance elsewhere by Lydgate and Gower respectively.[44] In this instance, while the vice characters of *Mankind* cannot directly claim Master Woode as one of their own due to his official authority, they can allude to other external examples where the kinds of character associated with this particular phrase are notorious vices. The episode subtly manipulates the legal specifics of whom one could explicitly slander as a moral offence and whom one could only target in a qualified, defensible way, while still achieving its goal of associating all those it names with a particular vice to an informed audience. Geck argues that those named as to be avoided were temporarily out of favour with national politics given their connections to nobles siding with the exiled king Edward and emphasises that traces of the three men not to be visited by the vices disappear from the records during the Readeption.[45]

43. Johnson *Staging Contemplation* 181 (see note 7).

44. Smart 'Notes (Continued)' 50.

45. Geck 'Dating and Prosopography' 38.

Perhaps their temporary loss of judicial positions in the changed national situation momentarily exposed them to public ridicule, while their previous office-holding would have made them targets to be very wary of publicly humiliating for fear of committing the offence of *scandalum magnatum*; hence they are included in the Worldling's lists, but only in a qualified way.

To understand *Mankind*'s naming episode in this manner – as carrying an allusive, non-literal meaning that links it to the defamatory tradition – is, in essence, speculative; the connection between the play and a context of defamation rests on a metaphorical reading of the naming and horse-stealing instruction. However, reading this scene and the naming of local men in this manner has been convincingly urged by other scholars of the play. Eleanor Johnson, for example, asserts that, at this moment of the play 'Titivillus names the local people whom the Worldlings should tap for assistance in the seduction of Mankind'.[46] She stresses that this scene succeeds in:

> Bringing eerily home to the audience their own social proximity to the staged drama before them. After all, the help that Titivillus and the Worldlings seek is financial support; the people they plan to tap are thus cast not only as coconspirators but also as victims who fall prey to sinful temptations themselves.[47]

Johnson refers to this episode as the 'calling out of the specific complicit men' and argues that when the play does this, it does so in order to remind the audience 'that by giving in to the Titivillian predilection ... for the debasement of language, they are, themselves, sinners who contribute to the debauchery of Mankind'.[48] This metaphorical understanding of the passage as marking out the named men as co-conspirators with the vices, labelling them as those who have 'fallen prey to sinful temptations', strengthens the connection drawn in this article between the naming scene and a defamatory tradition.

Allowing for a non-literal understanding of the scene, then, and bearing in mind that an audience watching *Mankind* at the end of the fifteenth century would be embedded within the culture of differentiated types of defamation outlined above; this audience in totality acted as witnesses to the play's public slanderous speech. The play thus implicates the audience in its potentially

46. Johnson *Staging Contemplation* 181.
47. Johnson *Staging Contemplation* 182.
48. Johnson *Staging Contemplation* 182.

defamatory content; their mere presence constitutes this as offensive language. If spoken in private the words would not significantly damage the men's reputations, whereas uttered in public they become widely enough known that they threaten to represent an established rumour. In this period, the existence of a rumour of wrongdoing was considered sufficient evidence for the courts to question the conduct of the subject of the rumour.[49] Whether individuals hearing these lines laugh, express disapproval, gasp in shock, or do not react at all, they have heard the words and so the play succeeds in involving its audience in potentially dangerous acts of idle, low, or excessive talk as opposed to diligent labour by their presence as spectators.[50] Moreover, the play is deliberately calling the audience's attention to this reaction and participation:

> Up until now it has been possible and even probable to laugh at Mankind, to enjoy the malefactions of the Worldlings, Mischief, and Titivillus ... But now, with this conspicuous reminder of the interpenetration of the world of the play and the world of the audience, the proverbial rug is jerked out from under our feet: we can no longer participate in the verbal fun of the bad guys without being aware that we are becoming one of them, that we are vulnerable to their seductions, and that this vulnerability – if not guarded against – will play out badly for us.[51]

The naming episode happens at a crucial moment of the play, just before Mankind falls into temptation because he mistakenly believes that Mercy has been hanged for stealing a horse, exactly the same action that the three vices are supposedly out committing. But if the three vices' 'robbery' is really of reputation rather than the actual theft of horses, then we, as modern readers, might have always misunderstood this section in exactly the same way as Mankind 'falls' for Titivillus' lie about Mercy being hung for theft of a horse. And, indeed, perhaps in the very same way those audience members who were wealthy enough to have good horses might also have misunderstood

49. Kaplan *Culture of Slander* 12–15.
50. Pamela King argues that the Worldlings' persuasion of the audience to join in with their rude Christmas Song at lines 331–4 has the same result; King 'Morality Plays' 246–7 (see note 3).
51. Johnson *Staging Contemplation* 182.

Titivillus' warning by being concerned over theft of their livestock. If so, then the episode tricks the audience on different levels. When the men named are associated with vice, the audience members who laugh because they understand the defamation joke or because they are not part of the ridiculed social class are guilty of vice for endorsing and thereby participating in defamation. However, the audience members who express concern rather than laughing, presumably some of the wealthy who own valuable horses or whose peers are targeted, are just as guilty; they reveal themselves to be as naive as Mankind (and possibly as us as modern readers) because they are more concerned about the consequences of the theft of their horses or other belongings. They are too worried about a potential loss of material possessions to realise that it is, in fact, their reputations as morally upstanding members of society that are under threat of exposure. If their chief concern is for their material possessions, as Titivillus tries to convince them it should be, rather than their good name, they show themselves to be guilty of a lack of care for their moral conditions.

Beyond the literal reading of the threat of horse stealing in the play, Paula Neuss has highlighted the metaphorical interpretation of this allusion. Neuss emphasises Mercy's earlier use of the horse as a metaphor for man's regulation of his moral condition in the lines:

> MERCY: Yf a man have an hors and kepe hym not to hye,
> He may then reull hym at hys own dysyere.
> Yf he be fede overwell he wyll dysobey
> Ande in happe cast hys master in the myre.
>
> *Mankind* 241–4.

This image is used again later when Mercy warns: 'Yf ye dysples Gode, aske mercy anon, | Ellys Myscheff wyll be redy to brace yow in hys brydyll' (*Mankind* 305–6). Neuss explains that then 'when Titivillus tells the audience to beware lest their horses are stolen he is speaking metaphorically: the Vices' idle language is the chaff that will feed the horses (their flesh) too well (with many words) and thereby gain control of their souls'.[52] When the naming section is understood as engaging in discourses surrounding defamation a further dimension is added to the metaphorical control of the vices over men's souls. Neuss explains that Titivillus' plan culminates in engineering Mankind

52. Neuss 'Active and Idle Language' 60 (see note 7).

into Mischief's 'bridle', the noose. I believe this analysis can be extended further: if Titivillus' command to the vices to 'steal men's horses' and the naming words of the Worldlings actually defame the men they name (claiming them to be guilty of each vice by allusion), then the episode in effect has also already braced each man in the bridle of his associated vice. The performative power of the words in the vices' slanderous verse is all that is needed in this context to effectively harness men's horses/bodies to get at their souls; by naming them the vices have taken the reputations they may have had, or have been expected to have, for being in possession of morally upstanding 'condicyons' (*Mankind* 908). The audience being warned about having their horses stolen should understand that in listening to the idle words of the vices they are metaphorically being fed chaff that will over-nourish their bodies and so entice them to surrender their souls to vice. However, at the very same time, in the vices' discussion of whose horses they will steal the naming words they use actually defame men, in the real world, under the guise of the act of going to steal their horses. Metaphor is translated, in a way, back into literal meaning because the words in themselves commit an action: not horse theft, but defamation. The vices' words steal souls by taking away reputations for impeccable morality; just as the Worldlings' act of physically going off stage supposedly to steal horses could literally deprive the men of their possessions or just as Titivillus' verbal warning could metaphorically alert the men to beware of listening to idle words in case their flesh is too well fed.

I would argue that the threat of horse stealing is designed to function both literally and metaphorically at the same time and that the defamatory content is designed to add another layer to this complex set of threats; ambiguity or confusion over which meaning is paramount seems deliberately incorporated in order to challenge an audience so that they must choose how to interpret the scene. The different interpretations of the passage and therefore the differing reactions to it in the audience could distinguish between those audience members who take it literally; those who heed Mercy's earlier metaphorical reading; and those who prioritise the defamatory aspect of the episode. Here, we might further imagine a scenario in which some of the audience laughs and some do not. If some laugh at the prospect of the 'horse stealing', the section then has the potential to reveal complex layers of identity and social alliance within its individual audience members. In laughing or not laughing, the spectators must consider whether their moral conditions have already been corrupted by idle words of vice, or whether they feel or express some concern for the state of their souls. Those who laugh at the vices ridiculing real men of high status, presumably a tempting source of laughter, show themselves to have succumbed to the corruption of idle words; whereas those who understand the horse-stealing threat metaphorically, and are in possession of a good soul not yet stolen by idle words, could choose not to condone the Worldlings' actions by not laughing along with their actions. As part of the audience hearing the words, though, they cannot escape the enactment of this shaming defamation, whether they are forewarned about its impact or not. However, it is possible that the presence of differing reactions in parts of the audience could serve to further tensions between spectators by heightening the sense of immorality in those who are laughing. If all laugh the audience shares a common identity, but if some laugh while others do not the controversy of the statement is affirmed and the audience might feel more divided. It would seem that a large portion of the audience, in deliberately different ways, fall for the temptation of malicious words just moments before the protagonist similarly falls for the idle, deceitful words of Titivillus that claim that Mercy has been hung for horse stealing. This use of defamatory language, the ultimate immoral, criminal use of words, is key to the play's central moment of temptation and fall for the audience, just as much as it is for the play's protagonist.

All or, indeed, none of the audience reactions imagined in the paragraph above may, in actuality, have been part of the Shrovetide performance of *Mankind* in 1471 – we can scarcely ever hope fully to recover an ephemeral moment of performance and spectatorship, especially one at such historical distance and without surviving witness accounts. However, the mere existence of so many possible ways to understand this passage – literally, metaphorically, defamatorily – argues for a diverse range of audience interpretations and possible reactions based on the differing identities, social statuses, alliances, and material possessions of each individual audience member. Naming real local men in an allegorical morality play during the devil and vice scenes is in itself provocative and controversial: the play is confronting the audience with a collapsing of the distinction between play world and real world. Thus it is possible that in this moment spectators might also be spectating the reactions of their fellow audience members, as well as the actors of the play, simply because the audience's reactions are *not* homogeneous. A moment of subconscious reaction to a provocative topical joke, such as laughter, could reveal something about an audience member to their fellow spectators; this part of the play has the capacity to expose and even alter both individual and communal relations in the real-world context of this provincial society.

Perhaps most importantly, though, the audiences' attention is drawn to their own reaction:

> Titivillus's role is not simply that of a tempter, it is also that of an enforcer, or even whistle-blower: he reminds all present that they accede to living in a world ... in which the powerful few invite, in effect, despair and malefaction into the larger social realm ... the calling out of the specific complicit men and our own complicity with them signals that the play has ambitions not only to reform the soul for better contemplative participation but also to reform the social world.[53]

The naming episode jars the spectator into an acute awareness of their individual conditions *and* their place within the wider social community in order to effect change.

It is also important to consider that the play itself offers a retrospective view of the defamation scene when the vices reappear onstage having been out on their 'stealing' mission. That an audience, at the moment of the naming episode, were made to realise the complicity of their fellow community members and themselves in vice, is further reinforced by the play's staging of the aftermath of the excursion. Johnson notes that Mankind's temptation by Titivillus while asleep, and the revelation of his vulnerability to despair having sinned, 'retroactively' shed light on earlier scenes deliberately to reveal to the audience how they had been 'invited to participate in them'.[54] In the play's equally 'retroactive' perspective on the defamation scene, at lines 612–49, New Gyse comes back on stage reporting that he and Mischief have been caught by the authorities and nearly hanged. New Gyse claims that he escaped because the hangman's noose broke while he was upon the gallows, whereas Mischief was imprisoned rather than hanged because he could recite his 'neck verse' – a Latin verse meant to prove that one was a cleric who could claim the benefit of clergy not to hang for a first offence. Luck, or craft, saves New Gyse, and the feigning of clerical Latin saves Mischief, from the secular courts. New Gyse, having related all this, then remarks: 'Alasse, he [*Mischief*] wyll hange such a lyghly man, and a fers, | For stelynge of an horse, I prey Gode gyf hym care' (*Mankind* 621–2). This last remark affirms the literal reading that the pair had been stealing horses when they were caught and nearly hanged. Nowadays

53. Johnson *Staging Contemplation* 182.
54. Johnson *Staging Contemplation* 181.

then also returns reporting: 'I have laburryde all this nyght; wen shall we go dyn? | A chyrche her besyde shall pay for ale, brede, and wyn' (*Mankind* 632–3). These lines have been understood as indicating that Nowadays has stolen from a nearby church, either the properties of the church, perhaps the Eucharist and wine, or cash or goods that will furnish them with money for food and drink. New Gyse remarks that Nowadays is a better merchant than he. Nought, appropriately, returns with nothing complaining that he will die if he cannot get some of the food that Nowadays has mentioned. Mischief then re-enters boasting of murder and manslaughter having killed his jailer and ravished the jailer's wife, but makes no mention of why he was imprisoned in the first place.

I would argue that this retrospective reporting of the night's activities also leaves room for both literal and metaphorical interpretation. Literally, Mischief and New Gyse stole a horse and were nearly punished at law, Nowadays stole from a church and Nought came home with nothing; all then profit by the food and drink that Nowadays gets from the church. However, New Gyse's lines about horse stealing are an exclamatory remark contrasting the seeming extremity of hanging with the slightness of stealing a horse; they fall short of a direct and detailed report of the offence, of the kind we get of the legal repercussions that New Gyse and Mischief suffer at the hands of the court. New Gyse's lines leave room for doubt, as does Nowadays' claim that he has 'laburryde' all night, and will now sustain his endeavours through the church. It is significant, given the distinction in the naming episode between the secular criminal offence of defamation and the moral, ecclesiastical offence with their respective punishments of hanging or, at the most extreme, excommunication, that one vice returns having been through the secular legal system, and one comes back unscathed and in profit from a church. New Gyse was the only Worldling who named three men he would visit and *did not* name anyone he would spare. If the reference to being hung for horse stealing is still also read metaphorically, his defamatory actions, in avoiding no one, have resulted in him being tried for slander. It may then be significant that the first man New Gyse named, Huntyngton of Sauston, was recorded as Sheriff of Cambridgeshire and Huntingdonshire later in the century between 1479 and 1480. At the time of the play's performance, Huntyngton was not yet, as far as we know, in an official position of authority; however, he was close to it, being of a social status and prominence to take up an official position in the near future. Perhaps the play's retrospective explanation of New Gyse's activities suggests that he trod too close to the line of who could and who could not be 'safely' defamed. It may highlight that where the other two were careful to name those they would spare, New Gyse did not state anyone he would avoid and included a borderline social superior first on his list of co-conspirators. Nowadays' list also included a man on the very cusp of official power, Woode of Fullburn, who became a Justice of Peace in November of 1471, the year of the play, but Nowadays knew to avoid him as a 'touch me not'.

Furthermore, if we likewise read Nowadays' return to the stage metaphorically, we might understand that he avoided the secular criminal offence and was not tried or nearly hung for it; but we might consider that he successfully defamed those private individuals who would only have recourse to ecclesiastical courts for redress. Hence, it would be fitting that Nowadays went to a nearby church but was not punished, rather he walked away in profit from his activities. Nought returns hungry but unscathed by any punitive measures, relaying no information about his activities, and is revived by Nowadays' profit from the church. It is possible that these outcomes offer a commentary on the discrepancy in punishment meted out by the two legal contexts for defamation, in which the leniency of the church or the ease with which it can be exploited is critiqued. The feigned benefit of clergy saved Mischief from his offence in a secular court; and Nowadays' visit to a nearby church, albeit perhaps unbeknownst to the church, sustains the actions of the vices collectively thereafter. That they come back from their excursions hungry and likely to die for lack of food might also symbolically relate to the premise of the horse-stealing metaphor. As observed above, in the horse-stealing metaphor the vices' idle language symbolically was the 'chaff' that overfed the horses/men's' flesh too well and thereby gained control of the horses/men's souls. That the vices come back hungry and without food then symbolises the accomplishment of their activities literally and metaphorically – their mischief has been managed by giving out their food/idle words.

If stealing from a church, or metaphorically getting away with the moral offence of defamation in the church-court context, is what sustains the vices, then the play suggests that the regulation of sins in the moral world is not functioning sufficiently. This message also suggests an earlier, parallel, scene worth investigating: the other explicit instance of defamation in the play, when Nought ridicules 'Pope Pokett' (*Mankind* 143). Early on in the play, when the Worldlings first meet Mercy, they ridicule him for his use of 'Englysch Laten' (*Mankind* 124), and Nowadays asks Mercy to adjudicate in a 'batell' between Nowadays and his wife, Rachel. Nought chips in that Rachel won the battle and he would venture a bet on it. Nowadays reacts angrily to this and tells Nought, in Latin, to kiss his arse. Nought's next lines, which Kathleen Ashley glosses as addressed to Mercy, are:

> NOUGHT Lo, master, lo, here ys a pardon bely-mett.
> Yt ys grawntyde of Pope Pokett,
> Yf ye wyll put yowr nose in his wyffys sockett,
> Ye shall have forty days of pardon.
>
> *Mankind* 143–6

Jambeck and Lee's 1977 article convincingly demonstrates that although this reference is possibly just 'a conventional, albeit indelicate, jibe at papal avarice', it is much more likely to be a reference to a contemporary figure: John Poket, elected prior of Barnwell Abbey, near Cambridge, in 1444, an office he held until his death in 1464.[55] Interpreting this as a reference to Prior John Poket is supported by the geographical proximity of Barnwell to the assumed location of the play's performance and the fact that on at least one occasion 'Prior Poket is directly linked in a judicial proceeding with another of the contemporary figures mentioned in the play – a "Master Alyngton of Botysam"'.[56] Jambeck and Lee also note that

> The appellation 'Pope', however ironical its intended purpose, appears to have been justified, for during the tenure of his office at Barnwell, Poket served as papal representative in several actions.[57]

This is another complex episode – Nowadays has just addressed Nought about an offensive remark that Nought made about his wife, Rachel. Ashley glosses Nought's following speech as addressed to Mercy, however, Jambeck and Lee understand the reference to Prior Poket as 'embedded ... in the scurrilous exchange between Nought and Nowadays'.[58] Mercy has not spoken before this point in the debate between Nowadays and Nought, and Nought has no reason to protest to Mercy that he has a pardon, whereas he does have a reason to rebut Nowadays' offensive put-down that Nought is an unwise fool and so should kiss his arse instead of talking. I would therefore argue, with

55. Thomas J. Jambeck and Reuben R. Lee '"Pope Pokett" and the Date of *Mankind*' *Mediaeval Studies* 39 (1977) 511–13, at 511.
56. Jambeck and Lee 'Pope Pokett' 512.
57. Jambeck and Lee 'Pope Pokett' 512.
58. Jambeck and Lee 'Pope Pokett' 511.

Jambeck and Lee, that the line is a retort from Nought directed at Nowadays. What further complicates this episode is that it insults Poket on two counts: it implies that he corruptly sells indulgences to evil people but it also suggests that sleeping with the Prior's wife is a way to get a forty-day pardon. This second jibe seems to parallel the joke that Nought has just made at Nowadays' expense: that Rachel, his wife, bests him in 'batell'. The lines further slander Poket because, since he was a prior, in reality he should not have had a wife. This episode, then, stages an offensive exchange ridiculing Nowadays and 'Pope Pokett' because of the conduct of their wives, for which Nought, the would-be offender, claims he has a pardon granted by Poket himself. Presumably, at this point Nought brandishes a stage prop to indicate that he has a pardon. An insulting exchange is characteristic of defamatory offences, and the use of mock-official documents is ubiquitous in the defamatory tradition. Furthermore, Mercy's commentary on the exchange, directed at Nought, explicitly labels it a sin of the tongue and questions the efficacy of the pardon: 'Thys ydyll language ye shall repent' (*Mankind* 147).

This episode is, in effect, a more direct and explicit defamation scene than the later naming section in that it does not rely as heavily on an allusive association between vice figure and named man; here Nought directly insults Prior Poket; except that, if we accept the scholarly dating of the play to the period 1464–71, then by the time the play was performed Poket was dead. It was not until the early modern period that defamation law was changed so that defaming a dead person was an offence; before then, at common law it was held that the offense died with the person.[59] Nought can technically legally get away with insulting Prior Poket if he is dead; besides which, he claims to have a pardon absolving him of sins in an ecclesiastical context. Mercy refutes this by telling Nought he will still have to *repent* for his idle words. It is significant that it is Nought who names 'Master Alyngton' as someone he will spare for fear of hanging, given that Poket was directly linked in judicial proceedings to Alyngton. It is also striking that Poket was associated with papal-level authority in the locality:

> Aside from the commonplace right conferred upon a prior to grant minor ecclesiastical posts to worthy clerks, a right granted to Poket by

59. Alastair Bellany 'A Poem on the Archbishop's Hearse: Puritanism, Libel, and Sedition after the Hampton Court Conference' *Journal of British Studies 34: 2* (1995) 137–64; Holdsworth *History of English Law* 5 206–7 (see note 26).

> Nicholas V on at least two occasions, the pope also placed a good deal of trust in Poket's ability to evaluate and judge upon diocesan issues which were locally sensitive.[60]

The link between Poket and Alyngton in real-life judicial contexts supports the reading of the Poket scene and the later naming scene as connected; in other words, it argues for the vices' naming scene as a defamatory one directly related to the defamatory naming of 'Pope Pokett'.

The Poket scene also provides a possible explanation for why Nought comes back from 'horse stealing' with nothing, when New Gyse was tried in a secular court and Nowadays profited from a visit to a nearby church: Nought has a pardon supposedly granted by an important church official, whether or not it is a forgery, which he can apparently claim as absolving him from sins of the tongue, as he does in his retort to Nowadays. Nought also insulted a dead person and so while he succeeds in labelling the church as corrupt, he is not technically liable in a defamatory sense. In the later naming scene, Nought agreed that he would avoid Alyngton, the Justice of Peace, and Hamonde, the escheator, and 'go' only to Patryke; a defamatory act but one for which he claims to have a pardon. The above interpretation of the naming episode and the play's retrospective explanation of it argues for Nought being the most shrewdly aware of the legal contexts of defamation, and thus the one who would get away with no redress from his 'stealing' or insulting excursions. If corrupt church practices appear to provide Nought with some means of escape from punishment, as Mischief's use of the neck verse also did, and if Nowadays profits from his church 'visit', perhaps we can understand these defamatory episodes cumulatively as condemning the ecclesiastical system for aiding and abetting the vices in their sins of 'ydyll language' (*Mankind* 147).

The significance of words to the wider moral message of the play has been recognised by scholars such as Paula Neuss and Kathleen Ashley. Indeed, Ashley has argued that the play is 'thematically and dramatically structured by a "battle of words"'. She suggests that the 'confrontation between good and evil is dramatized as a battle of good words ... against misleading or evil ones'.[61] Ashley notes the stylistic embodiment of this battle in the diction and rhyme-schemes used by the opposing characters. Other scholars have

60. Jambeck and Lee 'Pope Pokett' 512.

61. Ashley 'Introduction'; Ashley 'Titivillus and the Battle of Words in *Mankind*' 130. See also Neuss 'Active and Idle Language' 41–67 (see note 7).

highlighted the many other embedded textual and verbal forms included in the play. We might also add to this the visual reference to a defamatory tradition in the mock pardon that Nought brandishes while ridiculing 'Pope Pokett' (*Mankind* 144).[62] The syntax and rhyming of the naming episode as well as the deliberately balanced patterns of numbers of men (six to be visited, three to be avoided, with two to be visited and one avoided by Nowadays, then one to be visited and two to be avoided by Nought) and grouped locations (six in Cambridgeshire, with two groups of three clusters, and three in Norfolk) argue for this as a carefully constructed embedded verse.[63] While this may be part of the general urgency with which the play seeks to bring its moral message home to its local audiences, it is also possible that it has been intentionally designed with a specific function in mind, just as the mock court roll is in the episode which follows shortly after.[64] If so, its resemblance to the kind of slanderous verse fixed to the Mayor's gate in the 1418 Cambridge dispute complained of to the King's council, for example, is significant.

ꕤ ꕤ

I believe that it is significant for our understanding of early drama that *Mankind*'s performed, allusive, and implicit style of public ridicule in moral terms, which exploits precise knowledge of the nuances of both communal relations and legal contexts for avoiding defamation charges, is strikingly similar to the later examples of provincial libel found in the records of Star Chamber. By the end of the sixteenth century, defamation law had been redefined so that the libelling of any individual, private or holding public

62. Ashley 'Introduction'. The play's uses of Latin have been the subject of scholarly criticism, for example: Janette Dillon '*Mankind* and the Politics of "English Laten"' *Medievalia et Humanistica 20* (1994) 41–64; Charlotte Steenbrugge '"O, Yowr Louely Wordys": Latin and Latinate Diction in *Mankind*' *Medieval English Theatre 31* (2009) 28–56. Brantley and Fulton 'A Year without Kings' (see note 2) and Hutson *The Invention of Suspicion* (see note 13) address the multiple uses of legal documents within the play. Other forms that feature in the play are the sermon, songs, and the writing Mankind hangs around his neck, for example.

63. Marshall disagrees with Smart's suggestion that the names and locations could be altered to fit different areas of performance for a touring company based on the impact such a change would have on the 'metrical consistency' of the passage; Marshall 'Addressing the Audience' 193.

64. Brantley and Fulton 'A Year without Kings'.

office, was understood as a criminal offence. The kind of libel which had previously been tried in church courts as moral offences could then be tried, alongside those previously seen as *scandalum magnatum*, at the most high-profile prerogative court in the country: the Star Chamber. Under this redefinition, anyone complaining of being libelled could sue the accused for monetary damages, providing real financial as well as reputational incentive for taking the libeller to court. Thus during the seventeenth century the numbers of libel cases brought to Star Chamber from all levels of society increased dramatically, with James I's reign witnessing the height of a libel epidemic.[65] During the early modern period, provincial libel developed its own genre, and it is significant that this involved performance: whether the libel took the form of a verse read aloud, a mock ceremonial or ritual enactment, or a symbol posted up in public, these cases involved varying elements of performance and theatricality.

One example from 1601 will serve to suggest some of the similarities in form and content that might be found between the *Mankind* naming episode and this later phenomenon of performed provincial libel. In the case of Lincoln vs Dymoke, Henry Clinton, the second Earl of Lincoln, took his two nephews, Sir Edward and Tailboys Dymoke, and others to Star Chamber for libelling him in their performance of a stage play 'termed the death of the Lord of kyme'.[66] The Earl of Lincoln complained that

> The said Talboys Dymocke Roger Bayard Iohn Cradocke the elder and Iohn Cradocke the younger vppon a Grene neere adioyning to the howse of the said Sir Edward Dymocke at kyme ... hard by A Maypole standing vppon the said greene did ... present and acte an enterlude or play ... dyvers persons of the Neighbour Townes therevnto adioyning and of the howsehould servantes of the said Sir Edward being then ^& there assembled to heare & see the same In which play the said Talboys Dymocke being the then principall actour therein did first ... Counterfeite and tooke vppon him to represent the person of your said Subiecte [*the Earl*] and his speaches and gesture and then & there in

65. Steven W. May and Alan Bryson *Verse Libel in Renaissance England and Scotland* (Oxford UP, 2016) 6; Fox 'Ballads, Libels and Popular Ridicule in Jacobean England' and *Oral and Literate Culture in England 1500–1700* (see note 20).

66. *REED: Lincolnshire* edited James Stokes, 2 vols (Toronto: University of Toronto Press, 2009) *1* 271.

> the said play tearmed & named your said ... Subiect the Earl of lincolne his good vncle in Scornefull manner and as an actor then tooke vppon him to represent the person of your said Subiecte and in such sorte representing the person of your said Subiecte in the said play was there fetcht away by the said Roger Bayard who acted and represented ... in the said playe the person and place of the divell.[67]

Here we have a provincial play, acted before an audience made up of the local community under the auspices of the traditional summer games of South Kyme, which came to a close with the dramatic staging of the death of their elected mock lord. Within this play, we are told, a local man of considerable wealth and status, who was part of an ongoing local dispute at the time,[68] was impersonated, named, and then 'fetcht away' by the character playing the devil – these elements of the play were considered libellous in content. Although there is no evidence that the three N's of *Mankind* impersonated the men they named, though it is of course possible that they did, they certainly named those men and made out to take the men's 'possessions' for the devil. This is, one could argue, just one step away from actually taking away an impersonation representing the men themselves.

The Earl of Lincoln further complained that

> The said Roger Boyard in an other parte of the said playe did then and there acte & represent the parte of the ffoole and the parte of the vyce ... and then and there actinge the said parte did declare his last will & testament and ... in hearing of all the persons assembled to see and heare the said playe did bequeathe his woodden dagger to your said Subiecte by the name of the Earle of lincolne and his Cockscombe & bable vnto all those that would not goe to Hornecastle with the said Sir Edward Dymocke against him [*the Earl of Lincoln*].[69]

Not only did the play libel the Earl by having the devil take away the character impersonating him, it also associated him with the Vice and Fool character

67. *REED: Lincolnshire 1* 271.

68. Edward Dymoke and others were alleged to have riotously broken into the parsonage at Horncastle, which was owned by Lincoln, on 26 July (a month before the play performance) to claim 'divers duties of right' belonging to Lincoln (*REED: Lincolnshire 1* 271).

69. *REED: Lincolnshire 1* 271.

by bequeathing him the Vice's dagger. This is a material possession bestowed upon the target, rather than a horse taken away from him, but the object still serves to connect the man with the Vice who names him in the play. This account also demonstrates a similar kind of emphasis on the audience's role in the libel as I have tried to suggest for the *Mankind* episode. Here, the audience are specifically invoked as witness to the libel: the last will and testament of the Vice/Fool is explicitly done 'in the hearing of all the persons assembled to see and heare the ... playe'.[70] Their identity as an assembly to see and hear a play is one thing but they also *all hear* the libellous elements of it and this is a subtly different function from their merely being gathered to spectate a play. Moreover, they are directly implicated in the action by the content of the Vice/Fool figure's last will and testament: all those who would not go with the group of libellers to riot and occupy Lincoln's house and grounds at Horncastle, in other words those who did not take the side of the libellers in the dispute, were labelled as foolish by being bequeathed the Fool's cockscomb and bauble. As an audience member, if you were not on the side of the actors then you were on the side of the Earl and thereby also associated with folly and vice. The audience was being asked to react, to pick sides in this libellous performance, and their reaction would dictate how they were viewed by the rest of the community, both the actors and their fellow audience members.

Lincoln also complained that one of the actors played a minister and delivered a mock sermon while drinking a pot of ale at the end of the play; that the actors also sang a dirge song naming 'knowen lewde & licencious woemen'; and that they fixed a written verse libel about him to the maypole on stage directly below a picture of a bull, which represented his coat of arms. These last elements extend and diversify the libellous contents of the play and they take this example somewhat beyond the potentially slanderous episode in *Mankind*. However, they do indicate a similar inclusion of a mixture of written, oral, and visual forms – the sermon, song, written verse, and coat of arms – as we find used throughout *Mankind* and, in fact, in another Macro play, *Wisdom*.[71]

The case of the 'Death of the Lord of Kyme' is from a different time period and social context to that of *Mankind*: by 1601, libelling anyone, whether

70. *REED: Lincolnshire 1* 271.

71. Marshall's argument that *Wisdom* satirises the Suffolks is based, among other things, on the play's use of their heraldic badge as part of the livery of the vices; Marshall 'The Satirising of the Suffolks' 45–6 (see note 19).

private individual or public official, was a criminal offence, and hence the case came to be tried in the court of Star Chamber. The case is also post-Reformation and specific to the local politics of provincial South Kyme, Lincolnshire. However, the existence of a libel case involving a stage play which names its target and accuses them of vice through association with the devil and Vice/Fool characters, as well as pushing its audience to endorse the libel or be ridiculed themselves, suggests that the *Mankind* naming episode might also be understood as engaging in similar ways with its own culture of defamation. That the early modern methods of performing libel might be traced back to medieval dramatic traditions should also prompt us to reconsider the significance of libel cases as records of performance.

Lancaster University

Acknowledgements: The research for this article is part of a larger, ongoing study of the performance of defamation in the medieval and early modern periods by the author and as such has been presented at several conferences. I would like to thank all those who have listened to the ideas in development and offered advice, but I would particularly like to thank Professor John J. McGavin, Professor Meg Twycross, Dr Sarah Carpenter, and Dr Liz Oakley-Brown for their help at various stages of this work.

THE SUN IN YORK (PART ONE): Illumination, Reflection, and Timekeeping for the Corpus Christi Play

Meg Twycross

Having returned, somewhat belatedly, to research I did on the York Mercers' *Doomsday* pageant wagon for the Joculatores Lancastrienses' recreation for the York Festival of 1988, I have been ambushed by all manner of questions, some of which had not occurred to me in the hurly burly of the actual production.[1] One of them is, 'Why is there no provision whatsoever for lighting in the 1433 Indenture[2] or anywhere in the Mercers' accounts?' There is a regular entry for processional torches for escorting the shrine of Corpus Christi, but no hint that these were used in the pageant.[3] They were liturgical objects, intended solely for the procession, and were stored separately, with their 'castles' and banners, in the Mercers' Hall.[4]

1. 9–10 July 1988. Four pageants: *The Death* (Unicorns of Copenhagen), *Assumption* (Durham Medieval Players) and *Coronation* (York Lords of Misrule) of the Virgin, and *Doomsday* (Joculatores Lancastrienses). Played at four stations in Petergate, starting at 7 p.m. Associated with but not paid for by the York Festival. On the Durham Medieval Players' production, see John McKinnell 'Producing the York *Mary* Plays' *METh 12: 2* (1990) 101–23; 'The Medieval Pageant Waggons at York: their orientation and height' *Early Theatre 3: 1* (2000) 79–104 (about both pageant-waggon sequences, 1988 and 1992); also his edition of *Three Mary Plays from the York Cycle* (Medieval English Theatre Modern Spelling Texts; Lancaster: METh, 1988). See also my 'The Left-hand-side Theory: a Retraction' *METh 14* (1992) 77–94, reprinted in *The Materials of Early Theatre: Sources, Images, and Performance* (Abingdon and New York: Routledge, 2018) 27–4.
2. *Records of Early English Drama: York* edited Alexandra F. Johnston and Margaret Rogerson, 2 vols (University of Toronto Press, 1979) 55–6. This, together with the shorter indenture of 1526 (*REED: York* 241–2), is the most detailed evidence we have of the appearance of a York pageant waggon.
3. The torches are first recorded as being made (with castles and banners) in 1437 (*REED: York* 58), and were carried regularly thereafter. The Mercers are not recorded in the 1415 *Ordo paginarum* as walking in the torch procession.
4. *The York Mercers and Merchant Adventurers, 1356–1917* edited Maud Sellers *Surtees Society 129* (1918) 98 (1497).

There are two reasons why the question of lighting is important. The practical one is visibility. *Doomsday* is the last pageant in the cycle. Even with the most expeditious of performances and the most efficient organisation, somewhere on its journey along the pageant route, the sun was likely to set. In our recreation, which we timed for early evening along Petergate – the run of four pageants started at 7 p.m. – the audience had trouble seeing things on the lower deck of the waggon while the sun was going down, and in general when it had gone down. At the time we just found this vaguely annoying, and attempted to compensate with hidden lamps rigged up from a car battery – this was before the days of portable LEDs. Notes sent to Giorgio Vasari by a friend after the dress rehearsal of the Florentine *Annunciation* play of 1565/6 suggest that this was not a purely twentieth-century problem:

> *Lumi, lumi, lumi! Et habbiateci l'occhio, perché el mazzo non si vedi punto. E vi dico che e' non ve ne sará tanti che e' non paino pochi.*[5]
>
> Lights, lights, lights! And keep your eye on this, because you couldn't see the garland of angels at all. And I'm telling you that however many [lights] you have they will still seem too few.

Sheer visibility is important to a play. Apart from the spectacle (which as we shall see is thematic as well as affective), if you can't see what the actors are saying, it's much harder to *hear* what they are saying. If, as in our *Doomsday*, all your actors are masked, you need even more to see their body language and gestures.

The second reason is aesthetic and theological: divine radiance is so much part of any late medieval presentation of God. Painted images show Him surrounded by a glory or nimbus, with much use of gold paint and gold leaf. Stained glass formalises this into silver-stain sunbeams. This attempt to approximate radiance was even more pronounced, as it turns out, in theatrical images.

There are two ways of producing this radiance theatrically. One depends on artificial light, and lots of it. The much-quoted Italian *feste* in Florence, contemporary with the York Mercers' 1433 Indenture, featured hundreds of lighted lamps circling about God like stars and planets.

5. Notes to the producer (Vasari) on the Florence *Annunciation* play of 1565/6. Nerida Newbigin 'Greasing the Wheels of Heaven' *I Tatti Studies 11* (2007) 201–41 at 226 and 240.

> On this elevated platform is set a throne, on which a man of majestic appearance sits, in magnificent robes and with a crown on his head. From all these things it is deduced that he is the figure of God the Father ... Around him and by his footstool are arranged a multitude of little boys in due order, representing heavenly virtues. Around the throne and amid the children around the Father there are seven spheres, the smallest of which measures two ells in diameter, and around it another, two hand spans larger, and so on, and on them burn a thousand (*al.* more than five hundred) little oil lamps ... All this represents an imitation of the seven spheres of heaven, of the planets, of heavenly might and inextinguishable angelic light. Their creator arranged them wonderfully ...
>
> There on the upper platform, the venerable Father can be seen, around him, as we described above, burned more than five hundred lights. These lights moved endlessly to and fro, weaving in and out very fast, some going up and others going down.[6]

The accounts and inventories for these *feste* are full of detailed information about glass jars, oil, cotton-wool wicks.[7] The craftsmen responsible for the set devised all manner of ingenious ways of reflecting, diffusing, and diffracting the light, by shining it through flasks of coloured water,[8] and by covering

6. Florence 1439: Annunciation *festa*; Nerida Newbigin *Feste d'Oltrarno* 4–5. The quotation is in English because of the complicated textual history of the account by the Russian visitor, Abraham, Bishop of Suzdal. Even this is a composite account; see Newbigin's original for how the quotation is put together.
7. Newbigin *Feste d'Oltrarno* 81, 87–8, 93, 95, 96, 102 (mirrors), 107, 117, 121, 124–5 (1469: *nugola* and lights that can be switched on and off)), 130 (1470), 136 (lighting effects on aerial machines). The larger *pianete* were first constructed in 1430 (87–8). See also 75 (Neri de Bicchi's inventory, 600 glass ampoules, 1466/7); 76 'two pans for illuminating the planets'; 107 (1446), 117 (218 glass ampoules, 1464); 121 (600 glass light sockets [*luminegli di vetro*], 1466).
8. Newbigin *Oltrarno* 88 and note 117 (date 1438), also 76 'two pans used for illuminating the planets'. In this case the water was coloured with saffron. See Sebastiano Serlio in *The Renaissance Stage* edited Barnard Hewitt (Coral Gables: University of Miami Press, 1958) 33–5. For more on these techniques, see Philip Butterworth *Theatre of Fire* (London: Society for Theatre Research, 1998) chapter on 'Flame as Light'. As his title suggests, he concentrates on artificial lighting, whereas here I am largely investigating the manipulation of natural light.

every surface with gold leaf or tin,[9] and studding it with broken mirrors.[10] Ostensibly, the scene presents the dance of the heavenly bodies round God; theatrically, it fascinates and dazzles the eye. Note that these were a myriad of flickering flames, not the constant steady illumination of an electric bulb. As many people at the 2018 METh meeting, where this paper was first read, pointed out, this produces an entirely different theatrical effect: shadows are brought into play as well as light. We can only guess at the effect on an audience unused to steady powerful illumination; for us, when at the last station the cast of a previous pageant produced flambeaux and stood around our waggon, it was profoundly atmospheric.

The Florentine lighting depended for its full effect on being indoors, with the windows blacked out, as in a modern theatre or cinema.[11] Similar effects were deployed in Royal Entries, which took place outside, but often after dark. Commentators remarked on the fondness of the Low Countries for holding Royal Entries at night. When Charles V entered Bruges as a fifteen-year-old in 1515 through the main gate of the city, the official chronicler Remi du Puys noted:

> *Au deuant et a lenuiron dicelle porte estoient cinquante deux torches fichees en platz destain pour empeschier la cire qui fondoit de tomber sur les passans … grosses torches a double rencz iusques au nombre de quatre mille cinq cens qui estoit plaisir a veoir / car le iour tendoit a la nuyct et faisoit desia brun / comme il est pardeca la coustume de faire les entrees de nuyt. A raison (comme ie croy) du grant luminaire qui y est si prodigalement espendu.*[12]

9. Newbigin *Oltrarno* 74 (the Stella), 77 (a decorative *Nugola* or cloud machine). See Joseph Furttenbach the Elder on how to make the 'glory' from which God speaks to Moses so that a 'man who looks at it too closely would lose his sight'; *The Renaissance* 224–9.
10. Newbigin *Oltrarno* 96, 102, 107.
11. Newbigin *Oltrarno* 103.
12. Remy Du Puys *La tryumphante et solemnelle entree faicte sur le nouuel et ioyeux aduenement de treshault trespuissant et tresexcellent prince monsieur Charles prince des Hespaignes … En sa ville de Bruges* ([Paris]: Gilles de Gourmont, [1515]) sig. b i^{v}. Online at <https://www.bl.uk/treasures/festivalbooks/pagemax.aspx?strFest=0074&strPage=14>.

    On the effect of light in these entries and in society generally, see Élodie Lecuppre-Desjardin 'Les lumières de la ville: recherche sur l'utilisation de la lumière dans les cérémonies bourguignonnes (XIVe–XVe siècles)' *Revue historique 301: 1* (1999) 23–43. She points out how the magnates involved dressed to enhance the effect of the

> In front of and in the vicinity of this gate were fifty-two torches fastened in pewter platters to stop the wax dripping down on the passers-by ... [*Inside the gate there were*] great torches in double rows up to the number of 4,500, which were a pleasure to see, for the day was leaning towards night and was already dusky, as it is the custom there to make Entries at night. The reason being (as I believe), the great quantity of lighting which is so prodigally expended there.

When Charles' son Philip of Spain, as heir-apparent to the Netherlands, entered Antwerp in 1549, the culminating pageant he saw was

> *Vng Arch triumphal ... contenant en altitude ou haulteur .lx. piedz, & de largeur .xxxv. piedz. Sur ycelluy Arch ... lon voioit ... vng moult grandt rondt spectacle de couleur celeste, ayant pour son diameter .xx piedz, & en rondeur .lx. piedz, tant artificiallement par engin pictural painct a la semblance du ciel, que proprement il sembloit que ce fusse le ciel mesme, & ce principallement pour ce que auecques plus de cent lampes (comme estoilles scintilantes ou luysantes) ardantes en ycelluy, il se mouuoit & tournoit, sans toutesfois y veoir aulcun y attouchier.*[13]

> A triumphal arch ... 60 feet high and 35 feet wide. On this arch ... could be seen ... a very large round display, sky-blue in colour, with a diameter of 20 feet and 40 feet circumference, so artfully painted by the painter's craft to resemble the sky that it seemed that it was the sky itself, and principally because, with more than a hundred lamps burning within it (like glittering or shining stars), it moved and revolved without anyone being seen to touch it.

This lamp-filled sky was revolving round a figure of God the Father, accompanied by Virtues, conferring his blessing on a figure of the Prince. The

illumination, in rich colours and (especially) cloth of gold. Sarah Carpenter and I make the same kind of comment about costumes in masks and disguisings; *Masks and Masking in Medieval and Early Tudor Theatre* (Aldershot: Ashgate, 2002) 5, 315–16, though we do not discuss it at length, as we did privately.

13. Cornelius Grapheus (Scribonius/De Schrijver) *Le triumphe d'Anuers, faict en la susception du Prince Philips, Prince d'Espaign[e]* (Antwerp: Pieter Coeck van Aalst, 1550) sig. N ii. Online at <https://www.bl.uk/treasures/festivalbooks/pageview.aspx?strFest=0116&strPage=99>.

illustration of the pageant shows, as the description does not, that behind God was a large figure of the sun.

Royal Entries which took place in full daylight employed other techniques, but ones that seem to have been just as dazzling, if to different effect. Two of the earliest recorded (for the Continent as well as in Britain) were into London: Richard II for his Reconciliation with the citizens of London on 21 August 1392, and the Agincourt triumphal entry of Henry V into London on 23 November 1415. In both, with the pageant at the Little Conduit (*aquaeductus ad portam Pauli*), the King encountered a figure of God. In 1392, Richard saw a throne surrounded by three circles representing the Orders of Angels. Below them, angel choirs of boys and girls sang,

> *Supra sedebat eos iuvenis quasi sit deus ipse;*
> *Lux radiosa sibi solis ad instar inest.*
> *Flammigerum vultum gerit hic, niveas quoque vestes;*
> *Supra ierarchias celicas ille sedet.*[14]

> Above them was sitting a youth, as if he were God himself; a radiating light after the fashion of/in the likeness of the sun appertains to him. This one wears a flaming countenance [*vultus* = mask?], and also snow-white garments; that one sits above the celestial hierarchies.

For Henry V, the Londoners recycled the concept.[15] The tower of the Little Conduit (*aqueductus in exitu de Cheep versus sanctum Paulum*) was arrayed

14. Richard Maidstone *Concordia* edited Carlson translated Rigg (TEAMS, 2003) lines 327–30; online at <http://d.lib.rochester.edu/teams/text/rigg-and-carlson-maidstone-concordia>. It is not entirely clear what Maidstone means by *hic* and *ille*. These should distinguish between two separate people; but there *seems* to be only one figure of God. Perhaps Maidstone is distinguishing between the actor God (*iuvenis*) and the God he represents (*deus*)? Or perhaps he merely sees it as elegant variation? He has used it correctly in line 323 to distinguish between the choirs of boys and girls representing angels.

15. They seem to have done the same for the Entry of Henry VI (20? February 1431/2) but the description, and Lydgate's versifying of it, do not give enough visual details to make this certain: *indivisibilis Trinitatis splendor effigialis in celsissimo celi imperii throno residebat inter exercitus angelorum sibi ministrancium* ('the splendour in simulacrum of the Undivided Trinity was seated in the highest of heaven on the throne of sovereignty surrounded by an army of angels ministering to him'); see *Collection générale des documents français qui se trouvent en Angleterre. Tome premier, Archives de la mairie de Londres, du duché de Lancastre, de la bibliothèque des avocats et 1ere partie de l'Echiquier* edited Jules Delpit

as heaven with a sky-blue canopy with massed clouds surmounted by a golden archangel:

> *Et de sub canopeo in trono quodam effigies magestatis in corpore solari, et emissis fulgentibus radiis ultra omnia rutilat. In cuius circuitu celesti nitore choruscarunt archangeli, psallentes dulciter.*[16]
>
> And from under the canopy in a certain throne, a figure of majesty in sun-form [in the body of a sun] and sending forth dazzling rays, shone beyond everything. Around it in a circle archangels sparkled with a celestial radiance, singing sweetly.

Both of these, in their would-be elegant and allusive Latin, suggest that the radiance was coming from the figure of God himself; but the mention of rays (*Lux radiosa, emissis fulgentibus radiis*) suggests that the actor was sitting in front of a (rayed) sun covered with reflective material – probably gold leaf, or its cheaper variant, gilded tin[17] – which bounced back the light from an

(Paris: veuve Dondey-Dupré, 1847) 247. Another account says, 'And so rode he forthe unto the Lytylle Condyte. And there was a ryalle mageste of the Trynyte, fulle of angelys syngyng hevynly songys, blessynge ande halowynge the kyngys whythe thes resonys in Latyn wrytyn'; *The Historical Collections of a Citizen of London in the Fifteenth Century* edited James Gairdner *Camden Society Series 2, 17* (1876) 175 (*Gregory's Chronicle*) online at <https://www.british-history.ac.uk/search/series/camden-record-soc>. *The Historical Collections of a Citizen of London in the Fifteenth Century* edited James Gairdner *Camden Society Series 2, 17* (1876) 175 (*Gregory's Chronicle*) online at <https://www.british-history.ac.uk/camden-record-soc/vol17/pp161-177>. It is not even clear whether the 'ryalle mageste of the Trynyte' was live or a model: *effigialis* could imply either. Richard II sees an actor; Henry V sees an *effigies*, a 'representation' of God.

For the Entry of the Emperor Charles V into London in 1522, the scene was much the same but translated into an Assumption of the Virgin; Edward Hall *Chronicle* (London: Johnson and others, 1809; reprint New York: AMS Press, 1965) 639–40.

16. *Gesta Henrici Quinti* edited Frank Taylor and John S. Roskell (Oxford: Clarendon Press, 1975) 110.

17. As in the Florentine productions: Newbigin *Feste d'Oltrarno* 74, 77, 535. On methods of 'gilding' tin, see Daniel V. Thompson *The Materials and Techniques of Medieval Painting* (New York: Dover, 1956 reprint of 1936 edition by George Allen & Unwin) 66, 180–1; for more detail, see Cennino Cennini *The Craftsman's Handbook* edited Daniel V. Thompson (New York: Dover, 1960 reprint of 1933 edition by Yale UP) 60–3. See also Jill Dunkerton, Susan Foister, Dillian Gordon, and Nicholas Penny *Giotto to Dürer: Early Renaissance Painting in the National Gallery* (New Haven and London: Yale University Press and National Gallery, 1991) 175–6.

external light-source, presumably the sun itself. The vocabulary, particularly of the Henry V description, suggests light in movement: *coruscare* ('to flash, gleam, glitter', originally 'to move quickly, vibrate'), *rutilare* ('to gleam, sparkle, shine', associated with a reddish glow), *fulgere* ('to shine brightly, gleam', related to *fulgor*, 'lightning'), *radiosa* ('full of rays, radiant, resplendent; sending out rays'), *nitere* ('to emit light, gleam; to shine with reflected light, flash, glitter').[18] You could add to the dazzling effect by stippling the metallic surface so that the reflection was scattered.[19] Even more, you could make it move.[20]

The London suns may have revolved. (I reserve my argument here to a further study.) Later, France in particular provides a whole galaxy of rotating suns:

17 June 1493: Royal Entry of Charles VIII into Abbeville. The eighth pageant was a Paradise with the Trinity, '*notablement postée* devant un soleil *clair*, *tournant incessament* et entourée des neuf choeurs d'anges rangés en ordre par étages' ('strikingly placed before a bright sun, turning unceasingly, and surrounded by the Nine Orders of Angels arranged in order in stages').[21]

1 August 1510: Chateaudun, accounts for the *Mystere de la Passion: une livre et demye d'oingt … pour oindre les mouvemens du grant solleil* ('a pound and a

18. For these definitions, search the classical and medieval Latin dictionaries collected at the *Logeion* website <http://logeion.uchicago.edu>. These include the *DMBLS*.

19. Furttenbach is particularly keen on this technique: see *Renaissance Stage* 220–1: 'the entire interior of the cloud is lined with pieces of beaten brass or gold tinsel so cross marked and mottled that they scatter shimmering light from the candles', also 225. Though the intention is to make the reflected light shimmer, an added bonus is that you do not get a clear reflection of the back of the actor playing God. A gold-Fablon-covered cardboard halo reflects the head of the wearer precisely; it helps to confuse the image if they are wearing a gold wig.

20. Besides the records of revolving suns, later Renaissance stage designers suggest turning the sun from side to side: Furttenbach's *glory* for Mount Sinai was to be 'turned a little to the right and then a little to the left to send a beautiful splendor with shimmering beams towards the spectators'; *Renaissance Stage* 227.

21. François-César Louandre *Histoire d'Abbeville* 2 vols (Paris and Abbeville: Joubert and others, 1847) 2 6; cited in Louis Petit de Julleville *Les Mysteres* 2 vols (Paris: Hachette, 1880) 2 200. The quotation above varies between reportage and quotation.

half of grease, to grease the movements of the great sun').[22] This sun was situated in heaven behind God.

Sunday 30 April 1536: Bourges *Monstre* (procession advertising the *mystère*), the Heaven waggon: *Au milieu estoit ung siège fait en façon d'arc-en-ciel, sur lequel estoit assise la Divinité, Père, Fils, et Saint-Esprit, et par-derrière deux soleils d'or, au milieu d'ung throsne, qui turnoient sans cesser, l'ung au contraire de l'autre* ('In the middle was a seat made like a rainbow, on which was sitting the Godhead, Father, Son, and Holy Spirit, and behind, in the middle of a throne, two suns of gold, which turned without stopping, one in the opposite direction to the other').[23]

1547: Valenciennes *Mystere de la Passion: au paradis ung Ray dor deriere dieu le pere tournant incessanment* ('in Heaven, a ray of gold turning continuously behind God the Father').[24]

The York Mercers' 1433 indenture lists, among other gear for heaven, three pieces of red clouds with 'sunne bemes of golde & sternes for þe hiest of heuen'.[25] It sounds as if the sunbeams formed at least a part of their pageant-waggon setting for God, and that possibly they were attempting the same kind of effect, though static, as the Londoners were for Richard II and Henry V. The stylised sunbursts surrounding God in the stained glass from St Martin Coney Street now in York Minster (FIGURE 1) suggest what these might have looked like.[26]

22. *Compte du Mystere de la Passion Chateaudun 1510* edited Marcel Couturier and Graham A. Runnalls ([Chartres]: Société Archéologique d'Eure et Loire, 1990) 150 (fol. 190^{v}); see 26.

23. Thiboust *Bourges* 72–3.

24. BNF MS Rothschild 3010 folio B^{v}–1^{r} (foldout); image online at <http://gallica.bnf.fr/ark:/12148/btv1b55005972m/f13.item>. Information in cartouche on fol. B^{v}. There is no corresponding information in BNF MS fr 12356. 'One ray' sounds strange, considering the image, which shows a sunburst behind God.

    I am not suggesting by citing these Continental examples that there was a direct line of copying from one country to another (though there certainly was within countries), but that stage designers seem unsurprisingly to have come up with much the same solutions to the creation of special effects.

25. *REED: York* 55. Our interpretation can be seen by following the link at <http://www.medievalenglishtheatre.co.uk/URLSvol40.html>.

26. Sarah Brown *'Our Magnificent Fabrik': An Architectural History of York Minster c. 1220–1500* (Swindon: Royal Commission on Historical Monuments, 2003) 287–88.

FIGURE 1: God in a sunburst: York Minster window S 28, c.1450.
Te Deum window from St Martin's, Coney Street.
CVMA inv. no. 003768. © Crown copyright. Historic England Archive.

The Sun in York

All these outdoor effects seem to have involved golden, often moving, suns which would catch and reflect ambient and sometimes direct light; there is no mention of artificial lighting. So can we move a stage further and assume that in York, instead of relying solely if at all on artificial light, they also used the sun as a reflecting light-source – until it set, which would surely be quite late on at midsummer? This sends us off on a whole new line of investigation, about the direction and height of the sun over the course of the day, the orientation of the pageant route, and the timing of the individual pageants along that route. Then there are the technicalities: how could sunlight have been exploited as both a general and a focused light-source? And was there a point when it would have to be supplemented and finally superseded by artificial illumination? The pursuit of these questions led me down all sorts of unexpected path. Then Richard Beadle suggested that I should look at all the pageants which apparently called for specific light effects. This opened up an entirely new dimension, thematic as well as technically varied, and led, inevitably, to an article that was far too long. I have therefore split it into two parts. The first will deal with the practicalities of using the sun, not just as a light-source in general, but as a means of producing some dazzling special effects. It focuses on three especially interesting case studies, the *Nativity*, the *Transfiguration*, and the *First Day of Creation*. These then lead on to the questions not only of what they were trying to do visually, but also of what they seem to have been trying to convey thematically. The second part, forthcoming in the next volume, will ask how the specific setting (the pageant route in York) and its relation to the position of the sun at different times of day might have facilitated or possibly hampered the production of these effects. It also returns to my on-site experience of mounting two pageants (*Doomsday* in 1988 and the *Resurrection* in 1992) at roughly the right time of day along a stretch of the original route, in order to assess and explain some of the things we noticed about the lighting and its effects (usually unintentional, as this was not our major focus at the time).

Some of the God figures in the Great East Window (1408) have radiating sun-haloes: 15a (First Day of Creation), 15g (Seventh Day), 11e, 11h, 8f, 9h, 4e, 2j. The image of God as Alpha and Omega in the very top panel of the tracery (DD1) seats Him on a sunburst.

The Sun as Light-Source

The sun is of course infinitely brighter than any form of artificial light. It has always seemed strange, and almost self-defeating, that pageant-waggon plays insist from time to time on the sudden appearance of a great light, when they were performing in the open air in midsummer. What light could possibly override the light that was there already? If they used the sun, it would have to be concentrated in some form, which implies reflection or possibly refraction.[27] Conversely, since they could use the sun, it would be pointless to rely on other sources of light like torches or candles, even in reflectors, unless the scene were within a very enclosed and dark space (as possibly in the *Harrowing of Hell*). One is reminded, not irrelevantly, of the inefficiency of Joseph's candle when confronted with the light of the Infant Christ in St Birgitta's account of the Nativity.[28]

This argument is based on the premise, grounded purely in general observation of the data of medieval theatre, that if the characters say there is a light, then the stage staff would have tried to produce one. One could argue that this is a reverent if unworkable adherence to the text of the Bible (though in several cases it is an addition from a later retelling), and that the audience were simply expected to use their imaginations. The whole history of medieval staging, however, suggests the opposite. As we have already seen, they loved *devices*, and they appear to have risen to challenges.

The pageants in my case studies all appear to call for major light effects: moreover, not for an instantaneous thunder-flash like the *fervent* in the Digby *Conversion of St Paul*,[29] but for a sudden but continuing great light. In each of the following brief case studies the light first is not, and then is. Moreover, once it has appeared, it has to keep going. Would it be possible to produce these effects using the sunlight alone? And what would happen if the sun 'went in'?

27. They understood the technology: see Butterworth *Theatre of Fire* 63–78, though most of his examples are for condensing artificial light from candles, lamps, and torches.

28. For more on this, see below page 177–84.

29. *The Late Medieval Religious Plays of Bodleian MSS Digby 133 and E Museo 160* edited Donald C. Baker, John L. Murphy, and Louis B. Hall *EETS OS 283* (1982) 7, sd after line 182.

The Technicalities of Light

In order to assess this we need to consider the resources at their disposal:

1. A source of light: the sun.
2. The means to reflect, concentrate, and transmit this – primarily here reflective materials arranged in various configurations.[30]

First, a few simple things to do with light and reflection. Apologies to those readers who are well-versed in this very basic physics, but I found this structurally useful and often very revealing when I was trying to assess what I saw. It is quite complicated, not because it is difficult in itself, but because there are so many factors involved, any one of which may come into play on a particular occasion. I shall try to relate each to specific points as I go along.

Everything we see is due to the reflection of light from objects. One general definition of *reflection* is 'the throwing back by a body or surface of light, heat, or sound without absorbing it'.[31] For the layman this is slightly confusing because there are two other common meanings of *reflection* (besides the mental, ratiocination one), both of which describe its visible results: where it is used as the equivalent of 'reflected light' as in 'the reflection of the sunlight from the copper pan'; and the more everyday, 'An image seen in a mirror or shiny surface'. Incidentally, it is important to remember that we cannot *see* light: we can only see its effects. We know that the copper pan is reflecting light because it makes a lighter, copper-coloured patch on the wall. It never occurs to most of us that our image in the mirror is produced by light bouncing off *us* onto a supremely shiny surface and back towards us, or more specifically our eyes, again.

This is, however, important. Everything bounces light back to a greater or lesser extent – apart from ultra-black, which absorbs everything.[32] (The result

30. A fascinating treatment of the representation of reflection in art, which tackles some of the following questions but from the point of view of painting, is Jonathan Miller *On Reflection: Catalogue to the National Gallery Exhibition* (London: National Gallery, 1998).

31. This is the main definition from the online *Oxford Living Dictionaries* site: <https://en.oxforddictionaries.com/definition/reflection>. Uncharacteristically, the *OED* is not so helpful: 'The action of an object, surface, etc., in reflecting light, heat, sound, or other form of radiation without absorbing it; the fact or phenomenon of this; an instance of this', as it uses the verb *reflect* to define the noun *reflection*.

32. Several projects have attempted to produce a completely absorbent black. Apparently the latest and most successful is Vantablack, which is said to be capable of absorbing

of this is apparently, disconcertingly, that we can't see it.) It does not have to be shiny. The way in which the light is scattered from 'rough'-surfaced objects helps to create our sense of the texture of that surface.[33] But without reflected light we would not be able to see anything.

One result of this is our perception that things are coloured. The frequencies that are not absorbed and which bounce back to the rods and cones in our eyes are what makes us perceive them as a particular colour. So something 'red' is in fact rejecting (throwing back) the red wavelengths. This is mainly important to our experiment in that white bounces back all wavelengths. It is thus, in layman's terms, the most visible and the most luminous of colours. Hence in the Richard II Entry, God is wearing *niveas … vestes* ('snow-white garments'), and in the *Transfiguration*, the Mons stage-managers are told to dress Christ in *une robe la plus blanche que faire ce pourra* ('the whitest robe that can be made'). On the narrative level, this is because the Gospel says *vestimenta autem eius facta sunt alba sicut nix* (Matthew 17: 3), or as the York pageant says, 'His clothyng is white as snowe' (23: 97); in practice it adds to the impression that He Himself is emanating light. White retains this quality even after sunset, when there is little apparent light: a long time ago, before I was thinking about it technically, I observed that in the 1988 *Doomsday* production 'the Good Souls' (in contrast to the Damned, who 'became shadows outlined against the glow of hell-mouth') 'dressed from top to toe in off-white … were strangely luminous in the gathering dusk'.[34]

The subject is complicated by the type of reflection we are talking about. We see things and colours largely because of *diffuse* reflection.[35] (Medieval

99.96% of all light. The material looks like a black hole. Lights directed at it (from a torch, or a laser beam) just disappear. See for a demonstration <https://edition.cnn.com/videos/style/2017/03/30/watch-all-light-disappear-into-this-material-orig-tc.cnn>. Most black material, because it is the most absorbent, registers as an absence of light, but we can still 'see' it because it bounces back some surface light.

33. Miller *On Reflection* 15.

34. Twycross '"With what body shall they come?": Black and White Souls in the Mystery Plays' in *Langland, the Mystics, and the Medieval Religious Tradition* edited Helen Phillips (Cambridge: Brewer, 1990) 271–86, at 286, reprinted in *The Materials of Early Theatre: Sources, Images, and Performance* edited Sarah Carpenter and Pamela King (Variorum Studies; Abingdon and New York: Routledge, 2018) 281–98, at 295.

35. The Wikipedia entry on *Diffuse Reflection* is very helpful in explaining this, with diagrams: <https://en.wikipedia.org/wiki/Diffuse_reflection>.

scientists read this in a complicated variety of ways.)[36] We tend not to recognise this: in fact, most of us tend not to ask how it is that we can see things. However, some materials (mostly metals, but also some cloths, polished leather, glazes on pottery, beetles) throw back light in a particular way. In layman's parlance, these are 'shiny'. The smoother (and flatter) the surface the more apparently reflective, since the rays of light come back in the same relation to each other as they strike the reflective surface. This is known as *specular* ('mirror-like') reflection. If you hold a flat mirror up in front of your face, the light bouncing off your face is reflected directly back to you and you see it as a fairly accurate though reverse image.

More importantly for our current concerns, if you hold a mirror up to the sun, you are reflecting the light of the sun. If the reflection comes straight back at the spectator, they get the full effect of the sunlight: with a glass mirror, even dangerously. Even with polished metal or gold paper, the reflection of full sunlight will be so strong that you cannot look at it. If, according to the angle at which you let it strike the mirror, you reflect this light onto another surface, this will bounce it back in turn: we see it as a visible patch of 'light'. If the material of that surface is also highly reflective, it will bounce the sunlight back again directly enough for you to be able to bounce it back in turn onto something else, and so, theoretically, ad infinitum. (In practice the

36. There were two main theories, one which assumed that the eye itself sends out light which encounters the object and retrieves some of its essence (*extramission*), and the other that the object itself sends out something – the nature of what this might be varies from theory to theory – which is received by the eye (*intromission*). The subject is extremely complex. See David C. Lindberg *Theories of Vision from Al-Kindi to Kepler* (Chicago and London: University of Chicago Press, 1976); be warned, however, that, though fascinating, this is not an easy read.

The science of optics was known as *perspectiva*. Late medieval textbooks recognise specular reflection (called *lumen reflexum* by Bartholomæus lib. 8 cap. 29), and know that the angle of incidence equals the angle of reflection; and they recognise refraction (which Bartholomæus calls *lumen fractum*), when the light passes through but is bent by a transparent object (like water or a glass prism), but they do not seem to have had a term for or the concept of diffusion as such. Trevisa's account of specular reflection is worth reading (512). The standard textbook on optics was John Pecham's *Perspectiva communis*. The version I have used is published by Johan Petreius, Nuremberg, 1541, but there is a modern edition and translation by David C. Lindberg *John Pecham and the Science of Optics: Perspectiva Communis* (Madison, Wisconsin: Wisconsin UP, 1970). Pecham is better known to us as the Franciscan Archbishop of Canterbury 1279–92 who was responsible for the 1281 *Ignorantia sacerdotum*, translated as *The Lay-Folk's Catechism*.

sharpness of the beam deteriorates according to the minute irregularities in the surface of the reflectors.) You can direct the beam by angling each of your reflectors. Many of the light effects the pageants call for – for example, the Transfiguration – could be done in this way.

We see this most noticeably when the light is bounced off glass, but in the fifteenth century they did not have glass mirrors in quantity. Those that existed tended to be relatively small and convex, because they were made from a bubble of blown glass.[37] (There was also the technical difficulty of 'silvering' them, usually with lead, or a toxic mix of mercury and tin). One of the most famous representations of a larger one is the convex mirror in the background of the Arnolfini portrait by Van Eyck,[38] though there are many others.[39] But convex mirrors scatter rather than focus the light, because of the angle at which the incoming beams are bounced back: that is why the images in them seem distorted.

However, they did have various kinds of metal that could be polished to a high gloss, and could serve as either plane (flat) or curved mirrors.[40] The

37. See Sabine Melchior-Bonnet *The Mirror: A History* (London: Routledge, 2001) 14–15.

38. 1434; London: National Gallery, online at <https://www.nationalgallery.org.uk/paintings/jan-van-eyck-the-arnolfini-portrait>. Miller gives a series of examples of these paintings and how they produce their effects: *On Reflection* 30–3, 43, 74–6.

39. E.g. Petrus Christus 'Goldsmith's Shop' (1449); New York: Metropolitan Museum of Art, Robert Lehman Collection, 1975 <https://www.metmuseum.org/art/collection/search/459052>; Hans Memling 'Vanity' (c.1485), Musée des Beaux-Arts, Strasbourg: <https://en.wikipedia.org/wiki/Musée_des_Beaux-Arts_de_Strasbourg#/media/File:Hans_Memling_Vanité_ca_1490.jpg>; probably also the hand-mirror held by the Musée de Cluny Lady with the Unicorn in the tapestry on Sight: <https://upload.wikimedia.org/wikipedia/commons/d/d0/The_Lady_and_the_unicorn_Sight.jpg> It is usually assumed that in paintings, round hand-mirrors like this are meant to be made of glass: e.g. BL Additional MS 42130 (Luttrell Psalter) fol. 63^{r} bottom margin, at <http://www.bl.uk/manuscripts/Viewer.aspx?ref=add_ms_42130_f063r>.

There is of course a vast literature on the *speculum* and mirror images in philosophy and literature. Mirrors will become important thematically in the later stages of this article.

40. The surface of some metals has a particular molecular composition which becomes very excited when light falls on it, and releases energy as further light.

There was a specialist trade or profession of Polishers (*Furbours* or 'Furbishers') who largely worked on armour. This could be polished to a mirror-like brilliance: see the armour of St Michael in Memling's *Doomsday* (late 1460s, National Museum, Gdansk): see <https://en.wikipedia.org/wiki/The_Last_Judgment_(Memling)#/media/File:Das_Jüngste_Gericht_(Memling).jpg>. His breastplate reflects a plain from which the Dead

famous stage directions for the late-fifteenth-century Revello *Transfiguration* suggest the use of *uno bacille pulito che faz che l'esplendore dil sole che fere nel bacino venga sopra di Jhesu et verso li soy discipuli* ('a polished basin which causes the splendour of the sun which falls on the basin to come onto Jesus and towards his disciples' – note the distinction).[41] Presumably they were using the inside of the basin as a concave mirror to focus the light almost as a spotlight.[42] It is usually assumed that this was a barber's brass basin,[43] in which case the light reflected would have a warm golden colour: light reflected from 'coloured' objects shares in the 'colour' of the object, because more of that wavelength is being reflected.

Sunlight is freely available and universal; the sun is far enough away and radiant enough to illuminate that half of the globe which is facing it like an infinitely powerful floodlight. Not all sunlight reaches us directly, however. To begin with, it is scattered by the gases in the atmosphere, which produces a different quality of light when the sun is low in the sky.

are rising, and what looks like a Gothic church, possibly meant for the Holy City to which the Saved are being admitted on the left wing of the triptych. Originally this polishing was probably purely a side effect of getting rid of the rust from the metal, but it clearly became an aesthetic aim in its own right, and Netherlandish-influenced painters enjoyed the challenge of representing it. Miller reproduces Bermejo's 1486 *St Michael* painting (see <https://www.nationalgallery.org.uk/paintings/bartolome-bermejo-saint-michael-triumphs-over-the-devil>), which is a more complex twin of Memling's, complete with reflection on the breastplate: *On Reflection* 82, fig. 1. The armour of St George in the van der Paele triptych (c.1434–36, Groeningemuseum, Bruges) of Van Eyck has a more subdued sheen; <https://upload.wikimedia.org/wikipedia/commons/4/4e/La_Madone_au_Chanoine_Van_der_Paele.jpg>.

41. *La passione di Revello: sacra rappresentazione quattrocentesca di Ignoto Piemontese* edited Anna Cornagliotti (Torino: Centro Studi Piemontesi, 1976) 87, sd at line 5222. It adds, oddly, that *si el sole non lucesse abiate qualche brandoni et qualche altro lume* ('if the sun is not shining, have certain torches and certain other lights'). This is usually interpreted as 'if the sun has gone in', but using artificial light in these circumstances would be pointless, since the ambient light would still be stronger than torches. It might mean 'after dark'; or he may just be unthinkingly answering the usual objection.

42. Whereas a convex mirror scatters the light, a concave one concentrates it. For examples of this in use, see Butterworth *Theatre of Fire* 63–4 and 63–78 in general.

43. See e.g. Serlio 'When you need a specially strong light you put a torch behind a glass and behind the torch a barber's basin well burnished. This will reflect a splendour like the rays of the sun'; *Renaissance Stage* 34. Serlio is talking about indoor artificial light: the glass is a container full of coloured water which refracts the light of the torch and its reflection from the bowl.

(This has an emotional effect which I shall glance at later.) Then, as we have seen, everything that is not totally black reflects and re-reflects some light – buildings, trees, pavements, clothes, puddles of water – by what is known as diffuse inter-reflection. (It does not have to be 'shiny' to do this.) As a result of these, we are surrounded by what we know as ambient light. If we go round to the north side of a house when the sun is shining on the south side, it may be somewhat darker in the shade, but it does not become night. And you can still see your reflection in a mirror.

This is partly because mirrors, like other shiny surfaces, reflect ambient light as well as direct sunlight. We can still see that a surface (such as our pageant sun) is shiny, even on a dull day and in shadow; and it will still reflect light, though to a lesser degree, onto other shiny surfaces. This again is important in this investigation, because for considerable stretches of the route, as we shall see, the sun would have been behind or to the side of a pageant waggon, not directly head on to it: but there would still have been a glow from the reflector. God would still seem to be sitting in front of a shining sun, even if the shine were muted.

More particularly, even if the reflector is facing the sun, you do not need direct unimpeded sunlight to produce a reflection. When the sky is overcast,[44] the light of the sun is diffused through the water vapour of the clouds, and though some of it is bounced back upwards (which is why we can fly above the cloud cover and see the rain clouds as white, even if the plane is about to descend through it into a grey and possibly rainy day), most of it still comes through: the day is 'grey', not black.[45] A sheet of reflective material will

44. Technically, *overcast* refers to a sky which has 95% cloud cover. Anything lighter is *cloudy*.

45. It is difficult to measure the exact amount of sunlight getting through to us on a cloudy day, because the clouds reflect and refract it in a very complex way. Various standard grids suggest that the intensity of the light getting through to us can drop from around 100,000 lux in extremely bright sun, to 20,000 lux in the shade on the same day, to 10,000 lux on what is described as 'full daylight' to 1,000–2,000 lux on a heavily overcast day. But this does not adequately reflect the experience of reflection from the overcast sky, and is in any case much brighter than a sunny day indoors (the recommended lux levels for work vary widely) – where the sunlight from a window can still be reflected very brightly.

The change of seasons does not make that much difference: we should not equate cold with lack of light when the sun is up. Note that of the two London Entries, Henry V's was in November.

FIGURE 2: (left) 21 August 2018 – full sun; (right) 22 August 2018 – overcast. Greyscale does not give quite the right effect: the sky to the left is bright blue, and the whole image brighter if more contrasty; but the reflection is accurate. Photos: © Meg Twycross.

still reflect quite strongly, except that this time it is reflecting the light from the overcast sky, instead of direct sunlight. The quality of reflection will be different, that is all. (Even when it is raining quite heavily, as it is as I write this, outdoors will always be much brighter than indoors.)

This answers the question, 'What would happen to our pageant-waggon suns if the real sun went in?' The answer is that the light of the sun doesn't disappear – that only happens at night, or in an eclipse. The light striking the reflector is softer (i.e. less contrasty because diffused) but there is still enough to produce a glow. The photographs above (FIGURE 2) show the same sheet of metallic 'gold' Christmas wrapping paper propped up facing the sun on two consecutive late-August days. On the first day the sun was in a (temporarily) cloudless patch of sky at 14.11 BST at a height of approximately 44°. On the second day the sun was behind a grey heavily overcast sky with rain threatening (it did in fact start raining while I was photographing) at 10.20 BST at a height of approximately 35°.[46] Given the vagaries of the camera (and of printing), FIGURE 2 is a pretty good approximation of what we saw. All the circumstances of the second photograph should make it considerably darker and a light-meter reading[47] suggested there was a lot less light on the reflective material – on the first day it had gone right off the scale – but it still creates a considerable reflection. On the first day it was so bright you could not actually look at it.[48]

Blinded by the Light?

This suggests some interesting conclusions about the way an audience might experience the reflection. Even on a dull day you could read it as representing divine radiance. When the sun comes out, it moves from representation to illusion. The light is blinding: you cannot look at it. Even with a God-figure seated in front of and thus masking some of it, if the reflective 'sun' were sufficiently large it would be difficult if not impossible to look at him, especially if he were wearing a gold mask and halo and perhaps gold or white garments. (The white-painted door in the photographs gives some sort of idea of how much light might bounce back from a white surface, though here it is behind the gold paper, not placed in front of it.) And, an added bonus, he would be backlit.

Experiments conducted by an interdisciplinary team from Bristol on the effect of different kinds of artificial lighting on a medieval painting (Duccio's 1311 *Annunciation*) in which the figures were set against a background of gold leaf, suggested that under modern subdued artificial lighting conditions the reflective gold leaf appeared to direct the viewer's gaze away from itself to the

46. Latitude-wise, Lancaster is six miles further north than York. It thus makes a reasonable general comparator. Because it is 70 miles further west, the sun rises and sets 6 minutes later, but this is irrelevant to the experiment. The altitude of the sun on the first day compares with roughly 10.00 and 15.56 at York on 21 June; on the second day with roughly 09.05 and 17.15 at York. The heading is a different matter, which I shall come to in Part Two.

47. I do not include my light-meter readings here, because I am not sufficiently happy with their accuracy, but in general terms they support my observations.

48. This was confirmed independently by my companions (I did not have to prompt them).

(matt surface of the) figures it surrounded. The viewer looked automatically at the face and not the halo. But under the 'dramatic glow' produced by candlelight, the original illumination, the greater contrast in brightness between the gold leaf and the matt paint deflected the gaze even further, so that the viewers were not looking at the faces at all, but at a different, matt, area of the painting. 'One might speculate that this is the eyes being directed away from the faces (looking at them directly might have been considered irreverent).'[49] In bright sunlight this avoidance effect is intensified to the point of repelling all vision: the dazzle is such that you have to look away.

It may seem strange that in a pageant play the effect of gilding could be to deflect visual attention from the most important figure: but, as a taxi-driver in Sheffield pointed out to some of us when we were discussing the possible effects, one cannot look at the face of God directly, and even the prophet Muhammad only saw Him from behind a veil.[50]

In the Qur'an, when Moses asks to see God face to face on Mount Sinai, God replies, 'You will never see Me, but look at that mountain; if it remains standing firm, then you will see Me'; but 'when his Lord revealed Himself to the mountain, He made it crumble; Moses fell down unconscious'.[51] The Biblical equivalent to this is in Exodus 33. Moses asks to see God in his glory, and God replies *non poteris videre faciem meam non enim videbit me homo et*

49. In diffuse daylight lighting, this concentrated on the faces of the figures, whereas by beeswax candlelight, which was the medium by which this painting was meant to be viewed, and where the contrast appears to have been greater, it was directed away from the faces to the significant gesture of the Virgin's hand; Ute Leonards, Roland Baddeley, Iain D. Gilchrist, Tom Troscianko, Patrick Ledda, and Beth Williamson 'Mediaeval Artists: Masters in directing the observers' gaze' *Current Biology 17: 1* (January 2007) R8–R9. The authors assume that this effect was intentional: it is possible that at first it was merely meant to suggest divine radiance, and the artists discovered the secondary effect later. Many thanks to Pamela King for this reference.

50. The Qur'an, Surah 6: 103: 'No vision can take Him in, but He takes in all vision'. Also the Qur'an, Surah 42: 51: 'It is not granted to any mortal that God should speak to him, except by revelation, or from behind a veil, or by sending a messenger to reveal by His command what He will'. (These two verses were used by Aisha to rebut any idea that Muhammad might have seen God directly.) All quotations from *The Qur'an* translated M.A.S. Abdel Haleem (World's Classics; Oxford UP, 2004, revised 2015).

    Unfortunately we (Elisabeth Dutton, Olivia Robinson, and myself) did not ask the taxi-driver for his name, as we were so involved in the discussion, but I am extremely grateful to him for his observations.

51. Surah 7: 143.

vivet ('Thou canst not see my face: for man shall not see me and live'; Exodus 33: 20). He promises, however, to shelter Moses in a cleft in the rock, and to permit him to see the glory retreating. 1 John 4: 12 reiterates, *Deum nemo vidit* ('No man hath seen God at any time').[52]

Here what appears on the face of it merely to be a stage effect has become, whether accidentally or not, theological. That the York playwrights were aware of this is suggested by the Curriers' *Transfiguration*.[53] The Apostles are dazzled by the light emanating from Christ, and even more so by the shining cloud which envelops Him, and from which the voice of God speaks. When it has gone, Peter asks,

> A, lord, why latest þou vs noȝt se
> Thy fadirs face in his fayrenes? 217–18

transplanting Philip's words at the Last Supper, 'Lord, shew us the Father, and it sufficeth us' (*dicit ei Philippus Domine ostende nobis Patrem et sufficit nobis*; John 14: 8) to this episode. Christ replies (equally not in the play source) that no man may look upon the Father and live (223–4).

In the *Transfiguration* this effect was probably largely produced by supplementary means: I am not suggesting that the blinding reflection of sunlight was a permanent accompaniment of the Gods of pageant waggons. As we shall see, even if the day were not overcast, the sun was not always in the right direction, and the York pageant route had several right-angled turns, some of which would even put the waggons with their backs to the sun. But on occasion, especially when God was seated on an upper deck among the rooftops, a section of the audience must have experienced a small theophany of dazzling light.[54]

52. John deflects the topic to add *umquam si diligamus invicem Deus in nobis manet et caritas eius in nobis perfecta est* ('If we love one another, God abideth in us: and his charity is perfected in us'). There are, however, several characters in the Old Testament, like the parents of Samson, who are terrified that they are about to die because they have seen God (*et dixit ad uxorem suam morte moriemur quia vidimus Deum*; Judges 13: 22), but are permitted to live.

53. Based on Matthew 17: 1–9.

54. It would of course depend on the angle of incidence at which the sun struck the reflective surface and which of the audience were in the range of the angle of reflection. Out of doors, and with a large-diameter reflector (5 or 6 feet wide) this could be quite considerable.

Case Studies: A Great Light

The several pageants which call for a sudden great light are not solely interested in causing delight and wonder in the audience.[55] There are theological implications. Light has always been a figure for spiritual illumination, and the first two pageants I shall look at are theophanies: the Tile-Thatchers' *Nativity* and its attendant *Shepherds* (by the Chandlers); and the Curriers' *Transfiguration*.[56] Each was played in the full light of day. Each presents a slightly different technical problem; their iconography and the very few parallel staging accounts (none of these York guilds has left any meaningful records) suggest some possible solutions.

The *Nativity* uses the Brigittine topos:[57] in the gathering dark (difficult naturalistically, since the pageant was probably played from what is for us early morning to about midday), Joseph goes off to find 'sum light' for the stable (39). Returning with a candle (not mentioned in the script, but featured in the *Revelations*[58] and in some of the images derived from it), he sees from a distance a sudden light (78–9). Mary explains to him that it is the Star of

55. A reaction frequently emphasised by the Renaissance stage designers when writing about light effects. See especially Furttenbach in *The Renaissance Stage* 215, 224, 227.

56. I have only touched on the Saddlers', Glaziers', and Fustours' *Harrowing of Hell*, since Peter Meredith looked at it fairly comprehensively in 'The Iconography of Hell in the English Cycles: A Practical Perspective' in *The Iconography of Hell* edited Clifford Davidson (EDAM Monograph Series 17; Kalamazoo: Western Michigan University Medieval Institute, 1992) 158–86. He also deals with the York *Doomsday*, but purely from the point of view of Hellmouth.

    A Glazier is either a 'Worker in glass', or polisher (of metal): see *OED* sv *glazer* n., so might have a professional interest in reflection. Other pageants with possible light effects are the *Baptism*, the *Ascension*, and *Pentecost*.

57. *Den heliga Birgittas Revelaciones*: Bok 7 edited Birger Bergh (Uppsala: Almqvist & Wiksell, 1967) 86–9. Text online at <http://www.umilta.net/bk7.html>.

58. *Birgittas Revelaciones* edited Bergh, chapter 21: 3. *Qui cum intrassent speluncam, senex ille ligatis boue et asino ad presepe exiuit extra et portauit ad virginem candelam accensam fixitque eam in muro … 9. Neque candela illa, quam posuerat senex, quoquomodo lumen reddebat, quia splendor ille diuinus splendorem materialem candele totaliter annichilauerat.* The English version gives, 'and he went and lighted to þat maiden one candill, and festind vpon þe walle … And þare com so grete a light and brightnes þat it passed þe brightenes of þe son, and þe lightnes of the candill þat Joseph sett on þe wall might noȝt be sene'; *The Liber Celestis of St Bridget of Sweden* edited Roger Ellis *EETS OS 291* (1987) 486.

the Nativity (95–8), and implies, as in Birgitta, that the Child himself is the ultimate light-source (104–5); Joseph hails him as 'lemer of light' (111).

The images which derived from St Birgitta's *Revelations* became the dominant iconography of the Nativity in the fifteenth century,[59] and suggest both the effect that the playwright was trying to achieve and possibly how the staging achieved it (FIGURE 3). Sometimes light from the star is shown pouring into the stable through the hole in the thatch: 'þe ruffe is rayued aboven oure hede', says Joseph (14: 18).[60] It strikes the figure of the Christ Child who is himself lying in a bed of rays, which are supposed to be emanating from him: Birgitta says, *in momento et ictu oculi peperit filium, a quo tanta lux ineffabilis et splendor exibat, quod sol non esset ei comparabilis* ('in a moment and the twinkling of an eye she gave birth to her Son, from whom emanated so much inexpressible light and radiance, that the sun could not be compared to Him').[61] Presumably, as with the London pageants, this was produced by placing a reflective surface behind the Child, which one hopes was a doll, as He is usually shown white (which would produce the maximum intensity of scattered light, and would inter-reflect with the gold under him) and naked.

59. See Gertrud Schiller *Iconography of Christian Art: Volume 1* translated Janet Seligman (London: Lund Humphries, 1971) 78–80.

60. E.g. Baltimore: Walters Art Museum, Walters Manuscript W.174, fol. 17^{v} (Missal of Eberhard von Greiffenklau) detail at <https://art.thewalters.org/detail/8054/the-missal-of-eberhard-von-greiffenklau-2/> and see <https://art.thewalters.org/files/pdf/W174.pdf>. More sophisticated artists manage the perspective better to show the light coming from the star through the hole in the roof: BL Additional MS 35313 fol. 89^{v} (Hours of Joanna of Castile, this image by the Master of James IV of Scotland, c.1500), image online at <http://www.bl.uk/manuscripts/FullDisplay.aspx?ref=Add_MS_35313>, or BNF Ms lat. 9474 (Hours of Anne of Bretagne, Paris, Jean Bourdichon, 1503 to 1508) <https://gallica.bnf.fr/ark:/12148/btv1b52500984v/f111>. Both exploit the chiaroscuro of the night scene. One of the Nativity scenes in St Peter Mancroft, Norwich, shows the angels apparently tearing away the thatch to make a hole. Generally, however, the artists avoid the problems of perspective by showing the Child lying slightly outside the stable.

    The 1453 Barcelona pageant ordered from Joan Calom was to produce a very similar effect, save that the light on the Child was to proceed from a figure of God the Father in a vault on the pageant: Manuel Milá y Fontanals *Obras Completas* 6 edited Marcelino Menéndez y Pelayo (Barcelona: Verdaguer, 1895) 368–9; translated in *The Staging of Religious Drama* edited Meredith and Tailby 72. The Nativity scene in Great Malvern Priory (after 1501: CVMA N VI 2d) also has God the Father, surrounded by rays, in this position, as does the Leuven *ommegang* Nativity pageant.

61. *Revelaciones* 7 21: 8.

FIGURE 3: Morgan MS M.1003 fol. 75^{r}. © Pierpont Morgan Library, New York.
Book of Hours France, perhaps Paris or NE France, c.1465.
Image online at <http://ica.themorgan.org/manuscript/page/19/76920>.

The actor playing Mary must in some way not only have revealed the Child from under his cloak, but also uncovered His reflective bed. (This suggests that both were already *in situ* but hidden, and perhaps some kind of catch was tripped in order to uncover them. Usually He is shown as lying directly on the floor, though sometimes in an open manger.) The ambient light, which would also be reflected and diffused from light-coloured objects in the street,[62] should have been enough to create a glow, and probably simultaneously the Star was activated to throw extra light down on the Child.

Richard Beadle in his edition of the *York Play* suggests that the angel 'speaking to the shepherds and players in the following pageant' (*loquens pastoribus & ludentibus in pagina sequente*[63] – probably, as in the Brussels *ommegang*, positioned on the roof on the stable)[64] – also managed the lighting effects.[65] The light is said to be 'sudden', which suggests either a rapid tilting of a reflective surface or the opening of shutters on the star, or both. If the Angel-actor were to be holding or in some way manipulating the Star, whether it were a surface which reflected the sunlight or a light-box encasing candles or torches (though this sounds dangerously heavy),[66] he could direct its rays downwards through the hole in the roof onto the bed of reflective material

62. No shop windows, or other expanses of glass, however.

63. *Ordo paginarum*, entry for the Tilers' pageant; York City Archives MS E20, fol. 253^{r} [1415] A/Y Memorandum Book. Later alteration (possibly made 1422?).

64. Denis Van Alsloot *Triumph of Isabella* (Brussels 1615), London: V&A. See for illustration my 'The Flemish *Ommegang* and its Pageant Cars' *METh 2: 1* (1980) 15–41 at 25, reprinted (with the second part from 2: 2 (1980) 80–98) in *The Materials of Early Theatre: Sources, Images, and Performance* edited Sarah Carpenter and Pamela King (London: Routledge, 2018) 337–90 at 348; also online at <https://www.vam.ac.uk/ommegang/>, with zoomable image. This angel, however, carries a banderole with the words *GLORIA IN EXCELSIS DEO*, not the star.

65. *York Plays 2* 103 and 107, note to lines 95–105.

66. See Philip Butterworth's conjectures about the' great hed gildyd' of the Lincoln Cordwainers' pageant of Bethlehem, *Theatre of Fire* 75–6. That it was a 'great head' suggests that it was meant for God the Father. It does not sound very portable.

    Helen Bennett drew my attention to the figures displaying large pies, or perhaps bread 'shields', in front of the kitchen building in Joris Hoefnagel's *Wedding Feast at Bermondsey* (c.1569; sometimes attributed to Marcus Gheeraerts the Elder), now in Hatfield House; <https://upload.wikimedia.org/wikipedia/commons/b/bc/Marcus_Gheeraerts_the_Elder_-_Festival_at_Bermondsey.png>. The metal platters to which the pies are attached are hung round their necks on a sling like a saxophonist's, or a marching band's drum sling. She thought the Angel might carry the star in the same

FIGURE 4: East Harling, SS Peter and Paul: East Window chancel panel 4c, *The Nativity*. Photo © Meg Twycross

around the Christ Child. The stylised image of the Nativity in East Harling (?1462–65) suggests a possible arrangement of surfaces (FIGURE 4). The rays, or at least the tilt of the surface of the star which made it catch the light, could also later be directed at the Shepherds in the following pageant (15: 36–75).

How long was this light was meant to last? After Joseph formally welcomes him with 'Hayle, my maker, hayle Crist Jesu ...' (108–12), Mary asks the Child's permission to wrap Him in 'such clothes as we haue here' (121) and lay Him in the manger. He becomes more of a vulnerable human baby, and attention moves from the light to the tableau with the ox and ass, and the way that they not only acknowledge Him as their Lord, but warm Him 'With þare warme breth' (131). Did the manger also have a mattress of shining rays, as in the East Harling window? Was the immediate glow muted, possibly as the Star was repositioned?

Because if the pageants are acting in tandem, this suggests that the Shepherds are *following* the stable. The announcement of the Nativity may have been made by the angel on the roof of the preceding waggon.[67] With the 1615 Brussels *Nativity* waggon, the angel is definitely sitting facing backwards, facing the Shepherds who are following along behind. Was the star two-sided? Could it be tilted or swivelled horizontally on a stand, so that at one moment it would be pointed at the Child on the floor and then at the Shepherds in the next pageant? Did the Shepherds come round to the front of the Nativity waggon, or was it completely transpicuous so that they could access it from the back? Paintings usually show the stable with at least some remnants of walls, but all the *ommegang* illustrations (Brussels, Antwerp, Leuven) show it as completely open (FIGURE 5).[68]

way. The dishes reach from shoulder to mid-thigh, so must be at least 30 inches in diameter.

67. One might speculate that the Waxchandlers did not have a waggon of their own, if it were not for the fact that they hired a pageant house from the Bridgemasters from at least 1501–28: *REED: York* 188, 199, 211, 218, 226, 233, and 249. They did not hire one in the earlier years. There is no record of hire of a pageant house by the Tilethatchers, but this of course does not mean that they did not have one, merely that they did not hire it from the City. The same is true of the Curriers and their *Transfiguration* pageant.

68. Antwerp: whole image online at <https://www.rijksmuseum.nl/en/collection/RP-P-OB-44.139>. Brussels: Denis Van Alsloot *Triumph of Isabella* (see zoomable image at <https://www.vam.ac.uk/ommegang/>. Leuven: *Liber Boonen* (1594) fols 459v–460r; images not easily accessible online. See my 'Flemish *Ommegang*' *METh*

FIGURE 5: Jan Luyken *Omgang tot Antwerpen* (1685), detail: 'Bethlehem' with Shepherds, followed by Three Kings with star above roof. Original in Rijksmuseum Amsterdam, RP-P-OB-44.139. © Public Domain.

Experiments conducted with scale models in both bright and overcast sunlight confirmed that, in principle, this serial reflection works.[69] It also produced some unexpected side effects. The characters acquired a strangely luminous look as they were struck by diffused light reflected from both the star (above) and the manger (below). It was strongly reminiscent of the fill light created for television out of doors by a white or silvered reflector. This casts more (diffused) light on the face of the subject and softens the depth and sharpness of shadows. However, it went beyond this. When Mary was placed leaning over the Child, and so directly above the 'manger', the light from the gold paper on which He was lying was visibly reflected in ripples up her front, as if the Child itself were throwing out rays. If the stable on the waggon was indeed transpicuous, there would also be a fair amount of ambient light even

2: *1* 24, and Eddy Put *Stoet van grote en kleine levens: De Leuvense Ommegang in 1594* (Amsterdam UP, 2018) 148–9.

69. Links to the evidence for this are on the METh website at <http://www.medievalenglishtheatre.co.uk/URLSvol40.html>.

under the roof, though a slight amount of shade might have drawn further attention to these light effects by contrast.

My second example, the Curriers' *Transfiguration*, would have been played from about 9.30 a.m. to about 3.30 p.m.[70] Its plot centres on a major lighting effect. Christ goes up Mount Thabor with three chosen Apostles, Peter, and James, and John, and is 'transfigured before them' (*et transfiguratus est ante eos*; Matthew 17: 2). Matthew describes the effect as 'his face did shine as the sun: and his garments became white as snow' (*resplenduit facies eius sicut sol vestimenta autem eius facta sunt alba sicut nix*).[71] The script reiterates this:

> His clothyng is white as snowe,
> His face schynes as þe sonne. 23: 98

The Transfiguration was a late feast, and images of it are comparatively few, as it did not get into the standard liturgical picture-cycles (though it was in later versions of the *Biblia Pauperum*),[72] but several of those images we have give Christ a gilded face and sometimes hands, giving a very good impression of a possible stage effect (FIGURE 6).[73]

70. Dorrell 'Two Studies' 104.

71. Matthew 17: 1–9, the Gospel for the second Saturday in Lent; see Pamela M. King *The York Mystery Cycle and the Worship of the City* (Cambridge: Brewer, 2006) 73–4 and 85.
    Mark does not mention the shining face, but elaborates on the garments: 'And his garments became shining and exceeding white as snow, so as no fuller upon earth can make white' (*et vestimenta eius facta sunt splendentia candida nimis velut nix qualia fullo super terram non potest candida facere*; 9: 2), a practical detail which must have been felt as a challenge by the costumier.

72. See Kathleen Scott *Later Gothic Manuscripts 1390–1490: Part 2* (London and Oxford: Harvey Miller and Oxford UP, 1996) 90, #22 on Oxford: Bodleian Library MS Lat Liturg. f. 2, fol. 2^{v}, apparently unfinished. The feast was not promulgated in England until 1487 and 1489. Both the play and this miniature predate this; interestingly, it may have been a manuscript for a York patron, as it includes a suffrage for Archbishop Scrope. The Transfiguration would, however, have been known as one of the types in the later versions of the *Biblia Pauperum*, flanked by Abraham and the Three Angels, and the Three Children in the Burning Fiery Furnace (a commentary on Christ's theophany as the Three in One); the Prophecies refer to His light. See *Biblia Pauperum* edited Avril Henry (Aldershot: Scolar, 1987) 69 and 71.

73. Oxford: Bodleian Library, MS Laud Misc. 165 fol. 331^{v}, illustrated above, see Lucy Freeman Sandler *Gothic Manuscripts 1285–1385: Part 2* (London and Oxford: Harvey Miller and Oxford UP, 1986) #125 (pages 138–40); also BL Additional MS 62523 fol. 32^{v}

FIGURE 6: Oxford: Bodleian Library, MS Laud Misc. 165 fol. 331v;
William of Nottingham *Commentary on the Gospels*, English, this artist 1380s.

(Sarum Hours, London or Oxford, c.1460), see Scott *Later Gothic Manuscripts* 278, #100, image online at <http://www.bl.uk/onlinegallery/onlineex/illmanus/other/largeimage74698.html>. A later French version (Paris 1490s) is Glasgow University Sp Coll MSS Hunter 36–39 fol. 10v (Ludophus the Carthusian *Vita Christi*, translated Guillaume le Ménard, miniatures attributed to Jacques de Besançon); image online at <http://special.lib.gla.ac.uk/exhibns/month/dec2009.html>. Most images online come from the Eastern Orthodox Church (novice icon-makers are said to have been started on this image) or areas of Byzantine influence, and later from Italy. The Ingeborg Psalter, Chantilly, Musée Condé MS 1695, fol. 20r, has an early (c.1200) image with white robe and gold face (but not hands or feet).

An early-sixteenth-century example of the scene with heavily emphasised gold face and hands, almost as large and clumsy as oven gloves, is on the rood screen at

The Apostles are dazzled:

Petrus: Brethir, whateuere ȝone brightnes be? ...
It marres my might, I may not see,
So selcouth thing was neuere sene. 23: 85–8

Again, as with the baby of the Nativity and the God of the Entries, the light is imagined as emanating directly from Christ. The theologians say that He was giving the Apostles a preview of His glorified body after the Resurrection, and even, though this is disputed, of their own after the General Resurrection,[74] and the whiteness of his robe derived from this inner glory.[75] Theatrically,

St Andrew's, Westhall, Suffolk. See Eamon Duffy *The Stripping of the Altars* (New Haven and London: Yale UP, 1992; 2nd edition 2005) 45 and <https://www.flickr.com/photos/norfolkodyssey/2839695800/in/album-72157631358997080/>. The classic version in stained glass is in Window 7 at St Mary's, Fairford, Gloucestershire (?1500–17); chancel, south chapel, Corpus Christi Chapel, east window SIII; CVMA inv. no. 005032, illustrated (as Window 7) in *The Medieval Stained Glass of Fairford Parish Church* edited Sarah Brown and Lindsay MacDonald (Stroud: Sutton, 1997) Plate 7 and see pages 60–1. The Fairford programme is indebted to the *Biblia Pauperum*.

74. In the commentaries it was thought to be a foretaste of the *claritas* of the resurrected body (Matthew 13: 43: *iusti fulgebunt sicut sol*, 'Then shall the just shine as the sun'), though authorities disagree about the mode and implications. See Walafrid Strabo *Glossa ordinaria* on Matthew 17: 2: *Resplenduit facies. In exemplum futurae beatitudinis et claritatis, quam videbunt justi, prius sublatis impiis* ('His face shone: in example of the beatitude and brightness which the just will see, first having removed the unjust'; Migne *PL 114* col. 113), and on 2 Peter 1: 16, *PL 114* col. 691: *Transfiguratio Domini et claritas ejus signum erat resurrectionis suae et nostrae* ('The Transfiguration of the Lord and its brightness was a sign of His and our resurrection'). Aquinas *Summa Theologiae* Part 3 q. 45 art. 2 lays out the pros and cons. In Christ's transfiguration clarity overflowed from His Godhead and miraculously from His soul into His body, 'not as an immanent quality affecting His very body, but rather after the manner of a transient passion, as when the air is lit up by the sun' <http://www.newadvent.org/summa/4045.htm> (translation); <http://www.corpusthomisticum.org/sth4040.html> (original Latin).

    On the resurrected body in the *Doomsday* pageant, see my '"With what body shall they come?": Black and White Souls in the Mystery Plays' 281–98.

75. *Unde liquet quod claritas, quae foris per vestimenta Christi manavit, ab illa ejus interiore luce processit, quam nullus humani generis corporeus oculus potest intueri, sicut scriptum est, Deum nemo vidit unquam: I Joan. IV, 12* ('from whence it is manifest that the clarity which emanated to the outside through Christ's garments proceeded from his interior light, which no physical human eye can gaze upon, as it is written "No man hath seen God at any time" (1 John 4: 12)'; Paschasius Radbertus *Expositio in Evangelium Matthaei*, Migne *PL 120* col. 580.

however, the staging has again to rely for this effect upon reflection from an external source.

The white robe might not reflect the light so obviously as the burnished face and hands, because its woven surface is uneven and the light hitting it is scattered, but it will bounce back all the waves of the spectrum. We do not know exactly what Christ's whiter-than-white robe was made of, or how it might have been treated;[76] but note that it was intended theatrically to contrast with his normal pre-Resurrection garment of a dark red or murrey colour.

York is the only pageant in the English civic drama which treats of the Transfiguration, and we have no detailed pageant accounts for the Curriers (Leatherworkers) who produced it.[77] All we have to go on is the script; but from the evidence of that, their waggon seems to have been scenically complex, probably a double-decker, not only featuring a mountain, but also lifting gear for a shining cloud which descends and which apparently envelops Moses and Elias and takes them up (or at least hides them while they make their exit).

There are accounts and stage directions from later Continental plays which suggest how this might have been done (though they are all from fixed-stage multiple-setting productions). In the script of Jean Michel's *Mistere de la Passion* played at Angers and Paris in 1490,[78] and at Mons in 1501,[79] the stage directions specify that the mountain should be used as a changing room:

76. It seems unlikely that the materials used by fullers for whitening cloth (stale urine, fullers' earth) would have fluoresced in the UV of the sun, like cloth washed in some modern detergents. Thanks to Neil Hall for information on the chemistry.

77. There is no record of their renting a pageant house from the Bridgemasters, though this is course does not mean that they did not have one. In an undated ordinance in the A/Y Memorandum Book they complain to the Council that they are poor, and *chargez ouesque vne pagyne a tresgraundes costages & Importables* (*REED: York* 619), being less important and poorer than they used to be, which unless it is a ritual lamentation may imply that the pageant was a left-over from earlier more prosperous times.

78. Arnoul Greban and Jean Michel *Cy commence le mistere de la passion de nostre sauueur iesucrist auecques les addicions et correct[i]ons faictes par treseloquent & scientiffique docteur maistre iehan michel. Lequel mistere fut ioue a Angiers moult triumphantement et dernierement a Paris Lan mil quattre cens quattre vingtz et dix* (Paris: Anthoine Verard, 1499). Accessed online at: <https://gallica.bnf.fr/ark:/12148/bpt6k15112776>.

79. Gustave Cohen *Le Livre de Conduite du Régisseur et la Compte des Dépenses pour la Mystère de la Passion joué à Mons en 1501* (Publications de la Faculté des Lettres de l'Université de Strasburg 23; Strasbourg and Paris: Istra, 1924; London: Oxford UP, 1925) 177.

Icy entre iesus dedens la Montaigne pour soy vestir dune robe la plus blanche que faire ce pourra. Et vne face et les mains toutes dor bruny. Et vng grant soleil a rays bruny par derriere. Puis sera leue hault en laer par vng subtil contrepois. Et tantost apres sortiront de ladicte Montaigne hely en habit de carme & vng chapeau de prophete a la teste. Et moyse dautre coste qui tiendra ses tables en sa main.[80]

Here Jesus enters into the mountain to dress himself in the whitest robe that can be made. And a mask and hands [*gloves?*] completely of burnished gold. And a great sun of burnished golden rays behind him. Then he must be lifted high in the air by a cleverly concealed counter-weight. And then Elijah will come out of the mountain in a Carmelite habit and a prophet's hat on his head, and Moses from the other side holding his Tables in his hand.

When Jesus emerges transfigured, *se mettent les trois apostres en grande admiration.* The illustration purporting to be of the 1547 production at Valenciennes shows Christ in white with yellow-stained hands and face standing in front of a man-sized oval sunburst presumably covered with gold foil.[81] This suggests a kind of mandorla with a platform on which Christ stood to be raised unto the air by the *subtil contrepois*.

80. Michel Mistere de la Passion sig. h vir; online at <https://gallica.bnf.fr/ark:/12148/bpt6k15112776/f129.item>. The direction concludes *Et ce pendant parlera la magdaleine*: Christ's quick change is covered by a lengthy conversation on another scaffold between Magdalene and her companion.

    The stage directions by Greban are much shorter, though they suggest that the same effects were intended: *Icy doivent venir les habiz de Jhesus blans et sa face resplendissante comme d'or, et doivent estre Moyse et Helie devant Jhesus*; sd at line 13262, *Le Mystère de la Passion d'Arnoul Greban* edited Gaston Paris & Gaston Reynaud (Paris: Vieweg, 1878) 172.

    When Jesus vanishes, the stage direction reads *Icy decent iesus dedens la Montaigne pour retourner en ses premieres habillemens*; sig h vii verso.

81. BNF MS français 12536, drawing of 1547 production by Jacques Cailleau, who played several of the parts including the Black Magus. No comments on *secrets*. Transfiguration fol 156^{v}: <https://gallica.bnf.fr/ark:/12148/btv1b55005970q/f320>. BNF MS Rothschild 3010 online at <https://gallica.bnf.fr/ark:/12148/btv1b55005972m> dated as 1577. Gives highlights of stage effects for each *journée*. Transfiguration at <https://gallica.bnf.fr/ark:/12148/btv1b55005972m/f382>. For a description of the *secret* of the Transfiguration see fol. 191^{r} at <https://gallica.bnf.fr/ark:/12148/btv1b55005972m/f381.image>.

Here, as with our two Royal Entries, the radiance of the burnished mask and gloves and the dazzling whiteness of the robe were boosted by setting the actor in front of a reflective 'sun'. This again, like the suns of the Royal Entries, can be read as light emanating from Christ Himself. Judging from experiments with a model, it could in the right circumstances have been literally blinding – 'It marres my might, I may not see' – especially if one imagines the size of the reflective surface as being five to six feet in diameter. With a more overcast sky, it still multiplies the amount of light surrounding the figure. It acts like a television back-light, giving definition and depth to the figure in front of it (if it does not wipe it out altogether), but it also sets up an inter-reflection as the light striking the white robe from behind bounces back to the 'sun', and so forward again, like a gallery of mirrors. To get the full effect in York streets the waggon would have to be largely roofless, and the figure of Christ set as high as possible to collect the maximum amount of the light from the sky, and avoid the reflections of the surrounding buildings. There would need to be a structure at his back to accommodate the machinery which revealed the glory (possibly by raising it from behind the mountain) and lowered the shining cloud, but on the whole one imagines, reverting to the evidence from the *ommegangen*, a Mount Parnassus (Antwerp, Brussels – or less ambitiously, Furttenbach's Mount Sinai)[82] set in front of a Leuven *Assumption* backdrop (FIGURE 7).[83]

Around nine years earlier than the Paris performance, the famous stage directions from the Revello *Passione* suggest a more focused approach to the lighting and a slightly quicker change of costume:[84]

A worrying feature of the Valenciennes drawings is that in the post-Resurrection appearances, Christ seems to move in his own nimbus, but there is no hint of how He does this. The advertisement of the *secrets* for that day merely mention how he appears *les portes closes* (fol. 340^{r}). <https://gallica.bnf.fr/ark:/12148/btv1b55005970q/f517.item> fols 253^{v}–254^{r}, and <https://gallica.bnf.fr/ark:/12148/btv1b55005970q/f542> fols 266^{v}–267^{r}; also <https://gallica.bnf.fr/ark:/12148/btv1b55005972m/f643.item> fols 326^{v}–327^{r} and <https://gallica.bnf.fr/ark:/12148/btv1b55005972m/f670.item>, fols 340^{v}–341^{r}.

82. *Renaissance Stage* 238; '8 feet high, 5 feet wide, and 3 feet thick'. Here the top would accommodate Christ, but not Elijah and Moses.

83. Centres of gravity would have to be carefully calculated, but should be no worse than those we managed with our 1988 *Doomsday* waggon, 20 feet high with the lifting mechanism for God towards the back of the 8 × 12 foot waggon on its distinctly lightweight modern base.

84. See *La passione di Revello: sacra rappresentazione quattrocentesca di Ignoto Piemontese* edited Anna Cornagliotti (Torino: Centro Studi Piemontesi, 1976) xxiv–vi for the possible

> *Et quando Jhesu serà sopra el monte, sia uno bacille pulito che faz che l'esplendore dil sole che fere nel bacino venga sopra di Jhesu et verso li soy discipuli. Et alora Jhesu lassi cadere la soa veste vermiglia et rimanga in veste biancha. Et si el sole non lucesse, abiate qualche brandoni et qualche altro lume.*[85]

> And when Jesus shall be on the mountain, let there be a polished basin which makes the splendour of the sun which projects from the basin come onto Jesus and towards his disciples. And then Jesus shall let fall his scarlet[86] garment and remains in a white garment. And if the sun should not be shining, let there be certain torches and certain other lights.

A polished basin, acting as a concave mirror, focuses the light reflected on the object: effectively it becomes a spotlight or solar concentrator.[87] If the

dating. A colophon to the manuscript says *Anno Domini 1490, die 15 julij completum fuit hoc opus et cetera*. This presumably refers to the writing-out of the manuscript.

85. *Passione di Revello* edited Cornagliotti 87, sd at line 5222. After the dialogue between Christ God the Father, Moses, Elias, and Peter (5462), the following sd reads *Facto questo, facieno l'esplendore cum el bacilli. Et li discipuli di Ihesu cadeno tuti sopra lor facie in terra. Et Dio Padre, Moysès et Elyas se ne vadeno. Et poy Ihesu se vesta la roba vermiglia. Et apresso toca li discipuli soy sveglandoli, dicendo 'Su, su, brigata, li è tempo di andare'* ('This having been done, they make the glory with the basin. And the disciples of Jesus all fall on their faces to the earth. And God the Father, Moses, and Elias depart. And then Jesus dresses himself in his scarlet robe. And after he touches the disciples, waking them, and saying, "Up, up, companions, it is time to go."')

    The other stage directions which call for light are Gabriel at the Annunciation *intrando cum splendore magno* (981), Gabriel appearing to the Shepherds *cum luce artificiale* (1957) and to the Magi with a star (2052), the Star accompanying the Magi to the stable (2526, 2532, and 2549). There is nothing specific after the Transfiguration, and the play ends with the Resurrection and the immediate post-Resurrection appearances.

86. Vermilion can come in various shades: see Daniel V. Thompson *The Materials and Techniques of Medieval Painting* (New York: Dover, 2016 reprint of 1956 edition by Allen and Unwin) 106. In medieval art, Christ's everyday robes were usually shown as a darkish maroon.

87. It is to be hoped that, despite Archimedes' reputed feat (that he ignited a Roman ship attacking Syracuse by focusing burning-glasses on it), it was not reflective enough to set Jesus's white garments on fire. One feels that if it had, it would have been recorded among the other cautionary tales on the dangers of drama. On Archimedes, see his Wikipedia entry under 'Heat-ray'. Scientists have had a great deal of fun trying to

FIGURE 7A: Antwerp *Parnassus* waggon. Luyken (1685) detail. Rijksmuseum Amsterdam, RP-P-OB-44.139. © Public Domain.

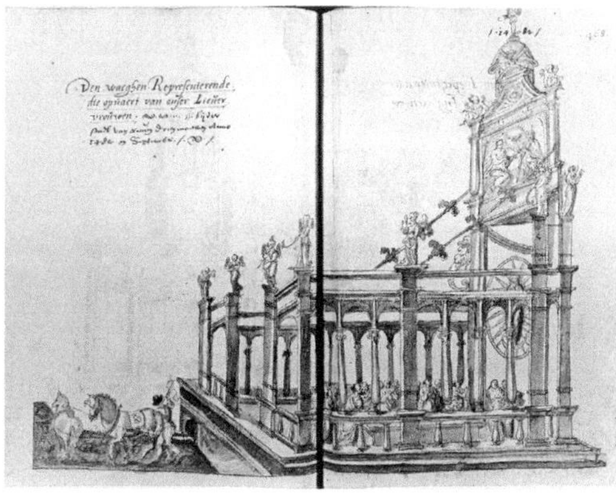

FIGURE 7B: Leuven *Assumption* waggon (1594). *Liber Boonen* fols 467^{v}–468^{r}. © Stadsarchief Leuven & M-Museum Leuven.

York pageant did use this supplementary piece of equipment, it must also have had a dedicated stage hand to find a different (raised?) vantage point at each station to manipulate the beam. In practice (again with a model) even if there is a 'sun' behind the figure of Christ, additional sunlight reflected from the front adds exponentially to the dramatic effect.

I will not deal at length with the *Harrowing of Hell*. It is the one which seems almost certainly to have depended on artificial light of some kind, and so is out of this remit. Peter Meredith wrote about this in depth as far back as 1992, and was of course interested in the effect of the sunlight and other

replicate 'Archimedes Death Ray' with mirrors: see e.g. <http://web.mit.edu/2.009/www/experiments/deathray/10_ArchimedesResult.html>. It has seemed slightly less improbable after the events at 20 Fenchurch Street EC3 in 2013; see <https://www.bbc.co.uk/news/uk-england-london-23930675>.

kinds of light-source on other pageants, including *Doomsday*.[88] He traced the angle of the sun on the *Harrowing* waggon at different stages in the performing day, assuming a roughly 3 p.m. start and a 10 p.m. finish for this particular pageant, and came to the conclusion that after the end of Coney Street 'artificial lighting of some kind must have been used for "interior" scenes'.[89] The reader is referred to his discussion for the details. One interesting point is that the imagined light-source and its effects are in two completely different places, and it would be difficult if not impossible for Christ physically to reflect enough sunlight (from a halo?) to illuminate an enclosed space in the waggon. The script allows for this, by very carefully suggesting that this light is a token, not an emanation: 'A light I woll þey haue | To schewe þame I schall come sone' (21–2).[90] This then leaves the way open for the light in Limbo to come from a completely different source.

It will have become apparent that when, in my two case studies so far, the scripts call for a great light, they do not mean a major all-over illumination of the kind that one might produce inside in the darkness of a theatre, but an impression of a sudden and in most cases long-lasting radiance emanating from a specific source, and faked, as it were, by the use of reflection.[91] Let me reiterate: we cannot see light, only its source and its effects. By sleight of hand you convince the audience (or they convince themselves), as with the London Royal Entries, that when looking at the reflection they are seeing the source. If

88. Peter Meredith 'The Iconography of Hell' 158–86. He deals with the York *Judgement*, but purely from the point of view of Hellmouth. Philip Butterworth also published a discussion of 'Hellfire: Flame as Special Effect' in this collection, 67–101.

89. Meredith 'Iconography of Hell' 179. Diagrams showing probable angle of sun on both end-on and sideways-on waggons, 178. He discusses the possible interpretation of the effect of different kinds of light-source, 180.

90. The Souls' reactions range from Isaiah: 'Nowe se I God þis same hath sende. | þis light comes all of Criste' (56–7) to Moses, who identifies it with the light of the Transfiguration: 'þat same light se I nowe | Shynyng on vs sarteyne' (93–4). The Adam of Chester is equally cagey: 'of this light *thou art author* | as I see well in sight. | *This ys a signe* thou wilt succour | thy folks that liven in great languor' (17: 3–6: my italics).

91. I am not here looking at the pyrotechnics of Hell, or the flames of fire of Pentecost in the Paris *Resurrection*, which sound dangerous in the extreme. These are startling and instantaneous and would burn themselves out quite quickly; see for the Paris example *The Staging of Religious Drama* edited Peter Meredith and John Tailby (EDAM Monograph Series 4; Kalamazoo: Medieval Institute, 1983) 107. This anthology is the starting point for a great many of my references, though I have then chased them back to the originals.

the light from the reflector surrounding the Christ Child shimmers on the face of the actor playing His mother, then we take it that He is the source of that light, disregarding the two stages of reflection that it has taken to reach Him.

The very first pageant, the Barkers' *First Day of Creation*, the obvious Alpha to *Doomsday*'s Omega, plays with the theme of reflection in a very interesting way. At first glance the subject may not seem particularly light-oriented, but the very fact that it has two different descriptions in the *Ordo paginarum*[92] (there are no titles in the York Register) hints at two ways of looking at the content, which turn out to be linked. The title in the Short List is biblical: *Creacio celi et terre*, 'the Creation of Heaven and Earth'.[93] In the 1415 list the pageant is described as *Deus pater omnipotens creans & formans celos Angelos & archangelos luciferum & angelos qui cum eo ceciderunt in infernum* ('God the Father Almighty creating and shaping the heavens, the Angels and Archangels, Lucifer, and the angels who fell with him into Hell').[94] The bulk of this narrative does not come directly from Genesis, but it enshrines the theologians' and the encyclopedists' tradition which links not only the figure of Lucifer, 'star of the morning',[95] but also the angels as a body, with the theme of light.

The commentaries pointed out that nowhere in the narrative in Genesis is it said when (or even that) God created the angels; but, following Augustine, it was assumed that this is implied by the creation of 'the heaven', and more directly by the creation of light:[96]

92. *REED: York* 16–26; Barkers (Tannours) at 17 and 25.

93. *In principio creavit Deus caelum et terram* (Genesis 1: 1). On the relation between the Long and Short Lists, see *The York Play: a Facsimile of British Library MS Additional 35290* edited Richard Beadle and Peter Meredith (Leeds: University of Leeds School of English, 1983) lii–liii. The Second List is in a hand associated with the Roger Burton, Common Clerk 1415 to his official retirement in 1432 though he kept working for at least two years after that. See my 'The *Ordo paginarum* Revisited with a Digital Camera' in *The Materials of Early Theatre: Sources, Images, and Performance* edited Sarah Carpenter and Pamela King (London and New York: Routledge, 2018) 104.

94. Hence Richard Beadle in his edition entitles it *The Fall of the Angels*. The *Ordo paginarum* entry is enigmatic: after *celos* it is written over an erasure, but there are no visible signs of anything else having been written under the erased patch.

95. Isaiah 14: 12–15. It became a commonplace to quote this in commentaries on the First Day of Creation: see e.g. Hrabanus Maurus *Commentariorum in Genesim Libri Quatuor* Migne *PL 107* col. 445.

96. Augustine *De civitate Dei* 11: 9: *Ubi de mundi constitutione sacrae Litterae loquuntur, non evidenter dicitur utrum vel quo ordine creati sint Angeli: sed si praetermissi non sunt, vel*

si ad istorum dierum opera Dei pertinent angeli, ipsi sunt illa lux, quae diei nomen accepit … Cum enim dixit Deus: Fiat lux, et facta est lux,[97] *si recte in hac luce creatio intellegitur angelorum, profecto facti sunt participes lucis aeternae, quod est ipsa incommutabilis sapientia Dei, per quam facta sunt omnia*[98]

if the angels belong to the works of God of these days, they are themselves that light which received the name of 'day' … For when God said, 'Let there be light, and there was light'; if by that light is rightly to be understood the creation of the angels, assuredly they were made partakers of the eternal light, which is itself the unchangeable Wisdom of God, by whom all things were made.

Thus they were the first of all creatures after the creation of 'the heaven': not the visible heavens, but the empyrean which, as the *Glossa Ordinaria* summarises Bede,[99] *statim angelis est repletum* ('was immediately filled with angels').[100] By God's division of light from darkness is to be understood the Fall of the Rebel Angels: *Intelligitur etiam hic angelorum facta diuisio. Stantes lux*

coeli nomine, ubi dictum est, In principio fecit Deus coelum et terram (Gen. I, 1); *vel potius lucis hujus, de qua loquor, significati sunt* ('Where Holy Writ speaks of the creation of the universe, there is no explicit mention of whether or in what order the angels were created, but they have not been passed over, for they are either signified by the name of *heaven*, where it is said, "In the beginning God created heaven and earth" (Gen. 1: 1); or, which is more likely, by the creation of that light of which I speak'; *PL 41* col. 323; Aquinas *Summa Theologiae* 1a, 61, 1: *nulla mentio fit ibi de angelis* ('but there is no mention of angels'; 204): <http://www.corpusthomisticum.org/sth1050.html> (Latin); <http://www.newadvent.org/summa/1061.htm> (English translation). Aquinas' discussion of the question is (naturally) comprehensive.

97. Genesis 1: 3.

98. *De Civitate Dei* 11: 9.

99. Bede *Hexaemeron*: *superius illud coelum … quia nimirum suis incolis mox creatum, hoc est beatissimis angelorum agminibus impletum est* ('that higher heaven … because indubitably, as soon as it was created, it was filled with its inhabitants, that is the most blessed orders of angels'); *PL 91* col. 14.

100. *Celum non visibile firmamentum sed empireum id est igneum vel intellectuale quod non ab ardore sed a splendore dicitur quod statim repletum est angelis* ('The heaven is not the visible firmament, but the empyrean, that is, "fiery", but intellectual, which is called not of burning but of brilliance, which was immediately filled with angels': *Biblia Latina cum Glossa ordinaria* (Strasbourg: A. Rusch, 1480); online at <http://gloss-e.irht.cnrs.fr/php/editions_chapitre.php?livre=../sources/editions/GLOSS-liber03.

cadentes tenebre dicti sunt ('For it is to be understood also here that a division was made of the angels. Those standing firm are called "light"; those falling, "shadows"').[101]

We have no records of the staging of the Barkers' pageant, nor, frustratingly, of the Chester Tanners' pageant which matches it in subject though not in detail. Likewise, accounts of parallel stagings (e.g. in France) all relate to fixed-scaffold productions which run seamlessly through the Six Days of Creation and thus have to present them all in the same mode. So *Le mistere du viel testament* (printed c.1500)[102] seems to depend on the drawing or lowering of curtains: for the creation of the heaven: *Adonc se doit tirer ung ciel*[103] *de couleur de feu auquel sera escript: Celum empireum* ('Then there must be pulled (down? across?) a heaven the colour of fire on which shall be written "the empyrean heaven"');[104] and for the division of light from darkness: *Adoncques se doibt monstrer ung drap peinct, c'est assavoir, la moityé toute blanche et l'autre toute noire* ('Then there must be shown a painted cloth, that is to say, one half completely white and the other completely black').[105]

A pageant concentrating solely on the Work of the First Day can, however, like an individual illumination, create its own scale and effects.

xml&chapitre=03_1>. See also Peter Lombard's *Sentences*; 2 vols (College of St Bonaventura, Quaracchi, 1916) *1* 315–16; Lib.2, dist 2, cap. 4: and cap. 5.

101. Peter Comestor *Historia scholastica* (Basileae: [Johannes Amerbach,] 1486) Book 1 chapter 3, sig a iii verso. Accessed online from <https://babel.hathitrust.org/cgi/pt?id=ucm.5316856714;view=1up;seq=14>.

102. The exact date of the *Mistere* is impossible to determine: it is a composite work. Its editor Rothschild says, 'Le *Mistére du Viel Testament* n'est pas une œuvre personnelle dont il y ait lieu de rechercher l'auteur; c'est une œuvre collective, qui a dû s'élaborer lentement pendant le cours du xve siècle': *Le Mistére du Viel Testament* edited Baron James de Rothschild (SATF: Didot, Paris, 1878) iv.

103. In French Royal Entries, the word *ciel* is also used of an awning or canopy carried over the king during his Entry.

104. *Mistére du Viel Testament* 2, sd at line 20.

105. *Mistére du Viel Testament* 23, sd at line 583. After the performance at Mons in 1501, these cloths were sold: Cohen *Livre de Conduite* 472–3. At its most schematic, see the illustration in BNF MS Français 316, fol. 28r, Vincent of Beauvais *Miroir historiale* (Paris, 1333), online at <https://gallica.bnf.fr/ark:/12148/btv1b10507212h/f61.item>; or BL Additional 18856 fol. 5v, Guyart des Moulins *Bible historiale* (Paris, c.1420), online at <https://www.bl.uk/catalogues/illuminatedmanuscripts/ILLUMIN.ASP?Size=mid&IllID=60211> though the latter shows the work of the Fourth Day.

I must resist the temptation here of trying to restage the whole play in my imagination, and will concentrate purely on the possible light effects, which were clearly spectacular. First God creates 'A bliss al-beledande[106] about me' (21), and then in the next two lines fills it with angels. *Bliss* here, rather than an abstract 'perfect joy or felicity', means something much more like 'a glory';[107] narratively the Empyrean, technically possibly the kind of 'glory' for whose construction Sabbatini and Furttenbach later gave instructions, a large light-box lined with reflective material.[108] They were dealing with indoor theatre and therefore discuss the siting of artificial lights. It is quite possible that in York, as in the London of the Entries, this pageant could have depended largely on the sun. At 4.30 GMT at the summer solstice this would be at 6° above the horizon rising to 14° an hour later,[109] striking the front of the pageant waggon full-face at the first four stations down Micklegate. (I provide more details about this in Part Two of this article.) If the waggon were a double-decker, as seems likely, and God and the empyrean heaven were on the top deck, then they would be picked out by the early light, whereas the

106. I am worried about the translation of *beledande* (which is the spelling in the MS), and possibly *beeldande* (1: 61), 'All blys es here beeldande aboute vs', with which it seems to have become confused. If we take *be-* as meaning 'around' (see *OED* sv *be-* prefix), as in *beset*, *besiege*, it would be a perfectly good equivalent of *circumducens*, in the sense of 'encircling'; see *OE* sv *lead v 1*. 'The word has always served as the usual rendering of Latin *ducere*'. The fact that the *be-* is reinforced with *about* is not unusual: Lydgate *Troy Book 3* 1497: He ... so sore was be-set With multitude of Grekis rounde about'; 'Many bulls have compassed me: strong bulls of Bashan have beset me round' AV Psalm 22: 12. *About* suggests something circular: see *MED* sv *round about adv*. 2(a): 'þe firmament is I-clepid heuene..and þe schap þerof is round a boute [L *sperica*]'.

    The verb *beeld* (build) as in 'I beelde þe here baynely in blys for to be' (1: 35) and 'In þis bliss sall be ȝhour beeldyng' (1: 38) means anything from 'create, establish' (transitive) to 'dwell, shelter' (intransitive). When Lucifer says 'Abowne ȝhit sall I be beeldand' (1: 87), he is thinking of changing his habitation: Isaiah 14: 13–14 (*In caelum conscendam, super astra Dei exaltabo solium meum; sedebo in monte testamenti, in lateribus aquilonis; 14 ascendam super altitudinem nubium, similis ero Altissimo*).

107. *OED* sv *bliss* n.3, translating '*gloria*'. *MED* sv *blisse* n 4 (a) '*Theol.* The splendor or majesty of God, divine glory; the splendor of heaven'.

108. *The Renaissance Stage* 173, 220–2.

109. Go to <https://www.timeanddate.com/sun/uk/york?month=6&year=2018> and choose 21 June. Click downwards-facing arrow to the left of date, and an interactive diagram of altitude and headings will appear. Move the sun and look at the time and data at the right-hand side.

lower levels, the main deck with the *ile* of Earth (1: 26), and one lower yet (under the waggon?) with Hell, would possibly still be in shadow because of the surrounding buildings.[110] On the other hand (depending on the possible starting time, which again I discuss in Part Two) it may still have been dark enough at the first few stations for artificial light to show up to advantage. By the end of the route, however, this advantage must have been lost.

Exactly what size and shape this 'bliss' was, and how it was instantly 'filled with angels', is irrecoverable. The likelihood is that it was circular.[111] It may, like the heavens of *Doomsday* and the Antwerp Entry of 1549, have revolved (and might even have been full of lights as well), and those angels which were not portrayed by human actors could have been models made of leather 'running on cords' as in the Cornish play of the Fall of the Angels,[112] in which case not only could they be used for a breath-taking mass dive – 'All goes downe!' (92) – but they could also be gilded with foil. But without documentation we shall never know.

The angels speak continually of brightness: the good talk of ambient light, which they attribute to God, the bad see themselves as its source. 'The bemes of my brighthode ar byrnande so bryghte' (50), and 'in a glorius gle my gleteryng it glemes' (82), boasts Lucifer, while his acolyte says, 'My schewyng es schemerande and schynande' (69). *Glittering* and *shimmering* suggest that a great deal of light-scattering gold foil, tinsel, and probably spangles went into their costumes.[113] Perhaps they also had metallic haloes, a more portable version of

110. And because it was probably an enclosed space (under the pageant waggon, if there was room?; 'In hell sall neuer myrknes be missande (1: 149): *Et divisit lucem ac tenebras. Divisit namque eas non solum qualitatis, sed et locorum distantia, lucem videlicet in superiore orbis parte diffundendo, in qua humana erat conversatio futura, inferiora vero ejus priscis in tenebris remanere sinendo*; Bede *Hexaemeron PL 91* col. 17.

111. York Minster Great East Window 15a–16a gives an idea of the usual format, but is not particularly helpful for the pageant: CVMA inv. No. 019001.

112. 'Let them (*Michael, Gabriel, and Lucifer*) fight with swordys, and in the end Lucifer voydeth and goeth downe to hell, apariled fowle, with fyre abowt hem, turning to hell, and every degre of devylls of lether and spyryts on cordys ruining into the playne, and so remayne ther. Nine angels after Lucyfer goeth to Hell'; *The Creacion of the World* edited and translated Paula Neuss (London and New York: Garland, 1983) 26, sd at 326. Manuscript written in 1611, but play older, possibly 1550s.

113. Both *tinsel* (sparkly cloth interwoven with metallic threads) and *spangles* (which we would call 'sequins', but with the hole at the top instead of the centre) are recorded in the *OED* and *MED* from the fifteenth century – at Gladman's Insurrection in Norwich

the sunburst behind Lucifer in the *Mistere du Viel Testament*;[114] maybe Lucifer's was star-shaped. Whether the shimmering was created by reflection from the sun, or from lamps would, as I said, depend on the start time of the play.

After Lucifer and his Angel have fallen, God suggests that some of the light has gone out because of them. He commands the surviving Angels to 'gyf lyghte To þe erthe, for it faded when þe fendes fell' (147–8). This is one of the most intriguing instructions in the pageant. Nothing in the Biblical commentaries hints at what it might mean, or how it is to be executed. Earth should be, as He says in the preceding line (146), 'vayne and voyde and myrknes emel' (Genesis 1: 2: *terra autem erat inanis et vacua et tenebrae super faciem abyssi*). The Angels seem to be called to enact a theatricalisation of *fiat lux*, for the next thing God does is to divide the light from the darkness, and name them *day* and *night*.[115] How did the Angels do this? Did they carry lamps in multifaceted reflectors?[116] Did they descend from the lighted upper stage to the darker lower stage and circle round the earth? Then how were the night and the day twinned in two (153)? Was the circle of the earth two- or three-dimensional?[117]

in 1445, his horse was 'trapped with tyneseyle'. Spangles were part of fashionable attire much earlier, but they were known as *bezants*; possibly they were once genuine Byzantine coins sewn on as ornaments. They seem to have been rather larger than our sequins. Because they were suspended rather than sewn down, they sparkled with the movements of the wearer. See Stella Mary Newton *Fashion in the Age of the Black Prince* (Woodbridge: Boydell, 1980) 37, 43, 46, 57, 115 note 36, 116 note 59.

114. *Adoncques se doivent monstrer tous les Anges, chacun par ordre, comme dit le texte, et, au millieu d'eux, range Lucifer, ayant ung grant soleil resplandissant darriére luy* ('Then all the Angels must show themselves, each one by Order, as the text says, and in the middle of them place Lucifer, with a great blazing sun behind him'; *Mystere du viel testament* edited Rothschild 3, sd at line 60.

For an idea of what massed haloes might look like, see BNF MS latin 920 fol. 320r <https://gallica.bnf.fr/ark:/12148/btv1b52501620s/f647.item>; also fols 179r, 180r, 182r.

115. This light, as the commentaries point out, is not our sunlight, as the sun had not yet been created, but something that produced the same effects of night and day. Some commentaries think that when the sun was created, this light somehow attached itself to it.

116. See Butterworth *Theatre of Fire* 66–8.

117. Painted images are of course two-dimensional, but some pageant waggons created three-dimensional worlds. The most striking are in Spain. In Barcelona in 1453, the priest Joan Calom was instructed to make a *Creation* pageant which featured, below the *nuvol* for God, *un gran mon rodó qui rodará* ('a great circular world which will revolve'); Milá y Fontanals *Obras Completas* 6 368–9; translated in Meredith and

If the former, was it vertical or horizontal? If the latter, did it revolve,[118] or did the lamp-bearing Angels dance around it, turning the apertures of their lamps away from the earth (and the audience) as they went round the back? Again, we cannot tell, and must resist the temptation to speculate further.

Because we are looking at practicalities, however, it is easy to disregard the fact that the spectacle meant something very specific. It would depend on the individual in the audience whether he were trained to recognise the theology behind the stage effects, or to see anything more than a striking metaphor in God's words to Lucifer, 'I make þe als master and m[e]r*our* of my mighte' (1: 34). Essentially the theology of angels as mirrors of divine light stems from Dionysius the Areopagite's *Celestial Hierarchies* and *Divine Names*.[119] It appears in its most popular form in the encyclopedias:[120]

> Denis seiþ in þis manere: an aungel is þe ymage of God and schewinge of hid liȝt, merour pure and ful briȝt, wiþout smittinge, wiþowte wemme

Tailby *Staging of Religious Drama* 71. It was, however, to be half water, a quarter starry sky, and a quarter land, and it does not say in which direction it revolved, vertically or horizontally – possibly as on a spit?

118. Which would not of course in pre-Copernican days have meant the same to the audience as it does to us.

119. Dionysius was introduced to the West by Hugh of St Victor, who translated him into Latin and commented extensively on him: text at *Commentariorium in Hierarchiam Coelestem S. Dionysii Areopagitae secundum interpretationem Joannis Scoti Libri X* Migne *PL 175* cols 923–1154. For an English translation see Dionysius the Areopagite *The Mystical Theology and the Celestial Hierarchies* translated by the Editors of the Shrine of Wisdom (Fintry, Godalming: Shrine of Wisdom, 2004).

120. The most compendious being Vincent of Beauvais in the *Speculum naturale* (Cologne: Hermann Liechtenstein, 1494) lib 1 cap 29 *Quid sit angelus: Dionysius de diuinis nominibus. prima imago dei est angelus manifestatio occulti luminis: speculum purum splendidissimum ac immaculatum declarans in se ipso sicut possibile est: bonitatem que est in abditis*. Chapters 33–6 concern angels and illumination. Here he is quoting 'the angel is an image of God, a manifestation of the invisible light, a burnished mirror, bright, untarnished, without spot or blemish'; Dionysius the Areopagite *The Divine Names and the Mystical Theology* translated by C.E. Rolt (London and New York: Macmillan for SPCK, 1940) 119, chapter 4, section 22.

An English translation of Dionysius is *Deonise Hid Divinity* edited Phyllis Hodgson *EETS OS 231* (1955). It ultimately leads to the mysticism of *The Cloud of Unknowing*. It does not, however, deal with the topic of the Orders of Angels, which seems to have got into popular culture via the encyclopedists and the *Golden Legend* and its derivatives.

> oþir defouling ... for he fongith by influens þe liȝt of þe godhede þat is in hit self incomprehensibil and ihid, and sendiþ hit forþ to oþir and schewiþ it and makeþ it iknowe to hem þat beþ lowere. And he is iclepid a mirour, for he is abil to receyue þe liȝt of God.[121]

Ultimately, this mirroring is aimed at us; it reflects 'the true light, that lighteth every man that cometh into the world',[122] which is transmitted to us down the hierarchies according to our capacity: *Unde illa lux eterna primo super angelos influit / & ipsis mediantibus ad nos descendit* ('And so þat liȝt þat is euerlastinge, first hit cometh vppon aungelis, and by aungelis it comeþ doun to vs').[123] The pageant God was not set in front of an image of the sun at random, possibly not even (though this is more likely) in general allusion to the Sun of Righteousness. Here, if I am right about the use of reflection, even the practicalities of a stage effect could give matter for thought to those who had the will and the training to consider the process by which the divine light was passed down to them. The pageant sun is an image-reflection of the real sun which is an image-reflection of the light of God.[124] Those without the training or the desire to ratiocinate this could still be thrilled and subliminally affected by its representation.

121. Bartholomæus Anglicus *On the Properties of Things volume 1* translated John Trevisa, edited Michael Samuels and others (Oxford: Clarendon Press, 1975) 62–3, book 2 chapter 2. This translates the original's *Angelus est imago dei / manifestatio occulti luminis speculum purum splendidissimum / immaculatum / incontaminatum / incoinquinatum ... quia diuinitatis lumen quod in se incomprehensibile est & occultum per influentiam recipiendo / & ad alios transfundendo inferioribus manifestat. Dicitur etiam speculum propter diuini luminis receptibilitatem* ... Bartholomæus Anglicus *De proprietatibus rerum* ([Lyons]: Peter Ungarus, 1482) sig. a5^{v}, Lib. 2 cap. 2.

122. Dionysius begins his *Celestial Hierarchies* by invoking this. For the handing down of this light according to our capacity, see Hugh of St Victor *PL 175* cols 941–2; Vincent of Beauvais *Speculum naturale* lib 1 cap 35.

123. Bartholomæus *De proprietatibus rerum* sig. a5^{v}, Lib. 2 cap. 2; Trevisa *On the Properties of Things* 62. Bartholomæus goes on: *& ideo lux per angelos ad homines processit*: Trevisa's text seems to have had *lex*, as he translates 'And þerfore by aungeles lawe cam to men' (62). Note that Bartholomæus seems to be thinking of a metal mirror, hence the insistence on lack of spots.

124. Dionysius *Divine Names* 87: 'For as our sun, through no choice or deliberation, but by the very fact of its existence, gives light to all things which have any inherent power of sharing its illumination, even so the Good (which is above the sun, as the transcendent archetype by the very mode of its existence is above its faded image) sends forth upon all things according to their receptive powers, the rays of Its undivided Goodness'.

And yet the whole thing must have started from practicalities – even if they were the practicalities of trying to express the inexpressible. We need to represent divine radiance: how do we do it? Painters use gold leaf, and we could try something similar: polished metal might be slightly less expensive. But doing it in daylight makes a difference. Those haloes aren't just shiny, they genuinely reflect the light. Let us try something even bigger, and sit God before a great metaphorical sun. But look at the way it reflects the real sun! Sometimes you can't even look at it. We could make it still more dazzling by spinning it, or focus the sunlight by using a brass basin – or even a whole system of polished reflectors. And so practical invention and theological metaphor advance hand in hand. Though the pageant builders and the theologians may only have been tangentially aware of this, they are both, in their separate ways, trying to do the same thing, and because their materials, however apparently different from each other (metal and mental images, visual and verbal metaphor), are well suited to the subject, they are obligingly leading those who work in them on from strength to strength. All the pageants I have looked at reflect this is their different ways. The result is what the medieval stage was particularly good at: meaningful spectacle.

In the next part of this exploration I shall look at the practicalities and possible drawbacks of using the sun in the specific setting of the York pageant route at that particular time of year. This involves an investigation of where it would be at particular times of day, and the angle at which it might strike the waggons at particular sections of the route. This naturally implies looking into the timing of the whole event, which leads to a consideration of their methods of timekeeping. I end by revisiting our on-site experience in 1988 and 1992 to reconsider, with the help of photos and video, what we found out, by accident rather than design, about the pros and cons of this freely available but intractable source of stage lighting.

Lancaster University

Acknowledgements: I am deeply indebted to and would like to thank the many friends and colleagues who have helped me to wrestle with this topic. A very long time ago, Nerida Newbigin loaned me the typescript of her edition of the *Oltrarno* accounts. More recently, Peter Meredith read the draft in its earlier stages and made helpful suggestions. Richard Beadle suggested that I should look at the other pageants which dealt with light, as a result of which everything started to fit together. The anonymous taxi-driver of Sheffield pointed out what immediately became the blazingly obvious and sent me off to the Qur'an.

Ghulam Yar and Heidi Stefania Hodkinson patiently explained the basic physics of light, and lent me books and videos. Heidi held up all manner of reflective objects and pointed them at other reflective objects so I could use both hands to take photos. Neil Hall lent me ultraviolet lamps and light meters. And Sarah Carpenter read each version as it came along, made encouraging noises, and pointed out where it did not make sense. It has all been and will continue to be an education.

Contributions for consideration should be sent to one of the editors:

Meg Twycross, Department of English and Creative Writing, Lancaster University, LANCASTER LA1 4YD, United Kingdom
E-mail: m.twycross@lancaster.ac.uk

Sarah Carpenter, English Literature, School of Literatures, Languages and Cultures, University of Edinburgh, 50 George Square, EDINBURGH EH8 9LH, United Kingdom. E-mail: Sarah.Carpenter@ed.ac.uk

Elisabeth Dutton, English Department, University of Fribourg, Ave. Europe 20, CH1700, FRIBOURG, Switzerland. E-mail: elisabeth.dutton@unifr.ch

Gordon Kipling, 3428 Park Avenue, MINNEAPOLIS, MN 55407, USA
E-mail: kipling@humnet.ucla.edu

Articles should usually be sent as e-mail attachments, preferably in a recent version of Word. See website for further information:

<http://www.medievalenglishtheatre.co.uk/submit.html>

Contributors are asked to follow the *METh* house-style (see website: address above). The language of publication is usually English, and translations should be supplied for quotations from all other languages, including French and Latin.